# LIGHTS & SHADES OF HILL LIFE

# LIGHTS & SHADES OF HILL LIFE

IN THE

AFGHAN AND HINDU HIGHLANDS OF THE PUNJAB

A CONTRAST

**F. St. J. GORE**

GYAN

*Published by*

Gyan Publishing House
5, Ansari Road
Daryaganj, New Delhi-110002
Phone: 011-47034999, 9811692060
E-mail: books@gyanbooks.com

*Distribution Network*
gyanbooks.com
India, USA, Canada, UK, Australia, France



ISBN: 978-81-212-8566-7 (PB)
First Published, 1895

2nd Impression 2023

*Printed at:* Gyan Press, Delhi.



**LIGHTS & SHADES OF HILL LIFE**
Author: F. ST. J. GORE

# LIGHTS AND SHADES

OF

# INDIAN HILL LIFE

OUR CAMP ABOVE PULGA (10.200 ft)

# LIGHTS & SHADES OF HILL LIFE

IN THE

# AFGHAN AND HINDU HIGHLANDS OF THE PUNJAB

## A CONTRAST


BY F. ST. J. GORE

B.A., MAGDALEN COLLEGE, OXFORD


*WITH MAPS AND ILLUSTRATIONS FROM PHOTOGRAPHS BY THE AUTHOR*


LONDON

JOHN MURRAY, ALBEMARLE STREET

1895

TO

HELEN COUNTESS HARRACH

TO WHOSE ENCOURAGEMENT

THIS VOLUME IS MAINLY DUE

# PREFACE

THE increasing interest that is continually being taken in that great dependency of ours which we call India, leads me to hope that the following pages may bring a little fresh light to those who are, unfortunately, unable to visit it for themselves; for even in these days of so-called enlightenment one still at times hears in England the cry of "India for the Indians"—that theory so plausible to the Western, but so meaningless to the Eastern mind.

An endeavour has been made, in taking these two valleys of one province alone of the vast continent, to recall how utterly different in race and nationality, religion and character, the inhabitants we know as "Indians" are.

What we call India has absolutely no meaning to any of the native dwellers within the area. It is a vast conglomeration of distinct peoples and nationalities, conquered by British blood freely shed, and welded together solely by the physical and moral strength of a superior race—a conglomeration which consists of some fourteen distinct races, speaking some seventy-eight different languages, and living in every possible degree of civilisation.

Politically, the native states alone, which cover only about one-third of the area of the whole, are governed by over two hundred princes totally independent of each other; while in British territory, where the Viceroy is supreme, such elements as Pathans and Bengális,

Sikhs and Tamils, Punjábis and Mahrattas, are controlled, each and any of whom has as much affinity for the other as oil has for water.

The races that pose most frequently in England as the "Indian" are the Bengáli and the Parsí. The former, as is well known, belongs to a subtle, versatile, and effeminate nation, densely populating a comparatively small part of the great continent, known as Lower Bengál. Possessing though they do the qualities of mind that enable them to pass the tests of English examinations, they are held in profound contempt by all the other peoples of India for their utter want of moral and physical backbone.

As we know him, this hot-house plant, the educated Bengáli, owes his existence solely to the presence of the British bayonets, and to the desire that English faddists have of trying Western experiments upon an Eastern people.

It is this Bengáli who is always clamouring for a greater share in the government that he has done nothing to support; it is he who is always ready to fill his newspapers with the iniquities of an "alien rule," and to shout the catch-words he has picked up of the "liberty of the subject" and the "freedom of the press"; while all the time he himself understands, far more clearly indeed than do his English teachers, that should ever the "alien rule" be withdrawn, his race will be the first to become again the hewers of wood and drawers of water to the hardy northern Mohammedans—a fine, bold, and manly people, who believe more in the virtues of a strong right arm and a fixity of purpose than in the criticism of the comparative values of Shakespeare and Milton.

The Parsí, on the other hand, of whom Mr. Dadabhai Naorojí, the ex-member for Finsbury, and Mr. Bhownagrí, the new member for Bethnal Green, N.E., are such excellent examples, have scarcely as good a claim to represent India as the English themselves have; for, like ourselves, they are aliens in race and religion, having come from Persia in small numbers only a century or two previous to our arrival upon the scene. Contemporaneously with the cession of the island by the Portuguese to the English the Parsís settled in Bombay, where they have established themselves solely as a trading community after the manner of the Jews. Under British protection they have made their mark as successful merchants and excellent citizens, but their insignificant numbers (not more than 89,000 in all India), as well as their eminently unwarlike character, prove that they cannot be considered as in any way representative of the continent at large.

It is between such varied elements as these that the English handful in India holds the scales. The magnificent *Pax Britannica* that enables the solitary traveller to walk unarmed through 2000 miles of country and 250 millions of people, has been bought by the blood of our forefathers, shed in a way that is plainly intelligible to all the dwellers in the land, and is sustained solely by the conviction they have that, if need arises, we are ready to pour it out as freely again.

The future of India must always be an uncertain quantity. With a population increasing by some twenty-five millions in every ten years, it is evident enough that, if the present state of peace and progress is to be maintained, a continually heavier burden will fall upon the 70,000 British bayonets who, alone among the now 300 million natives, represent the dominant power of the superior race.

The question is frequently asked, Are the natives more reconciled to our rule? is there any fear of another mutiny? The only answer that one can give, I think, is, that all really intelligent natives must be aware, quite as well as we are, that they have more to lose than to gain by turning us out. Often as they must feel the burden of the ruling power—and what child does not at times resent the parent's authority?—our worst enemies cannot but admit that the work done in India by the British is at least as honest as human nature can make it. The results of that work speak for themselves.

The real danger to India lies in the vast body of unintelligent natives who are flattered into impossible dreams by well-meaning but ignorant reformers from home. Each section of these natives has its own axe to grind, and they hope, in the upsetting of the present equilibrium, to possibly gain their selfish ends at their neighbours' expense. As long as we respect ourselves, the natives will respect us. The respect for the authority of a superior race is a sentiment that they have ever understood, and we shall have no one but ourselves to thank if, by overriding the well-matured opinions of its servants on the spot, the Home Government does anything to weaken the authority of the handful of white faces who in India are devoting their lives to the education and civilisation of so vast a mass of humanity.

No one can travel about India without a feeling of pride in what has been and is being done, as well as of gratitude for the kind and hospitable welcome that is offered him wherever he goes. To thank all would be impossible.

To my brother, Lt. Colonel St.George Gore, R.E., in charge of the Himalayan survey party, I owe previous visits to India in which we wandered off the beaten track, and lately three happy months under canvas amidst the magnificent scenery that Kulu affords. To Mr. W. Merk, C.S.I., who, as political officer, was charged with the taking over of the turbulent Kuram valley, I owe the Government's permission to cross the frontier with him, as well as the interest with which the society of so successful a frontier officer was able to invest my visit to that region; and it is but an inadequate return for all their hospitality and kindness to mention the names of Messrs. Philip and Vincent Mackinnon of Dehra, General Sir Henry Collett at Peshawur, the Shahzáda Sultán Ján, C.I.E., and the many officers of the Kuram force.

I am deeply indebted also to Signor Vittorio Sella, the well-known Alpine photographer, for the liberality with which he placed his great experience in working with the camera at high altitudes at my disposal. Any success I met with was, I feel sure, greatly due to my care in following his advice.

I have endeavoured, as far as possible, to avoid ground that has been gone over before, though I am fully conscious that there is nothing wholly new in the following pages. I can only trust that those who are much better acquainted with these valleys than I am, will pardon my attempts to bring these scenes again before the eyes of those who cannot visit them; for in these days, when incidents and information are poured so lavishly upon people's minds, it is only by constant reiteration, by dressing up an old subject ever again in new clothes, that any permanent impression can be made.

LONDON, *October* 1895.

# CONTENTS

## PART I.—KULU

### CHAPTER I



### CHAPTER II



### CHAPTER III

## CHAPTER IV



---

## INTERMEZZO

## PART II.—KURAM

### CHAPTER I



### CHAPTER II



### CHAPTER III

## CHAPTER IV



## CHAPTER V



## CHAPTER VI

# LIST OF ILLUSTRATIONS

The full-page plates were reproduced from the author's photographs by Messrs. Brunner and Hauser of Zürich.

## KULU

## THE SUB-HIMALAYAS



## KURAM

---

The illustrations in the text were reproduced from drawings kindly contributed by Count Ferdinand Harrach and K. M. Bernard.



---

## MAPS

# PART I.—KULU

## CHAPTER I

"It is no good your worrying, my dear fellow; when you have been in the Himalayas a little longer, you will learn that all this is a necessary part of the start into camp. It is the overture to the opera. You had better sit down quietly and wait. They will get under weigh all in their own good time." Then turning to the headman, 'O Jemadár Ji, what sort of jemadár are you? For two whole hours you have been arranging the loads and not one kuli has yet started."

"Sahib, all is now ready, but the mule-man has come and makes complaint that as he was driving the mules hither, the police caught them and have kept them back, because it is not lawful here in Simla for one mule-man to drive more than two mules. Without the mules, O Protector of the Poor, we are not able to divide the loads."

The mule chaudri (contractor) here advances to the verandah, and saláming low with both hands to his forehead, whines, "Sahib, the police are without doubt hard men. The mules were only being driven here with all speed for your honour's use, when the police seized them, saying that this was against the municipality's orders and not until this case is settled can the mules be released."

This new difficulty is too much for the curiosity of the crowd in the courtyard. They all leave their bundles, boxes, baskets, and tents, which everywhere strew the ground, and which they have been for hours trying to arrange in a portable form, and cluster round to hear the *dénouement* of the mule story.

For a while the babel is hushed in the new interest, till suddenly the jemadár, remembering for what purpose they were all got together, dashes at the kulis and with angry words and pushes drives them back to their work, where they squat down again upon the ground and play with the bundles, or wander to and fro lifting up each load with exclamations of pious horror at its weight, until a chaprassi (messenger), in a sudden access of zeal, pounces upon them and with voice and stick persuades them to take up their burden and walk.

Every one is talking; the chaprassis urging, the kulis protesting, the servants joining in voluble anxiety as they see the rough handling of some of the stores belonging to their special department. Even the chickens, resenting the new confinement in their round flat basket, cackle to the cook, who, staff in hand ready for the march, surveys them with a fatherly interest; while the ducks, sticking their long necks through the netting that covers the top, give vent to an additional quack of disapprobation.

Through all this confusion the mules wander, until they are seized upon by their big-turbaned Punjábi drivers to have their burdens slung over their backs. Three men grasp each side of the load, with a great amount of effort and mutual encouragement lift it off the ground, and with a supreme push roll the heavy tent over the mule's back, who, however, expresses his displeasure at this arrangement by taking a step forward at the critical moment, whereby the whole mass slips off over his tail, and is again deposited on the ground. A fresh volley of uncharitable and uncomplimentary language then breaks out on the part of the kulis, each of whom energetically explains that if it had not been for the others, etc., until a chaprassi's appearance cuts short the discussion and organises a new effort.

Upon this scene my brother St. George and I looked down from a Simla verandah on the morning of our start into the "Interior," as the inner ranges of the Himalayas are called: I with all the wonder of a new-comer, and he with all the knowledge, born of experience, that this entertainment has always patiently to be gone through on the first morning's march; after which, the loads being all settled and made up, there is no more difficulty, each kuli taking up the one that is allotted to him.

It was a glorious October morning, as indeed all October mornings are in India. The keen fresh air, at this height of 7000 feet, was gently warmed by the brilliant sun; above was the cloudless blue sky; while glimpses through the pine trees took one far down below into the deep valleys with their little terraced fields and peaceful villages, and through a gap in a line of hills the still lower plains of India could be seen stretching away into the morning haze. Everything seemed bright and sparkling in the clear dry air as we rode up on our ponies through the Simla bazár on to the mall on the crest of the ridge, and caught sight of the long line of jagged snow-peaks towards which, some hundred miles or so off, our jonurcy was to take us.

Off at last! The exhilarating delight of three months' camp life in the most beautiful scenery ahead of us, and all civilisation and care left behind! What more could one wish for? The very ponies seemed to share it as, pressing them with our knees, we cantered through the bazár and out on to the frosty road under the shade of Jakko.

Our destination was Kulu, for my brother was in charge of the Himalayan party of the Survey of India, and his work every winter took him to that valley, where his subordinates were surveying; some marking out the forests, and others some ground that had not yet been worked out in detail. My object in accompanying him was to take photographs, if possible, of some of the snows, whose bold outline fringes the horizon of every view northward in the Himalayas. Unfortunately for me, however, the "Himalayas," instead of being, as I was taught at school, a single mountain range, represented by a fat elongated caterpillar across the top of a map of India, are in reality a vast mountainous district some 1600 miles long, by at least 200 in depth. Range upon range traverses this belt, mostly in a north-west and south-east direction, but often completely broken up into a confused mass by the immense rivers that cut through them. The most curious feature of this mountainous belt is its sharp definition along the southern edge, for it terminates abruptly, nearly the whole way along, in a ridge varying from 6000 to 7000 feet, which drops sheer down into the lower country known, in distinction, as the Plains of India.

Standing anywhere on the summit of this outer ridge, you look south over the flat country, 5000 feet below, stretching far away into the hazy distance; while if you turn to the north, an endless series of ridges meets your eye, line upon line, none seeming very much higher than the ground on which you are standing, though a spur here and there may rise to 10,000 or 12,000 feet, and in the far-off distance, often over a hundred miles away, is a long array of snowy peaks, averaging mostly about 21,000 feet, but with peaks here and there reaching a height of 23,000, 25,000 and 26,000 feet above the sea.

From a distance these snows, standing up against the sky-line, look like one long backbone to the Himalayas; but they are not so in reality, for when you get closer to them you find them to be detached groups—often a great distance apart—so that it is extremely difficult to trace the watershed in the confused and broken mass of mountains.

The closer acquaintance with these high peaks, it must be admitted, is often rather disappointing, owing partly to the great elevation of the ground from which they are the outcrop, and partly to the hot dry atmosphere, which prevents the line of perpetual snow descending below 16,000 feet. For, as you march day after day through the Himalayas towards the snows, the valley bottoms

VIEW FROM THE FÁGU ROAD NEAR SIMLA

rise as well as the mountain tops, so that on arriving at the base of a 22,000 foot peak the traveller often finds that the valley that he is standing on is already some 10,000 feet above the sea, and that the summit above him is after all not much higher above his head than is often the case in Switzerland.[1]

And again, what a difference in the prospect: the Swiss village at the foot of its snow-peak has in most cases all the beauty and charm that green meadows and swarthy pine-woods and even fruit-trees can give; whereas our Himalayan valley of 10,000 feet is bleak and barren, with little sign of trees or vegetation, often only a stony waste, and should a few human beings here find a lonely abode, the villagers eke out a scanty subsistence from some little patches of buckwheat and a herd or two of hardy goats.

Into this maze of mountains our small party, consisting of my brother and myself, rode forth; and as we got clear of Jakko, we pulled up to review our army, which was of truly Oriental proportions.

Behind us stood our personal staff: the two ponies' saises, tall, wiry men, with the ponies' rugs and picket-ropes across their shoulders; our two gun-bearers, men of the mountains, carrying weapons to be used, in this peaceful country, against nothing more dangerous than the pheasant or the bear; and lastly, our two camera-men, whose knapsacks on their backs and tripods in their hands betrayed their ubiquitous nineteenth-century calling. These six

[1] These statements are confined to the central Himalayas, but the dryness of the atmosphere, as compared with Switzerland, is universal.

The summit of Mont Blanc is 12,333 feet above Chamonix.

| | | | | |
|---|---|---|---|---|
| ,, | Jungfrau is | 11,808 | ,, | Interlaken. |
| ,, | Monte Rosa is | 10,100 | ,, | Macugnaga. |
| ,, | Weisshorn is | 10,026 | ,, | Taesch. |
| ,, | Matterhorn is | 9,385 | ,, | Zermatt. |
| ,, | Salopant (23,240) is | 12,040 | feet above | Badrinath Temple. |
| ,, | Srikanta (20,130) is | 10,110 | ,, | Gangútri. |
| ,, | Nanda Dévi (25,660) is | 14,590 | ,, | Martóli. |
| ,, | Peak (22,000) is | 9,000 | ,, | Niti village. |
| ,, | Peak (18,000) is | 10,700 | ,, | Pulga in Kulu. |

men were our constant body-guard, and accompanied us wherever we went until the paths got too bad for the ponies, when the saises stayed behind to look after them.

Here come the advance-guard, stepping out briskly, staff in hand, and always well ahead of the main body, the four Mahomedan servants—cook, kitchen-boy, table-servant, and water-carrier. The twelve-mile stage is a joke to them, for they have packed all their goods into the kulis' baskets, and are marching light, with little superfluous flesh also to hamper them. With them goes a chaprassi to arrange about to-morrow's kulis, blue-tunic'd and brass-badged, his red turban giving him quite a martial appearance—"Sahib, salám."

Following at a respectful distance, as if conscious of his inferiority, comes the low-caste "sweeper," a mild Hindu, leading the two spaniels, Topsy and Nulty, who at the sight of us bark and struggle to free themselves from the hated chain. Another interval, and at last the main body, chaprassi led, straggles into sight, coming along the narrow road. The cavalry is represented by twelve mules, accompanied by their Punjábi drivers. Their heads are free from bridles of any sort, but their backs are burdened with great bundles of tents, bedding, mule trunks, tent-poles, etc. They file by, stopping whenever they get a chance, to nibble at the brown grass by the wayside, until the arrival of the muleman, with an imprecation upon their laziness, sends them jogging along the road, to the accompaniment of the rattling kitchen-pots upon their backs.

Close upon the heels of the cavalry follows the regular army, in the shape of ten kalassis (permanent kulis, who are Government servants in the Survey Department). These carry the survey instruments, and are trained to put up survey beacons, pitch tents, etc. They have five officers above them, the chaprassis, one of whom, however, is always on ahead making arrangements for the morrow, another is generally absent getting the mail, so that not more than three are often in camp together.

THE JEMADÁR, CHAPRÁSIS AND KALÁSIS

In rear of all, spreading over a long line, come the irregulars, kulis, some eighteen of them, carrying kiltas or baskets on their backs containing all the stores, etc. for three months; for little or nothing is to be had when once one gets away into the hills. The jemadár, the head man of all, walks patiently beside the last kuli, urging him to quicken his steps, and keeping his eyes open for anything that may have been left on the road; for the kuli, who has often been impressed against his will, has been known before now, when reaching a quiet corner out of sight, to deposit his load upon the road and disappear down the steep hillside, taking the shortest cut back to his village he can find.

The returns of the above parade show a number of fifty men, twelve mules, and two dogs; the only weapon of attack or defence, however, of the entire force consisted in a rusty old sword belonging to the jemadár, which was always carried wrapped up in his bedding on the back of a mule, except on state occasions when he was sent to the treasury for a bag of rupees. It was then buckled on, to the great honour and glory of the wearer. As this was the only military weapon of any sort I saw during my three months in the Himalayas, it deserves mention.

The road on which we marched out from Simla, for forty miles as far as Narkanda, is an excellent and very level path, made as the commencement of the famous Himalayan-Thibet road, of which such great things were prophesied, that have never been fulfilled, for the expected trade has been slow in coming. After Narkanda it degenerates into the bridle-path which is universal in these mountains, where wheeled traffic is absolutely unknown. Little care or money is spent upon these paths; they are mostly dependent for their excellence or the reverse on the nature of the soil in which they are made. Traces of the natives' idea of road-mending are always evident: wherever the road runs across a level bit of earth, he will cut the edges carefully, and sweep every pebble from off it; but fifty yards farther on, where the path crosses some rough and broken rocks, or plunges into the boulder-strewn bed of a ravine, there is not a sign of his handiwork to be seen.

From Simla to Narkanda this road, admirably laid out years ago by English engineers, scarcely rises and falls more than 1000 feet, keeping along the top of the winding ridge the whole way, with the result that there are no great heights to be seen above you. But if you are on a level with most of the surrounding mountains, you have here on all sides, straight down below, as steep as earth will lie, enormous valleys running in every direction; and your ideas of distance and size have to expand before you can realise the vastness of the depths.

As we rode along, in and out of the spurs, we looked down first into one valley and then into another, according as the path lay on the east or west side of the ridge, sometimes also crossing a narrow watershed, where the valleys drop steep on both sides.

A sharply-defined contrast is to be noticed in every view. On the hillsides facing the north, which, being shaded from the sun, retain more moisture, pine forests cover the slopes; while on the southern sides the treeless red soil is covered with short brown grass, and when the slopes allow it, little lines of terraced fields mark out the ground like the contours of a map. The midday lights over such a panorama are of course rather hard and ugly, for where the lines are wanting in a picture, one looks to the colouring to relieve it. But how can one describe the morning and evening on the same ground? As the sun begins to fall, all the brown, water-worn, herring-boned ridges on the bare mountain sides cast deep-blue shadows, as if to veil their nakedness; all the flat slopes seem to start into life as the ever-lengthening shadows reveal each little roughness; then a sudden softness comes over all the hard lines, the distance grows opal-coloured, through which the far-off snows flush pink for a moment, while the deep valleys at our feet turn indigo blue, passing almost suddenly into black, in the absence of twilight, and the stars begin to sparkle out of the frosty, dark vault above.

We reached Fágu, our first halting-place, twelve miles out from Simla, by 3 o'clock, and found our excellent servants ready with a cup of tea as we rode up to the Dâk Bungalow, which is here the sole representative of the somewhat large-typed name on the map. These few bungalows between Simla and Narkanda are so much used by picnic excursionists, that they are more like embryo hotels, and though they have none of the rustic charm they possess a good deal more solid comfort than the bungalows to be found farther on, where the stars often shine romantically down upon you through the cracks in the roof as you lie sleeping somewhat riskily on a three-legged bed.

But there were signs that the season was over, and that the gay Simlaites had departed to the more sober plains; for never a Sahib did we meet on our forty-mile march out to Narkanda, and the bungalow khansama's stores were scarcely able to meet even our modest demands.

I was up betimes next morning in my eagerness to get the first view of the new country, and as I stepped out into the fresh air the whole world seemed at my feet. I walked down to the edge of a little spur in front of the bungalow, and looked down into the deep valleys on both sides. Such a morning as this is one to dream of. The dark chill of night still covered the depths below, but here at this height the rising sun was lighting up, in its delicate way, all prominent points and ridges, while the valleys still remained in deep blue, till the long rays of gold, creeping slowly down the hillsides, picked out one by one the little villages set in their terraces of crimson amaranth. A cloudless pale-blue sky overhead, and all around a fresh keen atmosphere so clear and pure that the long line of far-off snows stood out white and sharp in brilliant definition; and above all the perfect stillness: not a sound could be heard but the muffled roar of the torrent far, far down below, echoing up out of the blue abyss.

I stood a long time listening to this intense stillness, and trying to impress the wonder of it all upon my memory, for it is quite impossible to photograph such vast extents. The camera would only pick out one little spot where one's eye roams unchecked from the depths below to the ridges above, which in step upon step lead up to the snowy summits upon the far-distant horizon.

I turned reluctantly back to the bungalow, in time to meet the table-servant carrying in a dish of tiny chops, off the little sheep of the country, and the inevitable, but excellent, curry and rice, which is the staple breakfast food all over India.

All was now in a state of activity on the terrace before the bungalow. The tents, not having been pitched, were still in their bundles, but the pots and the pans, the gun-cases and stores, the rolls of bedding and camp furniture, all had to be divided again into their loads, and apportioned to the new set of kulis, who sat in a long row, wrapped in their cotton sheets, which seemed to form but a poor protection against the keen mountain air. All went smoothly, however, this morning, and as we sat at our breakfast we heard none of the heated arguments of the previous day, and long before we had finished, the line of kulis and the burdened mules had disappeared round the spur, and were hurrying on to the next stage, a short one of only some two and a half hours' walk, to Theóg.

These stages are not very conveniently divided: they ought not to be much more nor much less than twelve miles; for that is about as much as a kuli can do, especially when one remembers that he invariably returns to his village again the same day. But the position of the bungalows has been no doubt mainly fixed at spots where the supplies of flour and rice are easily obtainable by the Sahib's retinue; for in India the retainers and kulis carry nothing with them, but buy each evening a few handfuls of flour from the local bunnia, who sits scale in hand before his large baskets of meal.

Sending our ponies on ahead, St. G. and I started off on foot, for we intended to make a detour from the road to a village

JENÓG

called Jenóg, which lies over a ridge and is quite hidden from the Theóg bungalow. It is a picturesque village, curiously enough rather Chinese in appearance, though its inhabitants have not a trace of anything Mongolian about them. The steep-roofed house belongs to the deóta, or village god. In most villages throughout the Himalayas there is some prominent house of this kind on which the inhabitants expend their skill in architecture and carving, and which they adorn with the horns of wild animals they have killed, from ibex and serow to the smaller karkur and chamois-like gural. Many of these god-houses are extremely picturesque, but though we frequently asked the people for what purpose they were used, we never satisfactorily found out. All we could learn was that the god *did* live in them; but at any rate he was not exclusive enough to prevent men and women living in the house as well.

In some villages which we saw later these god-houses are detached and more in the form of temples, and in these the nearest approach to a god that I could find was a stone smeared with vermilion. No objection whatever was shown on any occasion to our entering these village temples, which are more in the form of carved wooden châlets than places of worship. Most of them were quite unattended by any priests or officials, and except for the above-mentioned vermilion-smeared stone, we could find no emblem of divinity.

Indeed, the Hinduism of these hill men is sadly unorthodox, for though Hindus in name, and honouring the names of the Hindu divinities, they are practically demon-worshippers, whose religious zeal is in proportion to their superstition. The true believer is called upon to put his faith in Deós and Dévis, the divine beings, in Rikhis and Munis, those whose good deeds have earned for them a place in heaven, and in Jognis, the forest fairies, and Nág, the serpent god! But it is truly faith without works, for the chief effort required by their religion is the feeing of the holy man of the village, to prevent him calling down the wrath of the gods upon their many shortcomings. No doubt the priests live here, as often enough elsewhere, upon the ignorance of the people, and the curious processions of deótas at the fairs are all mysteries to work upon the superstition of the unenlightened peasant.

I had obtained as my servant a young fellow from the hills rather to the eastward of these parts, a Pahári Rajpút, one of the high-caste hill men. He had been excellently trained by a friend of mine in Mussoorie, and, with the extraordinary aptitude natives have for imitating what is shown them, he had evolved out of a nature of crass stupidity a fair amount of intelligence as long as he was kept within the lines of his training. He could skin birds with great skill; he knew every butterfly in the hills; he could make beds, clean guns, pack clothes, and with his beautiful eyesight, was a fair shikari; but ask him about his religion and his belief, or any other original subject, and his intelligence melted away, he stood before you a vacant idiot! Poor old Nainu! many a mile we travelled together, and useful servant though he was, I never discovered during the whole of our travels any indigenous spring of intelligence in the place where he kept his brains.

We took our photographs of Jenóg, and then climbed up the slippery grass hill to regain the road, whence a short walk took us to the Theóg bungalow, which being on the north side of the hill is prettily surrounded by pine trees. The jemadár approaches and saláms. "Sahib, all arrangements are perfect and the kulis are ready"; and as we approach the bungalow the jemadár marshals the kulis into line, and the usual evening ceremony begins. They have each earned four annas (4d.) for their day's work, and St.G., walking along the line, counts every four men, presenting the fourth always with one rupee (16 annas) for division, with the explanation to them of "Four four-annas, do you understand?" This always seemed to tickle the kulis immensely; possibly it was the flattery of considering them capable of dividing a rupee into four; still there generally was one amongst each four who had intelligence enough to explain how the trick could be done, and as long as they were in sight as they started back homewards, he could be seen demonstrating this mathematical problem to his wondering companions. Quiet, peaceable fellows all of them, obedient and submissive, they cannot lose their tempers, for they really seem to possess none.

The first institution that is forced upon the traveller's notice in the hills, is the system of Begár, or forced labour, a thorough comprehension of which is necessary for his daily comfort. It is no new thing, but has been the immemorial custom for ages as practised by the natives themselves. The right of the overlords to exact personal services from their inferiors has never been questioned in the East. In a less peaceable country than this district, the services of the peasants would have been exacted for warlike enterprises, but here, where fighting has long been unknown, the forced labour was mostly spent upon the roads—a thing most beneficial to all the inhabitants of the district—and upon facilitating the means of communication.

The Raja, moving from place to place, travelled literally at his subjects' expense. Notice was given to them that the great man was coming, and at each stage a small army awaited him, offering (willingly or otherwise) their services in whatever way he might command them. Supplies, wood, and water, were all requisitioned from the villages around, and it was, no doubt, with a lighter heart that the peasants next morning took up their lord and master's impedimenta on their backs, and carried them on to the next stage, where their neighbours were waiting to receive them.

After all, as long as it is not abused, this system is as good a form of taxation as any other, and has the advantage that, owing to the absence of all other means of locomotion, it supplies the only means of moving from one part of the country to another.

The first necessity in any civilisation is the freedom and possibility of movement and intercourse. From one end of the Himalayas to the other, excepting where the English have made roads up to their hill stations, not a wheel of any kind is to be seen, the tracks are mere bridle-paths, rough, steep, and stony; and though mules do penetrate from the plains to one or two places on the main tracks, yet they are never the property of the hill men themselves, but are only brought in by the Punjábi contractors in search of gain. Hence without the kuli to carry your baggage all movement would be impossible. The English have inherited this system, and instead of honestly recognising it as being a necessity, and working it on the Oriental lines but with English fairness, they have mixed up with it Western ideas of the "freedom and liberty of the subject," often to the utter confusion of the traveller and the native himself; and it is safe to say, that if some of the regulations which have been devised in their wisdom by the Assistant Commissioners for the prevention of compelling a native to do a fair day's work for a fair day's wage, were carried out in their entirety, all movement in Kulu would be impossible.

We pushed along next morning, for we did not wish to waste any more of the autumn days before reaching the snows, the fine weather generally breaking up about Christmas-time. Large herds of sheep and goats were frequently passing us on their way back from Thibet, whither they had been driven for summer pasture. These flocks belong mostly to Ladakhi and Thibetan merchants, who use them on their return journey to bring back the salt and borax which are found on the farther side of the Himalayas, and which are readily sold in India. Each animal carries about 16 lbs. in weight, slung over its back in bags; nor do such burdens seem in any way to inconvenience these active wayfarers as they walk along the rough paths, or scramble up the rocks in quest of a tempting mouthful. The excellent road as far as Narkanda continues almost on the level the whole way, keeping on the watershed between the deep valleys below. Curiously enough this ridge is no less than the watershed of India, for the water in the right-hand valley makes its way by the Giri river into the Jumna, and so into the Ganges and the Bay of Bengal, while that on one's left flows into the Sutlej and by the Indus into the Indian Ocean.

A night in the bungalow at Mattiána, and then a delightful day's march through some pine forests, brought us to Narkanda, which lies on the top of the ridge overlooking the main Sutlej valley, in which the great river flows some 5800 feet below. The full line of snows bursts upon one as one comes up to the little

HIMALAYAN TRANSPORT

gap in the crest where the Narkanda bungalow is built. A glorious view indeed, for the slopes in the foreground are clothed with deodars, through which, in places, the terraced cultivation and the homely villages are seen below, giving the landscape a more varied and picturesque appearance than is often found in the vast expanses one's eye is asked to take in in the Himalayas.

To any mountain-lover the contrast between the Himalayas and Switzerland is ever present, and no doubt there are parts of Kashmir where such comparisons are possible, but in the great central mass of the Himalayas there is an almost complete lack, from an artistic point of view, of the compact and finished Nature's pictures that one sees everywhere in the Alps. It is all on too vast an horizontal scale; the general absence of cliffs in the landscape, the drier atmosphere which browns the grassy hillsides, and the comparative scarceness of trees, all tend to produce a picture that, however grand in size, cannot compare with the broken lines and compressed variety that are crowded into the view in the homely Swiss highlands.

The beauty must be sought elsewhere—in the vastness and general high level at which we march day after day, which bring with them a sense of freedom that is akin to flying; in the gloriously pure and clear atmosphere, which allows the eye to roam undimmed over range upon range, until the hundred-mile-off snows stand clear and sharp before you; and above all, in the delight of being able and at liberty to go wherever you like, to pitch your tent where you like, with no exacting landlords to worry you, no guides and beggars to pester you, no trains to catch, and never a care upon your mind. Your little army is complete and self-contained, no matter how few in numbers, and you are marching through a magnificent country that is to all intents and purposes your own.

Every morning as you stand at your tent door in the keen fresh air, and look down into the deep blue valleys or up to the sharply-defined ridges which are catching the early sun, you feel again that the world is a beautiful place and that it is good to be alive to enjoy it!

Narkanda bungalow, with its khansama and stores, its well-swept rooms and spacious verandah, not to mention its service of blue Dresden china, was to be our last sign of civilisation, for we left the main track here, which leads up the Sutlej valley towards Thibet, and plunged into the narrow path that led through the forest straight down to the Sutlej some 6000 feet below.

The deodars just below Narkanda are, I think, the finest we saw anywhere. Fire, the great enemy of all Indian forests which

THE SNOWS FROM NARKANDA

so often causes such havoc in the hot, dry summer months, has spared these trees and also others at Bhagi on the Narkanda ridge, until they have grown to an enormous size. I endeavoured in vain to photograph them, but no lens would take in more than a very small part of their size, and I was forced to give it up. The tall rugged stems of these giants, weather-worn and battered, the upper parts of which alone are clothed by their dark plumes, are quite unlike the prim pyramids of the deodar in our English gardens, and a still more hoary look is given to them by the long streamers of grey moss and lichens which hang like beards down the stems, the growth of last summer's rains.

We were soon out of the forest, and exchanged its soft earthen path for a ravine of small boulders which served to carry the surplus waters, as well as weary travellers, down the steep hill. After an hour or two of this our feet were almost knocked to pieces, and we gladly left it to make an excursion with our guns after a covey of chikór partridges which had flown temptingly over our heads as we tumbled down the rough path. They come down from the hills above to feed on the terraced fields near the villages, and generally afford a shot or two, which, if successful, bring a welcome change to the evening's dinner.

We got on to our road again and floundered down the water-course of jagged stones set at an angle of 45° until at last the hamlet of Komarsen came in sight, and we halted for lunch under a big tree. The saises lead the ponies off into the shade and cover them with their rugs; Badulla, the table-servant, produces out of his basket some slices of cold meat and chupattis—for we have got beyond the reach of bread—which, with a little whisky and water, make up our midday meal. Rám Jas, the Brahman kalassi, who has constituted himself coat-carrier, brings up these necessary coverings after our hot walk in thin khaki-coloured cotton clothes, and we sit down to enjoy our well-earned rest.

Nainu and Raganáthu, the two gun-bearers, who form the remainder of our party, have already retired to a shady place and have lit a fire, round which they are all soon squatting. A pipe is made by taking the broad leaf of a creeper and bending it into a funnel-shaped cone, which is then pinned together with a pine needle. Into the wide end of this some black treacly tobacco is put, with a glowing ember from the fire upon it; this cone-shaped pipe-bowl being placed between the finger and the thumb of the closed left hand. Using the right hand, which is placed against the left, as a pipe-stem, Nainu takes two long whiffs of the fragrant weed with evident satisfaction, and passes the extempore pipe-bowl round the circle, where it is drawn upon in turn until its contents are burnt out. In this way they all economically get some satisfaction out of one pipeful, without the necessity—to them an impossible one—of touching another man's pipe with their lips. Natives never eat anything in the middle of the day, and mostly reserve their energies in this respect for their evening meal, but on the whole they eat far less than we do.

After a good midday's rest, we are ready again. It is wonderfully pleasant, is this continual glorious weather, this continual fresh air, this continual absence of cloud and wind. One is always hungry, one is always honestly tired at the end of the day, and, if the air is not too rarefied, one always sleeps well.

We have come to the conclusion that the water-course we have been marching down all the morning is a native road, for at Komarsen we struck into what was evidently an English-made one, which for the honour of our country we felt obliged to follow, though implored by the servants not to do so. The Public Works Department engineers, who stray into these out-of-the-way parts, have a passion for exhibiting their capacity for laying out roads at a minimum gradient, quite regardless of the somewhat elementary fact that the only advantage of a gentle gradient is to enable you to increase your speed upon it. Now as there are no wheels in the country, the speed is limited to one's power of walking, so these monuments of English engineering are never used by anybody, for the natives are so extraordinarily stupid, that they fail to see why they should be carried three miles out of the way in every two they want to go.

The servants, true to their instincts, went down the short cut, while we in our pride walked and walked, for what seemed hours, in and out of ravines, round projecting spurs and back again until we were almost giddy, all the time with the view of our little white tents pitched cosily in the hollow below, in front of which we could see our servants, long since arrived, spreading the tea we so

CAMP KITCHEN

much wanted. At last, as we never seemed to get any nearer, we put our pride in our pockets, and leaving the grass-grown road to its own wanderings, took the first short cut, and ran down to the camp, which was pitched at a delightful spot about a couple of hundred feet above the great Sutlej, that had been lying like a great green snake in the deep valley below us all the afternoon.

We found quite an imposing array of tents here, for St.G.'s babu or clerk had turned up with his complement in addition to our own.

Nothing can be more comfortable than well-arranged camp life in India, the chief factor in which is that best of abodes, the "field-officer's Kabul tent." No thin and flimsy hot-in-summer, cold-in-winter affair that we associate with the word "tent" in England, but a little house nine feet by eight, with an outer fly covering the whole of the inner tent, and keeping it both warm and cool, as required. The inner tent is thick and soft, and is lined with a yellow or blue rough cotton which takes away all glare, while the ground is covered with a bright-striped carpet. Laced to the end of the tent is a semicircular bathroom, which contains the portable washing-stand, etc., the tent itself being furnished with a camp-bed, a folding table and chair. Pockets are sewn into the tent round the sides, into which clothes or anything else can be put, and a ring of hooks surrounds the tent poles from which one's wardrobe most conveniently hangs. Nothing could be more convenient and cosy; there is just a place for everything, and everything is in its place.

The day ends soon after our arrival in camp. The table is spread, St.G.'s chair is brought into my tent, the lamp lit, and we sit down to an excellent *diner de Paris* of soup, a brace of roast partridges, curry and rice, and an omelet, served noiselessly and quickly by the barefooted Badulla. There is nothing to remind us that we are anywhere out of the world but the incessant thundering of the Sutlej outside. We stroll out after dinner into the lovely starlit night, to where the lines of mules are munching their hay as they stand picketed on the narrow terraces below our tents. All around are the numerous glowing fires of the servants, mule-men, chaprassis, kalassis, and saises; for each class at least, if not each man, has its own fire, at which they cook their chupattis of flour and water, and round which they squat. The tents are lit up by the flickering lights; the aromatic smell of the burning deodar wood fills the still night air, the roar of the great river below as it dashes over the rocks on its way to the far-distant sea rises and falls, while the big black mountains

LOOKING DOWN INTO THE SUTLEJ VALLEY FROM KOMARSEN

shut us in on every side, and make a frame to the picture before us; and as one lies in one's narrow camp-bed and all outside is hushed except the voice of the river, life seems to become a very simple and true thing, a feeling that Nature is our nearest step to God and Truth comes over us, till after the hard day's walk sleep creeps gently over our thoughts and blots out all.

I was up in time next morning to photograph the camp before the bustle of striking the tents began, but not before the kulis who had been sent down by the Rana of Komarsen had arrived. They squatted in circles round their fires, patiently waiting until the order should come for them to take up their burdens.

The peacefulness of these hill men is wonderful. They are much more like dwellers upon the plains than mountaineers, and though they have probably never even seen a soldier, and certainly have never heard a shot fired in anger, yet they accept the white man's orders with meek submission and obedience. The carrying of arms or weapons of any sort is a thing never dreamed of in these hills, for they have no danger from external enemies, and are too cowardly by nature to fight amongst themselves.[1] It is difficult to account for this want of manly vigour, which spreads through the Himalayas from Kashmír to the boundary of fighting Nepál. Probably they were originally plains men, who have gradually spread up the valleys, where, protected from all external foes, they have never been forced by any increasing want to forage for their needs. The soil is very fertile, and with the excellent climate, they have always had an abundance to satisfy the simplicity of life that they still retain.

A big river is a glorious thing, and we hastened down to the bridge over the great Sutlej, which here is narrowed between high banks, forming a deep, dark-green pool above a foaming rapid. In the many miles that it has come from the glaciers at its source, it has lost all the grey appearance of snow-water, and

[1] By the Arms Act of India, the carrying of arms of any sort by natives without a license is prohibited throughout British territory.

has acquired a curious solid green appearance, which is rather unlike a mountain river.

We watched long strings of wooden sleepers from the deodar forests up the valley, which were continually floating by, plunging and tossing down the rapids, and then resting a little as they eddied into the backwaters of the deep pools, until venturing too rashly they were caught again and swept along their downward course. Many seemed quite reluctant to leave their beloved mountains and clung despairingly to any projecting ledge of rock or bank of sand, until the next comer, somewhat ruthlessly bumping them off, drove them again into the deep water on their way to the hot and dusty plains, where for the rest of their lives they were to bear the continual burden of the Sahibs' iron horse.

We saw our retinue scramble down the precipitous bank and cross the river by the narrow native bridge that here spans it. Then they gathered themselves together on the farther bank for the steep climb of nearly 4000 feet that was between them and their night's rest, and we, mounting our ponies, led the army to the attack, and happily soon distanced them, for the dust made by the scrambling mules is at times suffocating.

The side of the mountain we were now going up was characteristically in contrast to the one we had come down from Narkanda. If the latter was shady and green with forests and vegetation, our present climb, being on the southern face of the hill, was over a bare and glaring slope, not a tree to be seen, only baked brown rocks and sun-dried grass for every step of the way. The path, a fairly good one, zigzags up in endless turns very steeply over this parched soil, on which, here and there, the trace of an Englishman's hand is seen in his endeavours to get some miserable saplings to grow in order to shade the passer-by. The few that have survived the burning summer sun seem to have become a prey to the active goats in search of food; for the improvident native has mostly taken the stakes with which they were guarded, to kindle the fire for his evening meal, wondering, no doubt, why the Sahib should

EARLY MORNING IN CAMP AT THE LURI BRIDGE

have been so considerate as to prepare fuel for him at such an out-of-the-way spot.

We slept that night at Dalársh bungalow, a solitary, lonely, tumble-down edifice of two rooms and a verandah, which stands, roughly speaking, on the brow of the first steep rise out of th Sutlej valley; and from here we were to march, at a somewhat more gradual ascent, to the top of the Jalaori Pass, two days farther on, from which we were to descend to the Kulu waters.

These little road bungalows have been built by the Government along the main roads through the hills. They are in various states of repair and mostly consist of two primitive white-washed rooms—possibly no ceiling—and a detached little cooking-house. For furniture they possess in each room a wooden bedstead, a rough native-made table and chair, and a printed set of rules governing the use and abuse of the Punjáb bungalows, duly signed by the Assistant Commissioner.

On arrival, the chowkidár, or village watchman, is sent for, who, after a considerable delay, produces the keys, unlocks the doors, and gives out of a cupboard the few odd plates and cups that comprise the table service, which have of course to be supplemented with your own. On leaving next morning, the Government visitors' book is brought, in which you enter your name, together with the inevitable growl about the general dilapidation and dirt of this Government institution, paying a charge of 8 annas (about 8d.) for each person so entered. It is an excellent and cheap system of facilitating travel, for a European is always glad to have a roof over his head, even though there is a hole in it; and on a few lines of road, where there are bungalows at every stage, tents may altogether be dispensed with, providing this road is adhered to.

We were glad to get away from this spot and to see the last of the hot Sutlej valley, for on leaving Dalársh the road goes over a crest and takes you into the upper part of a valley that leads up to the Jalaori—a valley well wooded, with immense slopes of terraced cultivation, testifying to the patient labour of hundreds of years.

These terraces where the ground is steep are often not more than six or eight feet wide, and will in places extend without a break, for a fall of two or three thousand feet, giving the whole mountain side the appearance of a cultivated garden. The lower terraces, where water can be brought to irrigate, grow rice and wheat, and higher up the hillside the green millet, the yellow pulse, and crimson amaranth form bands of colour that lead right up to the dark pine forests above.

On these vast slopes the hamlets, looking very small owing to the great distance they are below, are dotted about, evidencing the peaceful prosperity of the peasantry who dwell in them.

Incidents on such a road as this are few and far between. We walked or rode quietly along the track, which keeps along at this high level and does not drop into the valley, winding in and out of the spurs, which are as steep as they can be without being cliffs. Often in riding along, one's outside foot is dangled over a depth that makes one turn one's head away; but my tiny Spiti pony, whom we christened The White Rat, climbed like a fly up a window pane, and I gave up minding where my feet were, as long as he was satisfied about his own. These hill ponies think nothing of steps and loose boulders, and, I fancy, would mount a ladder without much difficulty, if put to it.

We camped again at Chawai, and next day continued on to Kót, the last village below the pass.

The country had been growing prettier and prettier; the broken ravines each contained a mountain stream, which was fringed with maiden-hair fern; the beautiful forests filled with deodar, tósh (*Pinus webbiana*), and kail (*Pinus excelsa*), with here and there a strip of crimson amaranth to give a dash of colour, formed many a pleasant picture.

We rode up the last steep rise into Kót somewhat late in the afternoon—for we had risen to a height of 7800 feet—and were

CULTIVATED HILLSIDE NEAR CHAWAI

delighted with the situation of the little wooden alpine village on its pine-covered spur, which juts out into the deep valleys on either side. A little carved wooden temple stands embosomed in some deodars of great age, and just above it the road bungalow is picturesquely placed, under the spreading pines.

We could not resist the temptation of spending an extra day here, especially as we were anxious if possible to get to the top of the pass soon after sunrise, in order that we might photograph the snows before the morning clouds had time to form upon them. It would have been impossible to get our camp under weigh at that early hour, so we gave the men a holiday; and at five o'clock next morning St.G. and I mounted our ponies, and accompanied only by our two gun-bearers and my camera-man, started away and pushed up the 3000 feet to the top of the pass in under two hours. Not bad going, for though the path is a good one, it is very steep in places. However, the ponies never stopped for a moment, and our men by taking all short cuts easily kept up with us. The morning air was chilly in the forests, for the sun had not yet penetrated them, and we looked in vain for a sight of a bear, though the many broken and overturned boughs of the evergreen oaks showed that they had not been far off; but our friend Bhálu is a great traveller, and moves rapidly from place to place, so that one is frequently disappointed in searching for him on his hunting-grounds. We reached the upper edge of the forest at last, and hurried in all eagerness on to the top of the narrow ridge, over which we were to see the promised land, Kulu.

It must be confessed that we were rather disappointed! The country is so enormous that though we had been marching for nine days towards the snows, they still were a long way off, and seemed indeed to be scarcely much closer to us than they did at Simla.

The summit of the pass is 10,600 feet above the sea, about the height of the Matterjoch at Zermatt, but unlike that pass it has no snow on it at this season of the year, the ground being covered with a short, brown grass. That we were not the first persons who had been here, was shown by the ruined forts which are built along the ridge, the walls of which can be traced in the heaps of stones that lie on the ground. How and when these forts were built it is impossible to say, but they exist in considerable numbers along these high ridges between the Sutlej and the Beás rivers. Except that they are on the tops of the ridges, they do not seem to have any strategic connection with each other, and it is difficult to realise against what people they could have been held. The height they are up, and the distance they are from any cultivated land, must have made the question of supplies very difficult, though they evidently provided themselves with water by catching the rain and the snow in the deep pits that are seen in the ground beside the now ruined walls.

The prospect from the summit is rather uninteresting, there being no very prominent peaks at all close, but the view over the forests through which we have come, with Kót and other little hamlets far down below, is very extensive. On the Kulu side of the pass the road drops into a narrow enclosed valley, which prevents any idea being got of the country beyond.

Still there was the glorious sense of height and freedom in the clear fresh air as we rested for some time on the stones of the ruined fort watching some beautiful monál pheasants, which, for their sins, have been burdened with the name of *Lophophorus Impeyanus.* They were feeding on the ground about a hundred yards below us, three hens and a cock, the latter in all the glory of his metallic blue-and-gold coat. In shape he is an ungraceful bird, being no true pheasant but more after the pattern of a turkey, still as regards his plumage he is the most gorgeous of all Indian birds. His head is ornamented with an upright tuft of shining green feathers. The head itself, neck, back, wing coverts, and upper tail coverts are all one sheen of dark metallic blue and green, while on his neck, by way of variety, a flush of copper-coloured feathers gives him a dazzling appearance. The hens are a modest brown.

AN EARLY START FROM KÓT BUNGALOW

We took our guns and crept cautiously down, making a long detour to get between them and the forest below; but most unfortunately, just as we were reaching our goal, a hen that we had not seen, flew up and with a shrill whistle alarmed her friends, who, with outspread wings, dropped down the steep slope into the protection of the forest below, long out of range.

We stayed two or three hours on the top enjoying the warmth of the sun, which now began to shine down hotly through the rarefied air. Even at this height in the Himalayas one often feels the thinness of the air—no doubt partly because of the extreme stillness of the atmosphere, which so rarely fans the exhausted climber. But it seems often to vary unaccountably with the day, and to be somewhat independent of the exact elevation one is on.

As we sat quietly identifying the snowy peaks on our map, a sudden crowing made us turn round, and there close to us was an old chikór cock, perched upon the highest stone of the fort, announcing himself in his pride to his lady friends below. Birds are unsophisticated in these parts, and have not yet learnt due respect for man. This familiarity was too much for us; so, slipping quietly down the hill, we went round to the side that he was overlooking and there flushed the covey, getting a nice brace of birds for our evening meal. Cold though it had been riding up in our sheepskin coats, we found our thin khaki cotton clothes almost too hot as we ran down through the woods to Kót again, leaving the path several times to make excursions after the chikór, which we met returning up the hill after their morning's feed on the villagers' crops. These birds, which in no way are to be distinguished from the French red-legged partridge, are great runners; and a large covey running uphill over broken and stony ground has all the appearance of a number of rabbits bolting in and out of their holes.

After an early breakfast next morning, the usual packing-up began, the rest of the previous day having put all the men into good spirits. All the bundles were laid out in lines on the little grass plot before the bungalow, while the kulis all squatted near awaiting the order to take them up, the mules seizing the opportunity of a few moments' freedom to wander about in every one's way as they nibbled the short sweet grass.

The custom of the country is that on giving notice, generally twenty-four hours previously, to the lumbadár, or headman of a village, he is obliged to supply you with the kulis you require, and, providing the number you ask for is not more than about twenty, they are generally forthcoming at the time you wish to start. They each carry any weight not exceeding 70 lbs., and are remunerated at the Government rate of four or six annas (4d. or 6d.), according to the length of the stage. In these mountain villages they do not take the trouble to send a messenger round to collect the kulis, but in the evening, as you stand at your tent door watching the brilliant stars sparkling in the dark vault overhead, with only the sound of the torrent far, far down below you to break the stillness, you hear suddenly a long-drawn call, "*āāā-o kuliāāā*," very melodiously shouted out into the dark night by the watchman standing on some prominent rock overhanging the valley. Away over the deep valley travels the call, telling the villagers that they will be wanted next morning. Again and again the call resounds, and now it is taken up by the villages beneath, until it is carried from hamlet to hamlet like a prolonged echo, which faintly dies away in the dark depths below us.

The whole scene is most poetical, and the simple homely lives of these peasants, who appear next morning obedient to the call, comes vividly before one. It was with reluctance that we started away from Kót and crossed the Jalaori Pass again; but we had to hurry on if we wished to reach the higher ground before the first snow fell, and a long march was before us till we got down to Jibbi, the first village over the other side of the range, when we might consider ourselves in Kulu, although the real Kulu valley lies some marches farther on.

HER MAJESTY'S MAILS

## CHAPTER II

THE district of Kulu, to which our steps were now taking us, has always been celebrated amongst Himalayan valleys on account of the romantic beauty of its scenery, as well as for the charm of its inhabitants, and there is no doubt that, as Himalayan valleys go, it fully deserves its reputation; and though it is visited by comparatively few travellers on account of its inaccessibility, in respect of alpine scenery it can quite hold its own with Kashmír.

The Kulu valley proper is composed of the first fifty miles of the river Beás, one of the five rivers of the Punjáb, and lies, roughly speaking, about one hundred miles due north of Simla, in the centre of the broken Himalayas. The main valley, running north and south, follows the Beás from its source to the point near Larji, where its course suddenly turns due west, and enters the native state of Mandi through a vast gorge, which completely bars any approach from this side.

A range of mountains commencing with 20,000 feet peaks and falling to 15,000 and 10,000 feet, closely borders this high valley on the western side, while the eastern bank of the Beás is fed by several large streams, which descend from more broken and still higher ground, including the Párbati, with its valley some 35 miles long, the Sainj, and the Chata, both of which latter meet the Beás at Larji.

The valley, thus shut in on all sides, can be entered only by crossing one of five passes, the lowest of which is 6700 feet high. Entering from the south, you have the choice of the Jalaori and the Bashleo Passes, both of which are 10,600 feet above the sea and are crossed by paths leading from the Sutlej valley into the waters of the Chata. There is not much to choose between these two, though the first is perhaps the best road, as well as the nearest for any one approaching from Simla.

From the west, which would be the easiest route to any one entering from the plains, two passes lead from Mandi state directly into the valley—the Dolchi, 6700 feet, which drops down to Bajaora, and the Babbu, 9400 feet, which brings the traveller directly into Sultánpur, the capital.

Few are likely to approach Kulu from the north, but there are two passes at the head of the valley, which lead over into the barren and desolate districts of Lahaul and Spiti; these are the Hamta, 14,500 feet, and the Rotang, 13,300 feet. All these passes are closed by snow in January, February, and March, while the higher ones are often not available until May or June. The east side of Kulu is completely shut in by a tangled mass of huge mountains, over 20,000 feet high, which border on the dreary

HOUSE-TEMPLE AT KÓT

wastes of Spiti, and over which no communication is possible even for the shepherds with their hardy flocks.

In the Rotang Pass the river Beás takes its rise, and, falling rapidly at first, meets its first village at Rala, and from there tumbles headlong through the high alpine valley. At Manáli, some 7000 feet above the sea, the area of cultivation extends as the fall of the river becomes less rapid, and from Nagar, 5700 feet, to Bajaora, 3300 feet, every available spot in the valley bottom and on the lower slopes of the mountains is devoted to the cultivation of luxuriant crops.

In the centre of this rich belt lies Sultánpur, the capital of Kulu, the only town in a district where the villages would be better designated as hamlets, consisting, as they do, mostly of a few comfortable peasants' houses clustered together.

It will thus be seen that the upper valley, above Nagar, has all the characteristics of high alpine scenery, while from there downwards the homely peacefulness of extended cultivation, the numerous hamlets dotted all over the valley, from the grass-thatched mud hut on the flat ground to the stone-roofed wooden chalet on the mountain side, all betoken the peace and prosperity of a people who, if their wants are few, have at any rate an abundance to satisfy them.

Somewhat distinct again in character is the valley of the Párbati, which joins the Beás valley in a narrow gorge a few miles below Sultánpur. This mountain torrent with its feeders flows through the district known as Wazíri Rupi, a long but narrow valley, enclosed on all sides by mountains of enormous size. The two gate-posts on either side of the mouth are over 12,000 feet in height, while the chain of peaks surrounding it rise to 17,000, 18,000, 20,000, and 21,000 feet as you go up the stream, forming a complete *cul-de-sac*, the only entrance to which is from the main Kulu valley, either up the Párbati torrent or over the high Malauna Pass.[1]

[1] Since writing the above I have heard from Colonel Tanner, whose beautiful monochrome drawings of these Himalayan peaks are so well known, that a passage

Shut in as it thus is on all sides, it is no wonder that Kulu was always regarded as the Ultima Thule of the Hindus. The earlier wanderers from the plains below, no doubt, made their way up here in search of an easier means of subsistence; but no great wave of immigration has ever been recorded, and the people as they are found now are no doubt the descendants of the original settlers. Cut off from their relations and co-religionists in the plains, they have naturally developed into a different people in appearance and in customs; but their own traditions go back into the dim distance of Hindu mythology, to an Homeric age when Purus Rám lived with the gods and ruled these valleys with their help and countenance. Coming down to a more reasonable date, we find that in Jagat Singh's reign, in 1660, the capital was transferred from Sultánpur to Nagar, and many immigrants came up from the plains to settle under his prosperous rule; and in Raja Maun Singh's time, at the end of the eighteenth century, the influence of the Kulu rulers spread from Lahaul and Spiti on one side nearly to Simla on the other.

But this prosperity did not last long. No great hold can be kept upon a scattered people separated by such lofty mountains and deep valleys. Internal dissensions caused them to fall apart as easily as they had been brought together; and the Sikhs from the Punjáb, without any great difficulty on their part, took over the government of the valley, granting the suzerainty of Waziri Rupi to an ancestor of the present Rai.

With the defeat of the Sikhs and the annexation of the Punjáb by us, this outlying portion of their dominions fell under our control without any disturbance in 1846, and since then it has been administered by an Assistant Commissioner, as a part of British territory. Only on one occasion have any troops of ours visited the valley, and this was some years ago, when a mountain

was made some years ago from Spiti to the head waters of the Párbati by a member of the Bengal Civil Service. The pass was described as very high and extremely arduous.

battery was marched through, partly to exercise the mules and partly to remind the peaceful inhabitants that such things as soldiers really did exist.

For many years after it came under our rule the valley was left entirely in charge of a native tehsildár, or magistrate, the Assistant Commissioner visiting it only during the summer months, and leaving again before the snow fell on the passes. During this short time he was naturally unable to visit more than the valley itself, although his political district covered an area of 6000 square miles of mountainous country, with a population of 100,000, embracing the countries of Kulu, Lahaul, Spiti, and Seoráj. Since 1870, however, the Assistant Commissioner has resided continuously at his post, to the great advantage of his charge; for, with the forest officer and an engineer, he is the sole English official in this area, which approaches in size that of Wales. Isolated as it is in the vast ranges of the Himalayas, this post of Assistant Commissioner in Kulu is an instance of the independent responsibility placed by the Government of India on the shoulders of its young officials—a trust which has produced, in the Punjáb alone, such names as Lawrence, Nicholson, Edwardes, and Lyall. The English character is certainly seen at its best in independent resource and action, and there are few responsible positions in the world where a man has such freedom to think out and carry out the ideas he has developed, as he has in these subordinate posts in the Indian Civil Service. It is the finest training-school for rulers of men that the world has ever seen.

Placed here in Kulu in charge of a population of one hundred thousand souls, belonging to different creeds, customs and languages, he is told to be their ruler, their judge, their guide, their friend, and above all to teach them by his example the full meaning of a white face. On the Kuram side of the Punjáb the subjects are warlike, and though here in Kulu the people are weak and peaceable, yet in both cases the same impartial judgment, the same tact is required to ensure success.

Nowhere is virtue more its own reward than in Kulu. The amelioration of his district and his people is directly in the power and under the eye of their ruler. He orders a bridge to be built one day, it is carried out under his eye on the next, and on the third day he and his subjects enjoy the benefit of it.

But though the responsibility is the same, how different are the conditions of life here and on the Frontier. A most delightful climate, temperate in winter and not too hot in summer, Nagar Castle, the Assistant Commissioner's home, at a height of nearly 6000 feet above the sea, is one of the pleasantest residences imaginable. The views down the broad Kulu valley on one side and up to the snow mountains on the other are all that the most exacting lover of scenery could wish for. Though far from the outer world, all the necessary comforts are obtainable and supplies are always at hand. The people around are gentle and well disposed, and the Assistant Commissioner travels from one end of his little kingdom to the other with no greater protection than the stick in his hand. Many things that make life pleasant are to be found in the valley: health, climate, scenery, and sport, all amid a quiet and peaceable population, who have much that is interesting about them, and who, though not always accommodating to strangers, are certainly far too cowardly to resist any demands made upon them by their white lord and master.

From the top of the Jalaori Pass, then, we looked over the mass of broken ground and confused ridges amongst which we were going to spend the next two months, and watched our long train of mules and kulis winding down the narrow path and disappearing into the wooded ravine just below us.

The top of the ridge, strangely enough, is bare of trees all along, the ruins of the forts standing exposed along the crest. Taking our guns we walked along this open ridge for some distance, to see if the chikór had yet come up to the high ground after their morning meal in the crops below, and found our friends the beautiful monál again at home. It seemed a pity to shoot such handsome birds, which are at the best but poor eating, and which are such an ornament to the ground they are found on. As it is, their numbers are sadly diminishing, owing to the persistence with which they are snared by the paháris, who, for the profit of a few annas, sell the gorgeous skins to some trader, who in turn carries them off to the plains to be converted into rupees. Here, as elsewhere, all lovers of Nature cry to Government to enforce a simple game law which would afford protection to birds and animals during their breeding season. Nothing can be more sad than the wholesale and unsportsmanlike destruction of animal life, in season and out of season, that nearly all over India is threatening the extermination of life in the jungles. Besides despoiling the jungles of their beautiful inhabitants, these would-be sportsmen are literally slaughtering the goose that lays them the golden eggs.

We ran down into the pine-woods after the kulis over the frosty ground, for at this height of over 10,000 feet the shady sides of the hills are chilly enough, and we were glad to warm ourselves by a somewhat rapid descent.

Our camping place this night was to be Jibbi, a little Road Bungalow some six miles from the top of the pass, and some four thousand feet below it, so that the descent on this side of the pass is more rapid than that on the side up which we had come. As we got down into the wooded glens the pine trees became finer, many an old weather-beaten giant blackened with fire standing beside the path, the forest having all the delights of a high alpine valley, in which the torrent below us increased in volume at every step, in its tumbling headlong course.

We halted for lunch in a pleasant glade where the sun broke through the trees, and were glad here, as always, to put on our coats before sitting down; and as we ate our frugal meal, the distant jingling of some bells announced the approach of that emblem of civilisation, the mail-runner. For some reason or other, his wand of office, all over India, is a short spear, the head of which is surrounded by a number of little bells. The spear, no doubt, is a weapon of defence against the attacks of wild animals, but the only use I ever heard for the bells, was as a peg upon which to hang that excellent tiger story, where the crafty beast lay nightly in wait for the jingling sound of the unconscious mail-man.

In the summer-time, before the snow has closed the pass, the mail-bag is carried over the Jalaori to Simla, each runner doing his few miles and then handing the bag on to the next, who comes down from his village and awaits it on the road. No guard of any kind accompanies it, but the inviolability of Her Majesty's mail seems never to be questioned, until, after passing through many rough hands, up hill and down dale, it is deposited on the floor of the Simla post-office.

The first hamlet we came to, a few miles farther down through the pine-woods, was Gaghi, a picturesque collection of wooden chalets, with shingle roofs, upon which great stones were laid, just as one sees in a Swiss mountain village. The ground about the village was terraced as usual, and the balconies and roofs of the houses were laden with the drying crops, great masses of crimson amaranth and yellow millet.

We stopped to watch the harvest operations. Four little black bullocks were being driven abreast, in the primeval fashion, round and round a central pole upon the smooth mud threshing-floor, wading through the yellow straw, and stopping now and then to nibble some prominent ear, until urged on again by the quick "Hutt, hutt" and simulated tail-twisting of the boy driver. Hard by, a woman was thrashing out with a long stick the tiny grain from a large heap of amaranth, which was in turn winnowed by a man who held the basket of grain aloft, and poured it gently from this height, whereby the chaff was scattered by the passing breeze, and the grain fell in one large golden heap.

They were much amused by my attempts at photographing them, no doubt wondering why on earth the Sahib was wrapping his head up in a black velvet cloth. They seemed, however, to

JIBBI

understand that they were about to be immortalised, for the women blushed and smiled in full consciousness of the stare of the lens, while the men stood, as usual, in a stiff row, as if about to meet their doom.

Nainu was invaluable on these occasions, for there is nothing that an ignorant native has more contempt for than ignorance in another of something he has just learnt himself. His language, it is true, would not have been quite in place in a West End studio, but it was to the point.

"O foolish ones, why stand ye thus in a row? Cannot ye see, O sons of asses that ye are, that the Sahib wishes to make your pictures? O you! stand here. Hold this stick so, and move not. Good! Another man is needed. Here, O mud-head, hold this basket like this, and let the grain fall gently to the ground. Enough, so. Let the women beat the millet. It is perfect. Now, all men, move not. Is not the arrangement complete, Sahib?"

Needless to say, the arrangement was much too complete, since any natural ease and grace they possessed was driven out of them by the stiff and wood-like positions in which they found themselves for the first time in their lives.

Photography is an excellent school for patience, for, after all has been carefully settled, one has often enough quietly to begin again at the beginning. Happily, in India, to the native at any rate, time is no object; and his chief wonder always seems to be that, after taking so long to get him into the right position, you do not keep him standing there for half an hour at least.

I spent some time in the picturesque hamlet taking photographs. The women, in strange contrast to those in other parts of India, were not at all shy, and were quite ready to stand and have their pictures taken, though rather disconcerted by the chaff of their fellow-villagers present. Some of them were quite good-looking, with well-shaped oval faces, but their rough, white blanket dresses had evidently been so long away from water that I was not tempted to make a closer acquaintance with them. For the benefit of more enterprising travellers, however, I don't mind divulging that the names of the two best-looking were Kuti and Nerki.

A couple of miles more, down through a beautifully wooded gorge, brought us to the Jibbi bungalow, which stands by the side of the torrent in a grove of magnificent deodars, a most picturesque spot. The hills rising steeply all round, being covered with forest, promised some good sport during the days we were obliged to spend here, as St.G. had the month's bills and accounts of his survey party to make out—a somewhat uncongenial occupation that kept him and his babu close prisoners for some days in the office tent.

I found the men had pitched my tent on a small patch of grass between a little stone chalet-temple and the bungalow, which together represent the 'town' of Jibbi. St.G. took up his abode in the bungalow, and the god not being at home, the temple was invaded by our servants, and soon the smoke of their fires was curling out from under the picturesque roof. These village temples, indeed, seem to be largely used as rest-houses by native travellers, for there are very few serais where shelter can be obtained by any one passing along these roads.

Nainu with my gun, Madho with my camera, and I with my stick, started out next morning to explore, first crossing the torrent upon a bridge formed of an immense single deodar, which had fallen across the water from its high bank. The swirling, rushing water beneath one is rather unsettling to one's composure on these occasions, and several times I found my hands groping downwards and my knees bending involuntarily in my anxiety to obtain a better hold on the log. Natives, with their shoeless feet, have an immense advantage on this sort of path, for every muscle of their bare feet can be brought into play to balance their bodies, while the flexible sole has not the fatal inclination to slip that is so frequent in a stiff leather shooting-boot.

The question of footgear is one of the most important on a

march like this into the Himalayas, as well as the most difficult to solve satisfactorily. Except when near the snows, the ground is always dry, but directly one leaves the path in search of game one has to traverse either rocks, which are often enough smooth, or what is still more dangerous, extremely steep slopes of short dry grass, on which, so slippery are they, a foothold can scarcely be kept unless one's boots are provided with a forest of good nails. Such nailed boots, on the other hand, are most unsuitable and dangerous upon the smooth rocks. I myself always wore the native-made leather chapplis—sandals with thick leather soles, fastened over the instep by a plat of straps, a chamois leather sock being worn over the ordinary sock, to keep out dust and dirt. Nothing could be more comfortable than these are on any rough or rocky ground, owing to the freedom and play they allow to the ankle, while, in order to give them a hold on the grass slopes, I put a row of projecting screws all round the edge of the sole. This is the way the Tirolese mountaineers nail their boots, and they, no doubt, have taken the idea from the chamois' foot, the centre of which, being a softer pad, prevents the animal slipping on a smooth rock, whereas the outside edges of the hoofs project in a sharp hard ridge, which clings to the crevice of a rock or cuts sharply into soft yielding earth, and by spreading or closing his toes the chamois is able to bring either of these footgears instantaneously into use, according to the requirements of the ground that he for the moment finds himself upon. The only alternative is to wear a good pair of nailed shooting-boots, and to slip on over them,

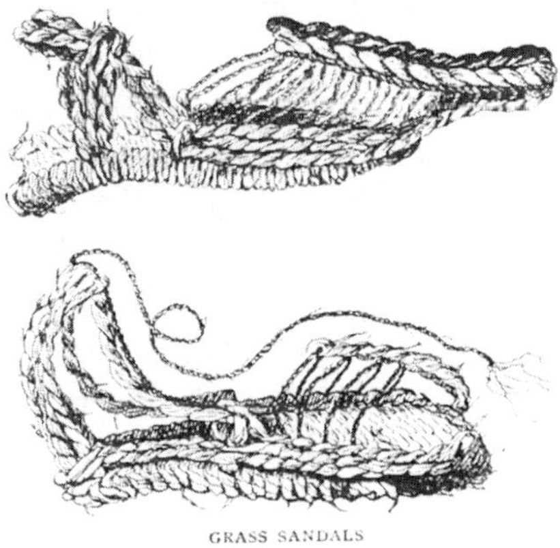

GRASS SANDALS

whenever you come to smooth rocks, a pair of the grass sandals that the natives themselves use, and which they so cleverly plat every morning that a new pair is required.

We soon found traces of the black kallidge pheasant (*Gallophasis albo-cristatus*), the cock of which is a handsome blue-black bird with a grey crest, more the shape of a fowl than the pheasant, after which he is indeed misnamed. It is useless to pursue these birds alone, for they would give a hare a start at running uphill and beat him, so we sat down while Nainu was sent back for the dogs, and before long the two spaniels came scampering up to us and were soon making the woods resound with their loud barkings. Then the race began. Encouraged by Topsy's and Nulty's tongues, which grew sharper every moment as the scent grew hotter, we hastened after them, already far above us. The forest was very thick and the hill-side most precipitous, but we scrambled up as one only can when in the pursuit of game, in all eager breathlessness, Nainu pushing and pulling, stones clattering, branches cutting, now turning to avoid a tangled mass, only to hurry up again with a supreme effort through the more open trees. "Look, Sahib, where the branches are thick—that big—" Bang! echoes the shot with a loud report under the enclosing trees, and down through the branches flutters the heavy bird. "Come here, Topsy, come to heel! Ah! Nulty, you brute, would you? Run quickly, Nainu, or there will be no supper to-night"; and soon he returns with the handsome bird, at which the dogs sniff admiringly. "Good old Topsy, good dog, Nult!" and we proceed more leisurely along the narrow forest path, until the dogs summon us for a renewed scramble.

Passing at times through little hamlets, we were far up on the mountain side by midday, and as I was sitting on a log eating my lunch, Nainu and Madho squatting at a distance polluting the fresh air with their noxious tobacco, an ominous rumble broke out amongst the high ground up by the Jalaori, and soon the slow but steady echoes, and an uneasy sigh of the wind through the tall pines, told us that the giants were warring up amongst the

DEODÁR CEDARS AT JIBBI

peaks, and warned us to seek shelter lower down. Before we had got far, an earnest of the coming storm swept down upon us in a chilly blast, which bowed the trees before the wreaths of cloud that, like scouts, rode upon the front of the now freshening gusts. Peal upon peal rolled down from above, at first in the glorious majesty of reverberating echoes, and then, all too soon, in the sharp and angry snarl which announces the near presence of the God of Thunder himself.

It was not a case of shelter, however, for the cold was very sharp at this height, and snow was falling not far above us, so we raced down, heedless of the heavy drops which fell upon us and the slippery paths, each of which now conducted its little muddy stream to feed the torrent below. A storm in the mountains is a glorious thing; no dwellers in flat countries can have any idea of the magnificent echoes awakened, which, repeatedly fed by new crashes, roll down the mountain side, only to be thrown back with a fresh roar from the steep hill opposite, until the whole air is trembling with the billows of sound. Long before we reached the bottom we were drenched through by the rain and driving mists, not to mention the steady stream which poured from the brim of my hat on to my knees at every step. By the time we got to the torrent, it was already thick and muddy with its swollen waters, and on stepping on to the big pine which served as a bridge, I was glad to have the help of Nainu's hand in crossing its slippery surface.

A change into warm dry clothes and a glass of whisky soon put me to rights, and as for Nainu, he also got rid of his soaking garments, for whenever I saw him for the rest of the day, he appeared in the garb of the primeval savage, with little on but the blanket, which formed, with the exception of his cooking pots and the suit of clothes that I had given him, his sole worldly possession.

The much-abused Indian servant has one great advantage over others. He never seems to exist unless he is doing something for you. The two words *ao* (come) and *jao* (go) sum up his daily movements. The first implies that you require his services, the next that he is to disappear off the face of the earth until next wanted. Where and how he eats or sleeps is no care of yours. No man has ever seen him eat, but there is a legend that the dark thing huddled up in a blanket outside your door, over which you stumble as you step out into the night air, is Narain Singh awaiting his next summons to the Presence.

On the march, however, the servants had their tents, the four Mohammedans chumming together, while Nainu, being a Hindu, preferred to lie down with his fellows, the kalassis. Never a complaint is heard, in hot weather or cold, in rain or sun, after a long day's march or a weary delay; he is always patient, always obedient, ready to do to the best of his varying ability his appointed task. Truly with all his little faults the Indian servant can only be called one gigantic success.

The storm rather unsettled the weather during our few days at Jibbi, and made us realise that we were still 6000 feet above the sea; but St.G.'s time was fully taken up with his accounts, while I wandered about and shot alternately with my gun and my camera lens. To my great regret, I had forgotten to bring some dust-shot cartridges with me, so as to get a specimen of each of the many new kinds of small birds I met with. The long-tailed blue jay and his orange brother; the little grey flycatcher with crimson wings, fluttering from rock to rock; the gorgeous smaller king-fisher one mass of crimson and sky-blue, sitting on a branch over a pool, or racing his bigger grey-and-white speckled relation in his swift flight down the stream; the tame little black water-bird with rufous breast and white top-knot, who never seemed to leave us; and the splendid flocks of Raja birds, little fellows, the males all scarlet and the females yellow, who seemed to catch every ray of the sun in their headlong course through the air—all these and many others became very familiar to us in our daily marches, but one needs to examine them once in one's hand in order to become really acquainted with them. To thoroughly enjoy a march of this kind one must make the acquaintance, if not the friendship, of all the life around one, both great and small, for it supplies a daily living interest, and is a study which never fails, but rather opens constantly new doors for further investigations.

One morning, on our return from a short absence from camp, we heard an immense tumult, and soon saw an angry gathering of villagers about the servants' tents. We thought nothing of it at first, until the interest which the disputants began to take in each other's female relatives proved it to be serious. "How now, O jemadár, what new arrangement is this you have made for our comfort?"

At these words the babel ceases, and the whole body turns toward us. "Sahib, these men, fools that they are, have come only to annoy us, who have given no offence; we drive them away, but they ever return with fresh complaints, so utterly without shame are they."

"Nay, Sahib, it is we who are true men, and our words are straight. Three seers of milk did the Presence's servants take from us, giving only payment for half a seer, but with many threats."

"What talk is this, thou liar and son of a liar? Is it not true that this man brought three seers of milk, and received payment for three? All our men, for they alone are true men, will bear witness that I speak the truth. Sahib, these men are wholly without shame."

Unfortunately for St.G. the witnesses are equally numerous on both sides, and both swear hard to the truth of their own and to the falsity of their opponents' case.

It is always difficult to find out whether it is the servants who are endeavouring to impose on the unsophisticated peasant, or whether the unsophisticated peasants are not trying to get the better of their natural enemies, hating as they do to have to supply anything at all to the passers-by. In such a case evidence on either side is wholly worthless, for each party votes straight, through thick and thin, and it can only be decided on the abstract principle, so universal in the East, that it is probably the stronger who are oppressing the weaker; and so the servants were condemned to pay up the defaulting threepence, because, wearing as they did the splendid brass badges which marked them as the representatives of Her Majesty's Government, they were, without doubt, in consequence the oppressors.

The weather cleared again next day, and as St.G.'s accounts were now finished, we made preparations to continue our march on the following morning down the valley. The mules had been sent back to Simla to avoid the expense of keeping them waiting; so chaprassis were sent out in all directions to scour the villages for kulis, for we needed a small army to transport our goods and chattels.

There was great excitement in the evening in the villages and hamlets lying in the hills above. No less person than the Devi himself had appeared, and was showing his anger by covering up the half of the full moon which ought to have shone brilliantly down out of the black sky. We stood out on the frosty night watching the eclipse, and listening to the weird howls and lamentations of the affrighted peasants. Conches were blown by the priests to fan the religious zeal, and their excitement went so far as to cause them actually to fire off a couple of shots. Surely it must have been a great harvest for the holy men. I gave Nainu an elementary lecture on astronomy next morning, to which he listened in respectful, if disbelieving silence, only remarking when it was over, "It is true, the Sahib lóg indeed know all things."

Next morning the usual difficulty in obtaining the kulis again cropped up when we wanted to start, the chaprassis not having been able to persuade a sufficient number of them to come down from their villages to do a day's work.

The whole question of Begár, or forced labour, cannot be judged without considering rather fully the position of the Kulu peasant or zamindár. These zamindárs have mostly very small holdings—

a few terraces near their villages, which they work with the help of their families, though in a few cases the zamindárs hold sufficient land to enable them to employ two or three labourers. These latter are practically serfs, and their remuneration consists of a few handfuls of grain daily, with the addition of one piece of puttu (homespun) and two pairs of shoes per annum. As is the case all over India, the zamindárs hold their land direct from the Government, the land being only reassessed at long intervals when the rent is fixed. Thus the zamindár is practically a peasant proprietor paying a small land-tax to the Government.

A collection of these zamindári lands, with a few hamlets upon them, forms the unit of area in Kulu, known as the kothi. These vary in size, some being large and containing several villages, while others are but sparsely populated, but all are compact and well defined. In the Upper Beás valley and Waziri Rupi there are altogether some twenty-three of these kothis or village communes. The headman of each hamlet in the kothi is the Lumbadár, who is generally chosen by the villagers themselves, and whose chief duties consist in seeing to the collection of the revenue, for which he gets a small percentage, and the carrying out of orders he receives for Begár.

Each kothi, in its turn, is presided over by a Neghi, who is the official really responsible for the rents, and for the behaviour of his charge. The office is hereditary, and is an esteemed one, for the neghi in many cases has several lumbadárs under him, as well as chowkidárs, the latter of whom perform the office of village watchmen. The neghi, besides collecting the rents, on which he also gets a commission, has to see to all arrangements for forced labour, to supply the needs of travellers with wood, milk, flour, etc., to obtain kulis for the transport of their baggage, and in general to furnish labourers for any Government work that is required on roads or bridges.

As far as appearances go, the neghis I met were in no way to be distinguished from any of the other villagers; but though in most cases intensely ignorant, they can generally read and write their own language.

The whole of the neghis, again, in Kulu and Seoráj are under the Tehsildár and his deputy, who live respectively at Sultánpur and Banjáur. These men are native magistrates, and have power to try civil and criminal cases, and to inflict as much as six months' imprisonment upon offenders. They carry out, under the Assistant Commissioner, the whole of the government of the district, and, as their name implies, are responsible for the tehsil or treasury. Both are strangers from the plains of the Punjáb, for no Kulu man has yet shown capacity enough for taking any real share in the government of his valley.[1]

It will thus be seen that the government of the country is extremely simple, and that the zamindár, beyond his nominal rent, pays no direct taxes, except the service he may have to render under the Begár regulations. This service, as has been said before, is from time immemorial, and though in itself it is no great burden, yet, unless very carefully adjusted, it may press with intolerable weight upon the individual.

Taking the claims of Government first, the solution of the problem was not difficult, and under the present system no works, unless imperatively necessary, are carried out during the months mainly devoted to agriculture. No call is made for forced labour, if willing labour can be found; and last, but not least, all labour is paid for at a fair day's wage. The traveller's claims, however, were not so easily adjusted, for even now they inevitably break down if any real demand is made upon them. His requirements consist of food for himself and his men, milk, wood, fodder for his horses and mules, with the addition of personal service in carrying baggage.

In the old days the Rajas simply exacted all these by force from the villagers nearest at hand, and as long as no organised system was laid down, the hardship on some zamindárs was in-

[1] See Appendix B.

tolerable, while others at a distance altogether escaped the tax. Again, men were often summoned from a distance of twelve to fifteen miles to a stage, there to await the traveller's pleasure for days, only to find in the end that they were not required, or if engaged, were taken on another twelve-mile march, only to be dismissed on completing the journey with but a poor recompense for their long absence from their fields. Likely enough, too, the peasant would be called away just at the time when his little plot of ground most needed his attention. These conditions have now been remedied by Government, by making out lists, so that each kothi is called upon in turn to supply kulis, and by organising the main routes into marches, for each of which a fixed charge is made for porterage; nor can kulis now be kept waiting beyond a certain time without extra payment.

All these arrangements seem sensible and workable enough, but where they break down is in the people themselves. Probably no peasants in the world are so well off as the Kulu zamindárs. Each grows enough food off his own little plot of ground to supply himself and his family with sufficient for the year. His little flock of sheep and goats provides him with milk and wool, which he spins himself into coarse thread. This is then woven by himself into long narrow strips of homespun, which furnish him with clothes and blankets. Tobacco he grows for his own consumption. His sole need of money is to pay his trifling rent to the neghi, and this he obtains by the sale of his surplus rice or wheat to the passing Lahaulis, or possibly the disposal of his small patch of opium to the Punjábi traders.

The consequence is that the Kulu peasant has little incentive to do a hard day's work, even if it is fairly paid for. A more enterprising people would be only too delighted to see travellers entering their country, bringing money and trade; but not so the Kulu zamindár. He seems to throw every obstacle he can in the way of the traveller obtaining even such necessaries as milk and flour, while he obstinately refuses to sell his honey, his eggs, and his fowls, for which he is offered liberal payment. This unwillingness to sell or trade seems to be a part of the Kulu character, for it is only under Government compulsion that the lumbadárs will supply sheep for payment or grass and wood for the traveller's use; and it is a curious fact that all the shops in the valley are kept by strangers from the Punjáb, Sultánpur, the capital, being almost entirely peopled by them. The very Bunnias selling flour to the servants at the end of the day's march, do not belong to the valley, and it is almost an impossibility to obtain a peasant's consent to part with his spare blankets or his quaint jewelry, no matter how liberal a price is offered him.

The result of all this is that, if it were not for the Government's enforcement of Begár, no work at all could be carried on in the valley, no roads made, no bridges built. Offer what he would, the traveller would not be able to obtain even the necessaries of life, for there are, of course, no local shops; he could not either move a step, for no one would carry his baggage or bring grass for his mules.

Such being the case, forced labour and forced supplies, both of which are fairly paid for at fixed rates, are justly exacted by the Government, the neghi of each kothi being obliged by law to comply with the demands made upon him. In practice, however, numerous difficulties arise. The neghi's excuse is that he has not received sufficient notice; the lumbadár announces that there is no milk to be had; a miserable sheep is brought for the stipulated four rupees, and is falsely declared to be the best they have. If any complaint is made to the Assistant Commissioner, he expresses his regret, but excuses himself by saying that he also continually has the same difficulties. In the meantime the traveller wastes a day of his precious leave, or goes to bed after a meagre supper.

If the Kulu people will not take any share in the trade of their country, and there arises a demand for it on the part of sufficient travellers, the present system will inevitably go to the

TEMPLE AT MANGLAOR

wall, and be replaced by a race of foreign traders and contractors, who will effectually prevent the people of the valley from ever having any share in the increasing prosperity of their country.

After waiting some time for the rest of the kulis, we decided to start at once, leaving a chaprassi behind to bring on the rest of the baggage when a sufficient number of men had been found. It was delightful to be on the move again.

The path continued steadily down the valley, and all too soon the delightful alpine character of the mountain sides began to grow less; we broke out of the dark pine-woods into the more open valley, where the hillsides were brown and bare, and where the peasants were busily scratching their terraced fields with quaintly-shaped ploughs. With the hot sun behind our backs the whole way, the views all day were flat and shadowless, without any variety to cause especial interest. About midday we reached Banjáur, whither the seat of the local authority has been moved from the village of Plách, high up on the hill opposite.

Banjáur is now the residence of the Naib Tehsildár, for whose benefit quite an imposing array of buildings has been erected. An excellent two-storied, gabled stone villa, worthy indeed of Upper Norwood, holds the great man himself, while alongside is a large, low, stone Tudor castle, enclosing courtyards for the treasury, the police station, and post-office. The half a dozen policemen lounging about are but the nominal guard of the treasure, for, as serious crime is wholly unknown in Kulu, the policeman's lot, here at any rate, is indeed a happy one. The buildings look well built and comfortable, but strangely out of place in this non-urban land. St.G. and I walked up to them, and were received with many saláms by the Tehsildár, after whose health we tenderly inquired, and then proceeded to discuss the crops and the season before we came to the important question of presenting the treasury warrant to him to draw pay for the men. We came to the conclusion that the Naib Tehsildár of Banjáur has a "soft billet," and when other professions fail, we determined to remember it as one well worth applying for. We had a further six miles of tramp however to-day, so we tore ourselves away, and continued our march down the valley.

About a mile below Banjáur a stream comes in from the right, down which the path leads from the Bashleo Pass, the two roads here uniting and continuing together on into Kulu. We hesitated rather about taking an upper line of road which branches off here, and leads through Plách over a ridge into the Sainj valley, and then over a second ridge into the Kulu valley at Bajáora. This would be a more interesting route, and in summer be cooler than the lower road, but in places it is almost impassable for ponies, and for us would have been disagreeable, owing to the cold caused by the late break in the weather. We therefore followed the path which keeps mostly along the torrent, except now and then where a projecting cliff causes it to climb up, only to descend again where the valley widens. Scarcely a tree is to be seen about here, and there is little to charm the eye in the monotonous red-brown colouring. A bold bridge, however, thrown across a narrow gorge just before reaching the end of our day's march, added a little interest to the proceedings.

Manglaor bungalow we reached early in the afternoon—a poor tumble-down little place, a great part of the roof being off, which would have been inconvenient had it rained. We strolled up to the little temple on the hill just above—a quaint building with some interesting wood-carving, the whole being in better repair and more carefully kept than most of the temples we had yet come across. There was no one in attendance, and we searched for the god, but, as usual, he was not to be found at home, until at last from within the inmost sanctuary Nainu unearthed a round vermilion-smeared stone, which he assured me was the Deóta himself.

I turned with more interest to some living goddesses who, hearing of our arrival, had come with Kulu boldness to have a chat and to see for themselves. The fame of Kulu ladies has spread far beyond the Himalayas, and many a fair one from the valley has reclined upon the couches of the emperors of Delhi, and gazed from out of the white marble halls of the palace across the great Jumna and the glaring plains towards the distant hills, high up in which her sisters perhaps stood up to their knees in water, planting out the young rice in their narrow terraced fields, to the sound of merry laughter and boisterous jokes.

The women greeted us with cheery saláms, asking questions whence we had come, and whither going. Simple peasants on their way to the hillsides to cut grass for the cattle at home,

KULU SILVER ENAMELLED NECKLACE

they carried ropes over their shoulders and sickles in their hands, and laughed heartily as I bade them stay to have their picture taken. Tattered and dirty as they undoubtedly were, there was a great charm in the unconscious frankness of these simple girls, which was all the more refreshing in this womanless Eastern land. Their voices were soft, and their gentle manners winning, as with a half-shy smile they chaffed me for wearing a ring on my finger, it evidently not being the fashion here for the male sex to burden themselves with a signet. In spite of the poverty of their clothes, they wore a great quantity of silver necklaces, prominent among which were the regulation silver and blue enamel *plaques*, on which the rude outline of a god is traced, which are universally worn by men and women in Kulu. Their olive throats were well set off by the strings of coral which mixed with the silver, while here and there a rough green turquoise added a little colour to their otherwise somewhat sober appearance. Masses of earrings hung from a little silk cap which covered the upper half of the ears and thus supported the weight, and though somewhat disfigured by nose-rings, they happily were not well enough off to wear the little gold leaf-shaped ornament, which, hanging from the nose of many Kulu women, so mars the otherwise pretty lines of their mouths. I asked them in vain if they would part with any of their curiosities, but with true Kulu feeling they refused to sell, especially setting a high value on the coral, which they said was a rarity in these parts.

I am afraid that the Kulu women have been often condemned for their immorality, and though in truth chastity is not looked upon here, as in other countries, as a valuable quality, yet those who know them best, and have time to consider the conditions under which they live, find it easy to forgive their laxity and want of continence, which has but little in common with the gross deceits or greedy desire for gain, often found in many more civilised communities. As will be seen later, the marriage tie has not the same binding effect on either the men or the women as is given to it by more cultivated races; and before condemning the women, it is necessary to look to the men, under whose charge they are.

Probably owing to the ease and comfort of life, and absence of any danger to call forth his manly qualities, the Kulu peasant has developed into a very lazy and ignorant member of society. Unselfish labour is to him a thing unknown, and hand in hand with his want of education and low moral tone goes a certain cunning, which is chiefly used to escape and evade any duties that he may be called upon to perform. Essentially an agricultural people, the man is seen at his best when at work in the fields, though here, as elsewhere, a great part of the work is done by the woman, who, in truth, is simply looked upon as a labour-saving machine,

PEASANT WOMEN AT MANGLAOR

and who is mostly valued by her husband in proportion to the amount of work she is capable of performing. We met afterwards in the valley a man who was pointed out as an exceedingly clever fellow. He bought a wife cheap, for some eight or ten rupees, broke her in to be a useful worker at home and in the fields, and then sold her to the next comer for double the money. This seemed to be his profession indeed, for he was then in process of educating the third.

Easy-going and dissolute as the men undoubtedly are, with no moral feeling or public opinion to keep them straight, but on the contrary with plenty of leisure and opportunity at the many fairs, where, intoxicated by a plentiful supply of *lugri*, they indulge their passions, what encouragement is there for their wives to remain faithful? Married, in the first instance, simply for money considerations, disgusted by the flagrant infidelity of her husband, a Kulu woman sees little harm in throwing herself into the arms of a lover for whom she has formed a real and natural attachment. Marriage to her is certainly no romance, but rather an estate of enforced labour; what surprise can therefore be felt if under these circumstances she abandons herself to the dictates of a heart that Nature has provided her with?

From Manglaor we trudged down the narrow and treeless valley, now somewhat monotonous in its brown winter tints, another twelve miles to Larji, passing no villages, only here and there a scattered hamlet; for the country is large and the inhabitants are not as yet numerous. We arrived in good time, for the march had been downhill all day, only to be met by the chaprassi we had sent on, who informed us that the neghi declared that he would be unable to furnish us with the kulis that we required on the morrow, but that he had sent men up to the villages scattered amongst the hills, and hoped to have them ready on the following day.

It is no good fretting about delays in the East; they come, indeed, with a punctuality worthy of a better cause, whether welcome or the reverse. We waited therefore a whole day at Larji, and before the end of it were convinced that, if human nature is the same here as elsewhere, it must be an enormously difficult thing to gather unwilling men together from such scattered hamlets perched high upon the mountains and often separated from each other by valleys several thousand feet deep.

The little Larji bungalow, which, with a few huts, represents the dignity of the place, stands near the bank of the Sainj river, some half a mile above its junction with the Beás, and is shut in by high hills all round, so that one gets but little idea of its situation at the junction of the three rivers. The great Beás creeps in almost unnoticed through the narrow gap in the high surrounding cliffs that is scarcely to be noticed on the right hand side of the accompanying photograph. The great gorge through which the Beás escapes from Kulu, and which prevents all access up its valley from below, is seen in the middle of the picture. We walked down to the actual junction of the rivers, and could from there realise the stupendous heights on either side, which enclose the narrow pass, and afford no place for life except to the solitary cormorant sitting on his rock watching the pool, or to the swift night flights of the countless flocks of wild-fowl on their autumn and spring journeys to and from the plains below.

The bridge at Larji is a very good specimen of the sangha bridge, made by the natives all through the Northern Himalayas. The principle of the cantilever, or bracket, is one of the oldest as well as the newest as applied to bridge construction, the brackets sticking out from each bank in the sangha bridge, being in reality but the half of one of the great Forth Bridge diamond-shaped cantilevers. The brackets in the sangha bridges are formed by building three, four, or even five tiers of deodar logs into a solid masonry abutment, where, for greater strength, the courses of stone are tied together with wooden beams. As will be seen, the greater part of the masonry is resting on the top of the deodar logs, which penetrate almost as far into the buttress as they pro-

THE SAINJ RIVER AT LARJI

ject. This mass of masonry is simply the weight to counterbalance the corresponding pressure on the point of the bracket of the actual bridge itself, which is formed by joining the extremities of the brackets with several long deodar logs, on which the decking is laid. To gain strength, it is the thin end of the log that is buried, leaving thus a greater thickness of wood for the fulcrum of the lever, on which the weight naturally falls. These bridges, everywhere met with, are excellent examples of a good design well carried out, and in most cases they are very well built by the natives, who have all the necessary materials at hand.

We spent the day lazily, strolling up the narrow Sainj valley on a wretched apology for a path in the morning, and in the afternoon making the cliffs around re-echo with our rifles as we tried to disturb some cormorants fishing in the river some five hundred yards below us. As fishermen, we always considered these birds legitimate prey, ever since we cut open one that we had shot, and found his crop and stomach literally full of fish of the smallest kind.

We had now finished our downhill, since the next march was to take us up the Beás into Kulu proper; and a most uninteresting march it turned out to be. The necessary kulis arrived in the morning, and soon the long caravan was winding up the steep hill opposite, on the path which was to take us round into the Beás valley high above the river cliffs. As Larji is 3100 feet above the sea, and Bajáora, at the end of the twelve miles' march, only 500 feet higher, the road continues the whole way at a dull level along the monotonous slope of brown winter grass. Not a tree is to be seen on this sunny western-facing slope, nor, for some reason, are any signs of inhabitants to be met with, though on the other side of the river, which is, as far as Bajáora, a part of Mandi State, villages and cultivation stand dotted amongst the trees which there find moisture enough to subsist. These great bare slopes of the Himalayas must look vastly different in June and July, when the summer rains have banished the brown in favour of a brilliant clothing of green. St.G. and I varied the monotony of the march by making a deep descent to the river below us, in pursuit of a flock of duck that were idly resting, after their long night flight, on the waters of a green pool. Nainu and Raganáthu were sent to do the driving, and we posted ourselves in the most advantageous positions; but, needless to say, after circling in a tantalising fashion round our heads just out of shot, they took their course straight down stream and were soon lost to view.

About half-way along this march the road crosses to the other bank of the Beás on a fine sangha bridge of 150 feet span, and then continues along the flat cultivated valley-bed as far as Bajáora. Many signs of the hotter climate were everywhere visible, some of the villages being more like the wattle, daub, and thatch-roofed huts of the plains, while the rich golden crops of standing maize took the place of the millet we had met on higher ground.

Bajáora, indeed, has quite a civilised look in its wide open valley. Besides the bungalow, a well-built house belonging to Colonel Rennick stands on the knoll formerly occupied by an interesting old fort, from which a beautiful view of the richly cultivated ground is seen stretching across the river-bed to the steep high mountains rising opposite. Colonel Rennick's farm buildings, the regular rows of the tea bushes which are cultivated here on a small scale, the well-kept roads along which trees have grown into an avenue—all tend to give the place a very homely and cared-for appearance.

In spite of all these peaceful characteristics, Bajáora is celebrated everywhere as being a very lair of leopards. Indeed, the Bajáora leopard must be a regular source of income to many Indian editors, for his doings are weekly chronicled in detail in the columns of their papers, no doubt by some observant correspondent who has never been near the spot. I feel therefore that I should not be doing Bajáora justice if I did not repeat the lie that the bhísti told me the morning after our arrival. He vowed by all his gods that, as he went down into the ravine at dusk to fill his water-skin from the stream, he met an immense leopard in the path, which, he declared, was only driven off by repeated blows of his (the liar's) staff.

As a matter of fact, it is as easy for a leopard to conceal itself about Bajáora as anywhere else, for these animals can hide almost in a tuft of grass, and the many ravines running down here from the mountains behind no doubt encourage them to come and pick up a good meal off a stray dog, or any sheep that has not been securely housed for the night. But during a fortnight's stay at Bajáora later, in the course of many a walk home of an evening after a day's black partridge shooting, we never had the good fortune to become any better acquainted with "Mr. Spots," although we continued daily to read of his doings in the newspapers that were brought up to us from the plains below.

SILVER MIRROR-RING

## CHAPTER III

In consideration of the fact that November had already begun, we decided to push on at once to the higher ground, leaving the lower parts of the valley for a later visit. Our preparations were soon made, for we simply discarded everything that was not absolutely necessary. Delightful as it is to be surrounded by many camp comforts on low ground where transport is to be obtained without great difficulty, such paraphernalia become an impossible burden to the Sahib who directs, as well as to the kuli who carries, when anything like a beaten track is left.

We sat down therefore to overhaul our baggage. As every reformer is confronted with a mass of detail every particle of which seems of vital necessity to the machine, so each and every article of our baggage stared at us in mute amazement at the supposition that it of all things could be dispensed with, and our only safety lay in seizing several of the prominent necessaries and rushing off, leaving the remainder to be sat upon by our servants until our return. When all, however, is said and done, it is astonishing to find out how many "real necessities" there are, and, in spite of all cutting down of weights, it is scarcely possible for a traveller to march into the hills with less than ten kuli loads of baggage.[1] We thought, indeed, considering our bulky photographic and survey kit, that we were rather lucky to start out of Bajáora next morning with only twenty-five men between us. We took one

[1] See Appendix C.

tent for ourselves, one for the servants, of whom only Badúlla and Abdurrahmán, the two Mahomedans, accompanied us—one to cook, and the other to serve. Nainu and Raganáthu, of course, came as gun-bearers, and my camera was carried by the usual man.

We had decided to visit the Párbati valley, which is the main feeder of the Beás on its eastern side, the scenery of which St.G. had heard much praised. It is a *cul-de-sac*, but we hoped to vary our return by crossing the Malauna Pass, by which we would descend on to the upper waters of the Beás, and so return down the Kulu valley.

Wazíri Rupi, the silver country of the Wazírs, through which the Párbati flows, is so called from the silver mines in the valley, which from time to time have been worked, but which now do not repay the labour spent upon raising the ore to the surface. In area this district is almost exactly the same as its neighbour the Upper Beás valley; but owing to its wild and mountainous character, its population is only about a third of the other, which includes Sultánpur, the capital, in its 36,000 inhabitants. In 1840, Wazíri Rupi was given by the Sikhs as a grant to the ancestor of the present Rai of Kulu, by whom the revenues are still enjoyed, these amounting at the present time to roughly a rupee per head of its 12,000 inhabitants. Its chief interest, to the native mind at any rate, are the hot springs at Manikarn, about twenty-five miles up the Párbati river, which are visited annually by hundreds of pilgrims in expiation of their sins. While humbly, however, confessing our sins too, we were anxious also to push on beyond Manikarn, to get at last near the snows that we had so long admired from a distance.

We made rather a late start from Bajáora, not getting off until eleven o'clock, for the difficulties of any new arrangement are always very forcibly impressed on the native mind, and the change in the composition of our party caused prolonged anxiety to the jemadár and his underlings. It was quite a new experience to find ourselves in the flat and open valley at Bajáora, riding along the level path, well shaded with carefully tended trees, which winds through the cultivated fields. The harvest was in full swing; the rice fields had already been stripped of their crops, and in every village we passed could be heard the thud of the pole that crushed the grain from its husk. The tall maize still stood, awaiting the reaper's sickle, and affording shelter to the jackal startled by our approach. The midday sun was hot on our backs, and to escape the heat we cantered our ponies sharply along the two miles of road which leads up the valley to the bridge over the Beás, just at its junction with the Párbati.

The native's instinct for idling is excessively strong, and such an untoward incident in his day's journey as a bridge to be crossed is always an excellent excuse for a halt. The result is that the approaches of a bridge in India are always littered with the refuse of many a camp, piles of dirt line the road on either side, while the sanitary arrangements would, if judged by the smell, compete with any Venice canal at low tide on a hot summer day.

We did not draw bridle until we got well into the comparatively pure atmosphere on the bridge, where we paused to admire this marvellous structure—an iron suspension bridge, made with wire rope and rods brought out all the way from England, every bit of which must have been carried on men's or mules' backs one hundred miles at least through the mountains. Surely a magnificent example of the way not to do it, especially when the materials for the excellent native-made sangha lie all around on the spot. It is commonly known as Duff's Bridge, and the legend runs that a Mr. Duff, who formerly resided in the valley, on entering into his family inheritance in Scotland, wished to leave behind him some grateful token of his happy life amongst these people, and started this bridge to enable the yearly pilgrims to cross the troubled water in peace and safety. Needless to say, the bridge had not made much progress when Mr. Duff's grant was exhausted, and after a long delay the Government was forced to take up the work and finish it, at a sum fabulously beyond the original estimate.

However, ours was not to reason why, so we trotted on into the narrow gorge through which the Párbati flows almost unnoticed into the Beás, and experienced all the delight that one does in turning out of the hot and dusty Rhone valley into the narrow Vispthal, as we left the open Kulu valley behind us.

The path was good, though narrow, and well trodden by the bare feet of thousands of pilgrims. In places it has been blasted out of the face of the cliff, which left, indeed, but little spare room for the White Rat, who had grown unconscionably fat during his idle time at Jibbi. I have learnt to consider a road passable where there is width enough for the White Rat and one of my legs, but it is unpleasant at times to be called upon in addition to lean out over the precipice in order to avoid bumping my head against the projecting rock, under which the Rat, in the happiness of being only three feet high, complacently jogs. As one surveys the torrent below one on these occasions, one begins to wonder whether the sais has remembered to tighten the girths this morning, or whether that girth buckle which was sewn on at the last village is likely to hold out.

Little could be seen, for the mountains rose steep on either side as we wound along above the tumbling, tossing torrent, which bounded from rock to rock with all the activity of true alpine water. At about three o'clock the river seemed to bend more to the east, and as the valley opened out a little, this seemed to be the spot on our maps where we wished to camp. Another half-mile brought us to a small hamlet, where we hailed a villager, "O Budha, this village, what is its name?" "Sahib salám, Chong is its name." We consult our maps. "Why, Chong must be up on the hill behind us." "Yes, Protector of the Poor, Chong is on the hill above." "Then this must be Chani?" "It is, as the Presence says, Chani." "How, O man of little sense, can it be both Chong and Chani?" "The Sahib knows all things: it is, indeed, as he pleases." No wonder map-makers in this country have a difficulty in putting the right names to the villages!

We settled the matter by choosing a level spot under some fine old walnut trees, just above the torrent, and there sat down to await the arrival of the kulis, who were still far behind.

It is a mistake to outstrip your baggage in this way, for the discomfort of having no shelter when you arrive is great. We amused ourselves, however, lying on the ground and watching the troops of monkeys coming down the hill on the other side of the torrent to drink. Gambolling and springing from rock to rock, whole families made their way down to the water, the old grey-headed father screeching and showing his teeth at any young bachelor who was rude enough to approach the ladies of his retinue; the anxious mother, with her latest Benjamin absorbing all her care, as with fond arms he clung round her neck; the younger members of the family lagging behind to enjoy a game with their neighbours, or to make love to any one foolish enough to listen to them. Every movement betrayed their idle inconsequence. We could not resist the temptation to fire a rifle at a large rock on the top of which a number were sitting gazing at us with a monkey's senseless curiosity. As the bullet splashed against the rock such a scramble never was seen; family ties could not stand the strain of the instinct of self-preservation, and husband and wife, brother and sister, lover and lass, scattered in all directions at their best speed, only to halt after a few lightning springs and pour forth their angry chatter at being thus rudely disturbed. Truly the monkey occupies a contemptible place in the scale of animal creation. He is the incarnation of unfulfilled promises.

At last the kulis came up, and we were soon warming ourselves driving in the tent pegs, while Badúlla crouched over his three-stoned kitchen-range and tempted us with savoury odours. We slept well to the tune of the rushing waters, and rose next morning early, as we had a double march of fourteen miles to Manikarn before us. The keen morning air seemed fresher every step we took up the valley, when suddenly on turning a corner a glorious view burst upon us. There were our snows at last, soft and clear

LOOKING UP THE PARBATI VALLEY NEAR CHANI

under their morning veil, standing majestically at the end of the valley. The jagged peaks projecting from the glaciers seemed to us an enormous height, towering above huge cliffs of rock which rose out of the blue hollows before us. The long beams of the morning sun were just surmounting the high ridges on our right and streamed down the buttresses, making alternate bands of light and shade; while out of the deep dark gorge ahead of us rushed the bounding torrent, bringing news from the glaciers we so much wished to approach.

We continued up this beautiful valley all the morning, every step taking us nearer our longed-for snows. The path is excellent all the way to Manikarn, rising and falling in pleasing variety, but keeping on the whole not far above the bed of the torrent. Few villages are passed on the road, most of them being on the heights above, so that there is rather a wild and lonely feeling about this alpine valley. The forest, through which at times we made our way, bore traces of last year's fire in the many blackened stumps, and what is worse, in the poor young saplings standing scorched and gaunt, extinguishing all promise of future recovery. It is in this destruction of all the young growth that the forest fires do such incalculable damage, and surely the Government deserves the support of every provident man in its endeavour to preserve the forests for the benefit of future generations as well as the present. It is essentially a Government work to prevent the wanton destruction of its resources. The ignorant villager cannot be expected to look beyond his immediate selfish needs. His cattle need to graze in the forest, and he who tends them needs a fire to light his pipe. It is in gratifying such apparently natural wants as the above that the great havoc is caused. In the hot month of May, before the rains have begun, the sun blazes down day after day, scorching and withering everything under its burning touch. The earth, dried up under its influence, pours out during the night the heat it takes in during the day, until the surface of the ground is one vast tinder-box, and it only needs an ember from the shepherd's fire or the spark from the herd's pipe to fall upon the dry brown grass, for the consuming fire to burst into life. Many are the complaints of the interested and the short-sighted at the Government rules for closing absolutely the forests during those hot dry months, but no unprejudiced person can visit a Government forest, where these rules have been strictly enforced for the last ten or twelve years, without appreciating the enormous improvement that has taken place, especially in the young growth.

The majority of St.G.'s men were surveying the forest areas in Kulu with a view of supplying the Government with exact data upon which to base its decisions; and it is sincerely to be hoped that the Government will back up the forest officer in charge, in his endeavours to prevent the present inhabitants from destroying the wants of future generations in the gratification of their own.

At noon we reached the village of Pautla, which lies in the enclosed valley, just opposite to where the Malauna stream issues out of the narrow and inaccessible gorge which prevents access to that solitary village from this side. A way has been found indeed, along the cliffs, but it is so bad in many places, owing to there being scarcely any foothold on the narrow ledges on which the track is carried high above the torrent, that the shepherds themselves scarcely ever make use of it. Here we met Mr. Senior, one of St.G.'s assistants, who had just returned from the high ground at the head of the valley, and whose newly-drawn maps we examined with interest, for they naturally corrected in many respects the only other map of this part of the Himalayas that up to now had been in existence. These are the much-abused sheets of what is known as the "Indian Atlas," which, on a scale of four miles to the inch, cover the whole of the continent inclusive of the Himalayas.

This map has been compared, by certain recent explorers, with General Dufour's beautiful maps of Switzerland—needless to say, to the great detriment of the former. Such comparisons surely

SUNSET NEAR MANIKARN

display a misconception on the part of the critics, for the two maps were produced under totally different circumstances. Switzerland was accurately and carefully surveyed by a large staff of surveyors going with great patience over every inch of the ground. No money was spared to produce a highly finished and accurate representation of what is, after all, an infinitesimally small piece of country in comparison with the great Indian continent. The Indian sheets, on the other hand, were executed some forty or fifty years ago. As far as the Himalayas are concerned they could never have been intended for anything else than sketch maps, where, in one season, a single European surveyor was set to fill in the details of a vast number of square miles of mountainous country, a few of the chief peaks of which alone had been triangulated. Working in this hurried way, it was quite impossible even to visit many of the valleys delineated; the leading peaks only could be ascended by the surveyor, from which the country below was sketched in to the best of his ability. Another difficulty arose from the fact that the maps had to be sent home to England to be engraved, so that those to whom this important work was entrusted had absolutely no personal cognisance of the nature of the ground they were set to draw, while they were completely out of touch with the surveyors themselves, who alone could have helped them.

Under such difficulties as these, the wonder is that these maps are as good as they prove to be. They have done their duty for the last forty years, and if the modern traveller, as is only natural, wishes for a more detailed and expensive survey, surely he can ask for it without disparaging the men who, forty years ago, did the best they could with the little money at their command. The want of money, in map-making as in everything else, is the root of all evil, and any one who could devise a means by which the surveyor's work could be more speedily brought into the hands of the public, would deserve the thanks of the Government, as well as those of impatient travellers.

After a cup of tea with Mr. Senior we saw our baggage transferred to the shoulders of the new set of kulis (for the march from Chani ends here), and then pushed on up the narrow valley, which was too much enclosed on either side to give one any idea of the surrounding country. The snows that we had so much admired coming up the valley, we were told by Mr. Senior, were not the main range after all, but a spur running out from it, separating the Manikarn from the Malauna valley, and the highest peak of which, Papidarm, is just upon 18,000 feet.

Needless to say, the weather continued quite perfect, and the crisp alpine air, as we made our way up the gorge, blew with ever-refreshing sweetness in our faces. Just before reaching Manikarn the valley closes quite in, and the Párbati comes tumbling down the ravine in a series of beautiful falls, which send the spray in white clouds high into the air. A rough wooden bridge leads across to the right bank of the river here, and as soon as we got to the head of the gorge the quaint little cluster of brown houses and temples known as Manikarn burst suddenly into view. Wedged in on both sides by enormous precipitous hills, there is scarcely foundation room for the fifty or sixty houses that compose the village; nor are they left here in peace, for the roaring torrent disputes the possession of even this little narrow strip with them. A curious feature is the deep dark shadow cast all day long over the village by the immense heights opposite, a shadow that only disappears for a short hour at sunset, when the light streams straight up the narrow valley. As we approached the village a strange smell of sulphur everywhere filled the air, while the steam rose all about in clouds from the numberless boiling springs that here bubble out of the ground. A most curious and original little place altogether, and one well worthy of a visit even to those travellers who have no sins to wash away in its steaming pools.

We marched straight to the little bungalow—a long, low, white-washed building, innocent of windows, which stands within a few paces of the torrent; and soon were endeavouring to dispel some of the gloomy chill of the rooms by kindling the blazing logs on the

The Hot Springs

MANIKARN

hearth. Long before we had unpacked our kit and changed our things, the sun had set behind the high hills, and the sudden Eastern darkness had fallen like a pall upon the little mountain village. As we stepped out on to the verandah into the chill night air, the stars sparkled in all their brilliance along the narrow strip of black sky which forms the roof of this confined gorge, while the roar of the torrent immediately before us was so deafening that with difficulty could we hear each other speak. A strange mystery seemed to be floating in the air—the mystery of the respect paid by thousands of weary pilgrims to this sacred spot. How many poor creatures, before now, had made their long journey up here, perhaps from the farthermost part of the great continent, burdened with some great sorrow, and, though tired and footsore, yet lay down on this their first night in the happiness of having attained their goal, and in full and faithful hope of the blessings to be derived on the morrow from a bathe in the sacred water. The faint aromatic smell of the villagers' fires, wafted up upon the evening air, seemed like the incense to the shrine where countless wayfarers had, to the best of their simple ability, fulfilled the beautiful words, "Come unto me all ye that are weary and heavy laden, and I will give you rest."

The spirit of the place even penetrated to the phlegmatic Nainu, for as he prepared my bed he broke out, "Has the Sahib seen the water? It is so hot that even the hand cannot be held in it. Without doubt, Sahib, this is a very good place, for there is no need of buying wood with pice. Flour, rice, pulse, chupattis, all things can be cooked in this water, and there is no need of fire. To-morrow we will cook our food in the water that the Nág has made hot, but Rám Jas says that the water will not cook the food of Badúlla and Abdurrahmán, because they are Mussulmans. The place is indeed good for Hindu people, and surely the Sahib will be pleased to stay here the morrow."

It was well that we decided to wait here a day, for when the morrow came, the god-despised Badúlla and Abdurrahmán were the only servants to be found, so we ate our breakfast in peace, and then sallied out in search of adventures.

In the fresh morning air the steam from the hot springs rose everywhere in white clouds as we strolled along the bank of the torrent. The chief source seems to be at the lower end of the village, where the boiling water is conducted to various rough baths formed by digging square pits in the ground and banking them round with stones; but there are so many of these bubbling, boiling streams flowing down just here into the glacier torrent below, that it is difficult to find out how many separate springs there are. In the village itself there are several other sources, which feed the covered bath enjoyed by the women and the better classes; but the most sacred place seems to be just under a red flag close by the edge of the torrent, where only the higher castes are allowed to go.

Here we found some of our errant ones. Rám Jas, the Brahmin, who when clothed and in his right mind occupied the somewhat humble position of coat-carrier to us, "sat by the side of the bubbling water" in the centre of an admiring crowd. His raiment consisted of his black elf-locks hanging down his bare back and a small pocket-handkerchief where most needed. In his hands he held a book—upside down, for he could not read—in which he was so absorbed that the bystanders no doubt imagined him already half-way to heaven. A little farther on, Nainu and Anandi, also in the airiest of costumes, were crouching over a steaming pool, into which they had cast their little bags of rice, which was being cooked for their morning meal.

"O Nainua, how is the water this morning?" "Bará achchhá, Sahib, see how hot it is. Does the Sahib know where the hot water comes from? No, Sahib, the people here tell other words, that Párbati (the goddess) once did bathe here in the river with Mahadéo, and as she laid her earrings upon the bank, Nág (the serpent god) did come and steal them, carrying them to his home beneath the earth. Mahadéo was then very angry, and made

THE HOT SPRINGS AT MANIKARN

much complaint, until the gods also were angry, and with one accord threatened Nág unless he gave back the jewels. Then Nág snorted with rage, blowing the earrings out of his nostrils, where he had hidden them, with such force that they flew through the earth to Párbati again, and from the holes they made ever since the hot water has come. The words must be true, Sahib, for see here is one of the holes."

We walked on, looking for a good place from which to photograph the village; but so confined was the space that it was with great difficulty that we found a ledge to stand the camera on. We visited the covered baths on our way back through the village, and found them to be large enclosed sheds built over a square of steaming water. They were not altogether inviting, for in addition to the sulphur there was a strong human smell about them, which hung in the hot and heavy vapour that rose everywhere from the surface of the water. Everything was damp and clammy, dripping with the condensed steam, so that it was a relief to get into the fresh air again.

On returning to the bungalow, to our intense astonishment we met a stranger in our chaprassis' uniform, who salámed in a grave and reverent fashion. "Gracious heavens, it's the jemadár!" we exclaimed, unable to control our laughter. "O jemadár ji, what have you been doing to yourself?" But no answering smile came back from his grave face, for he was in sober earnest. "Sahib salám! The Presence remembers that a year ago my brother, the son of my mother, being very ill, died, and then in my grief I vowed that no knife should cut my hair or my beard until my sorrow should be past. Now, O Protector of the Poor, in this holy place I have laid my sorrow down, for I have bathed in the water, and will mourn no more for my brother who is dead." The jemadár had indeed transformed himself. Yesterday his thick black beard and moustache and his flowing hair gave him a rough unkempt look, hiding almost all his features; to-day he stood before us, with his head and face clean shaven, almost painful in his nakedness!

Poor old jemadár, he seemed in general to take life rather sadly, for he was given to very few words, and a smile scarcely ever passed his lips.

We came to the conclusion that if we stayed here much longer our servants would all turn into saints and fly away to a land where they would no longer have to serve the Sahib, so we gave orders that they were to be ready next morning for another march up the valley.

We heard from the neghi that the path beyond this would not admit of the ponies being taken; we therefore decided to leave them here with their saises, together with everything that we could possibly spare, so as to march as light as possible. We knew that we would be obliged to return to Manikarn and could then pick up all that we had left behind.

It was with great difficulty, however, that our six men tore themselves away next morning, seeming to consider us very heartless for not allowing them another day to idle here; but we were inexorable and insisted on their starting before us, with the fifteen kulis with whom the neghi had provided us.

Immediately on leaving Manikarn we scrambled over a small cliff which shuts the village in at its upper end, and descended again into the narrow valley, up which we continued for the whole day's march. It was quite a relief to get out of the little sunless village, buried in the shade of its immense cliff, and to find ourselves in this beautiful sunny valley. Here at last we had reached the true alpine scenery, and nothing in Nature could be more charming than this nine-mile march between Manikarn and Pulga. Here was the picturesque village standing on a knoll, surrounded by its terraced fields and shaded by a clump of magnificent deodars; here were the vast pine-woods sweeping down the steep mountain side into the very torrent rushing below; here could be seen the alps and rocky precipices above; while at the head of the valley, in the clear atmosphere, glistened the dazzling snow-fields never yet defiled by man's feet. An hour's walking brought us to Uchieh village, in the neighbourhood of which are the best silver mines in the valley, but these we had not time to visit; and then the path, which had laboriously climbed to this height, dropped again with great rapidity until it reached the torrent itself, which just had before seemed so far below.

The neghi, who had come with us, stopped here to superintend the rebuilding of a small timber bridge which had been swept away in the last melting of the snows. Some half a dozen men were very leisurely dragging the logs into their places, a somewhat heavy job, for they had no appliances of any kind to assist them. Except at this spot where the bridge was washed away, I think it would have been possible to have got our ponies along the road as far as Pulga. In one or two places, however, rocks overhang the path, which would prevent any large pony passing, but possibly these too might be successfully negotiated by removing the pony's saddle, to enable him to scrape underneath. But a pony would not be of any great assistance on this march, for the path so continuously rises and falls that very little of it could be done with any comfort on horseback. It is rather a tiring march, as a whole, on foot, for as the torrent continually flows through narrow gorges, the path with provoking regularity is forced to climb over them in a series of gigantic steeplechases. We passed continually large flocks of sheep and goats returning from their summer on the high alps whence the first falls of snow had driven

THE TAIL OF THE FLOCK

them. The sheep were not unlike the lop-eared Bergamesque animals that are met with so often in Southern Switzerland, and the shepherd who walked at the tail of the flock urging on his charges with sharp whistles, invariably had his bosom full of the latest additions to the herd who were as yet too young to brave the perils of a Kulu path.

About half-way another village is seen picturesquely hanging to the opposite mountain side, a cluster of brown chalets surrounded by terraced fields; but beyond this no habitations are seen until we reach Pulga, which is the highest village in the valley. A good hour's walk through a well-wooded ravine along the banks of the rushing torrent brought us at last to a more open space, where Pulga lies a few hundred feet up, on the left bank, surrounded by magnificent deodar forests. The glorious snows here burst upon us all round as we hurried across the sangha bridge, which, stepping from boulder to boulder, carries the path across the water up to the village above. We raced at our best speed up the steep path to catch the last of the setting sun, and as we reached the first houses, the immense snowy mass appeared at the head of the nála, just above us. It almost took one's breath away to see the great mountain towering so close, 11,000 feet above us, for up to now we had marched through such confined valleys that we had little idea of our near approach to the snows.

The sun had already, at half-past three, dropped behind the high ridge above the village, and threw a shadow over the picturesque wooden chalets and homely farms that made up the foreground; the dark pines rose in steep tiers on either side of the nála, forming a V, within whose arms rose the great white mountain, glistening and sparkling in the sun like a thousand diamonds. The whole shape and appearance of the scene recalled to us the Jungfrau from the lower Lauterbrunnen valley, except that here we were much closer to the snows.

We gazed for a long time at the great glaciers and pure snow-fields, every detail of which was sharply defined in the clear atmosphere, and watched the ever-lengthening shadows cast their

PULGA

purple veils across the white expanse. Then we went up through the village into the pine-woods, where the Forest Bungalow stands somewhat shut out from the beautiful views that surround it. The chowkidár brought the key of the well-built little house, and we were soon trying to make ourselves comfortable and keep out the cold by piling logs upon the hearth. It was an extremely chilly evening, for Pulga is 7200 feet above the sea and it was the middle of November, besides which the squirrels had filled the bungalow chimneys with their nests, so that the smoke poured in volumes out into the room. We tried in turn all the fire remedies that we had learnt in our youth, first stuffing wet handkerchiefs into our mouths, then as the tears streamed down our cheeks, lying upon the floor to get the clearer air, only to find that in this somewhat uncomfortable position the draught nearly blew our heads off. Finally we retired discomfited, and shivered on the verandah, while Badúlla carried out the smoking logs and with many anathemas threw them on the ground outside; and as soon as the atmosphere of the room regained something of its pristine purity and chilliness, we returned and sought to warm ourselves, internally at least, by swallowing some soup that Abdurrahmán now laid upon the table for our dinner.

We had sent for a man who was supposed to know the mountains about here from being the best hunter in the village, and after dinner a little dark thick-set fellow appeared, who answered to the name of Jakhi. He was dressed in the ordinary woollen pantaloons and blanket tunic of the country, and expressed himself willing to lead us wherever we wished. After a long conversation with him, in which he frequently stated his opinion that it was too late in the year to go on to the higher grounds, we agreed that he should take us up next day to the alp above the forest, from which point at any rate we would get a clear view of the surrounding snows.

We had the usual difficulty here in buying a sheep for our men, none of the well-to-do villagers caring to part with theirs, and it was only on our reminding the neghi that he was bound to supply the required animal in return for our rupees, that a miserable specimen was produced for our inspection. A primitive balance was then made by hanging a pole by its middle to the branch of a tree, from one end of which the sheep was suspended, while from the other, most happy-go-lucky weights were hung, in the form of large stones, which were said by the vendors without fear of contradiction, to be of the specified weights. These occasions are made great functions of; all the servants collecting in a circle, in the anticipation of getting a free meal, while the villagers, on their side, assemble to throw every difficulty in the way of a settlement of the bargain. Every one has his word to say as to the merits and demerits of the unfortunate beast which is the centre of attraction, the servants indeed having little scruple in looking the gift horse very narrowly in the mouth. We wished our people to have one good feed at any rate, before starting for the higher ground where the cold would be great; but it is, in reality, a doubtful benefit to give meat to natives. They are so unaccustomed to the digestion of it, that a sudden and somewhat liberal supply is apt to upset even the most robust of them; for when called upon next morning to exert themselves, they approach with downcast countenances, announcing to the Protector of the Poor that they have a pain in what, for want of a more polite phrase, we must call the Usual Place.

Next morning saw us start up into the forest with lighter hearts and lighter baggage, as we had again reduced "the necessaries" in order to take as few kulis as possible on to the high ground; for it was settled that they should stay with us to fetch wood and water, and as we had no tent to offer them, they would have to make the best of it and sleep out in the open.

Jakhi led the way up a narrow path, zigzagging through the splendid trees, and ever mounting higher and higher. The morning was a heavenly one, with rather a keener and drier feeling in the air than is usual in Switzerland at these heights, and perhaps owing to the rarity of the atmosphere, the sun beat somewhat fiercely down on us whenever we crossed an open glade. Our men were in excellent spirits, the hardy villagers making light of their somewhat heavy burdens as they stepped from rock to rock with their grass-shod feet, or mounted steadily up the more slippery pine-needle-strewn forest path, and frequently the forest resounded with their merry laughter. We saw but little all the morning, for the trees shut out all distant views, but by the lie of the ground we made out that Jakhi was taking us up the steep ridge that forms the left bank of the Pulga nála.

After about two hours' steady ascent, we halted to examine some fresh tracks of bears which had evidently been digging there that morning. The Himalayan black bear, so well known by the white crescent on his chest, though a night feeder, is frequently to be met with in the daytime, especially in November, when he is searching the forests for acorns, which, with the wild raspberries and any summer fruit, form his chief vegetable food.

We told the kulis, therefore, to continue quietly up the ridge, making as little noise as possible, while we, taking our rifles, followed Jakhi down into the ravine up which we went, in the hopes of coming across any bear that the kulis above might have disturbed. Fortune, however, did not favour us, and after a hard scramble we emerged out of the upper limit of the forest on to a brown knoll; and there straight opposite us, not a mile away across a ravine, stood the great snowy mass with its hanging glaciers pouring like waterfalls from the icy basins above.

We almost shouted for joy as we rushed to the top of the knoll, for here we were indeed amongst the snows at last; and it did not take us long to decide to camp on this spot, at any rate for the night, at this height of 10,200 feet, for the forest was only half a mile below us, from which the kulis could get as much wood as they liked, while Jakhi knew of a spring that was not frozen down in the ravine below us.

Nothing could exceed the beauty of the scene around us. The

snow-covered ridges came down to within a few hundred feet above us. The whole of an immense snow mountain rose to a height of 18,000 feet just across the head of the Pulga nála in our front. Below us was the blue depth of the Párbati valley, at the head of which stood a great rocky cone, marked on the map as $M_4$ 19,000 feet. On the opposite side of the Párbati, facing us like a great wall, were the buttresses of Papidarm, whose jagged peaks rose in fantastic shapes out of the upper snow slopes which were supported in turn by the cliffs underneath.

Long before we had drunk our fill of this glorious amphitheatre, the men had pitched our tents and the kulis were bringing up dry logs from the forest below in preparation for the coming night; for as soon as the sun dropped over the ridge above, we knew that we should be dependent on the fire for any warmth in the place. We spent the short remaining daylight in the photographer's unfailing resource of overhauling our kit and seeing that all was in order, for it is only by continual attention to these details that the many unforeseen dangers to the negatives can be with certainty avoided.

Night closed in with wonderful rapidity, and after our evening meal we strolled out, away from the glare of the camp fire before our tent, to try and impress the position we were in on our feeble memories. Wrapped as we were in our sheepskin coats, the marvellous stillness of the air prevented us from feeling any cold at all. Everything around was full of the mystery of night. Our great white mass of eternal snow, though scarcely visible in the bright starlight, stood like a giant above us, seeming to crush us into insignificance by the vastness of his ghostly presence. The distant roar of the many torrents, set free from his glaciers by the day's hot sun, rose up from the ravine below out of the intense stillness. It was difficult, when standing here surrounded by the whole majesty of Nature in the heart of the Himalayas, seemingly so far removed from all earthly surroundings, to realise that we still held in our hands a line that bound us to the hurrying and

FROM THE RIDGE ABOVE OUR CAMP (11, 200 ft)

bustling civilisation, with all the narrowness and littlenesses which form so great a part of modern life.

We turned to walk down to our men, who were gathered round an immense fire of their own, and whose animated discussion on the price of flour showed that, in spite of a square meal off the Pulga sheep, all was yet well. With true Christian charity, we had stripped ourselves of any garments that we could spare for the benefit of our servants, whose wardrobe is necessarily somewhat scanty. My contribution was a pair of woollen stockings to Nainu, and to Madho, the old camera-carrier, a flannel shirt. Never was virtue more its own reward, for Madho ever after wore the garment in native fashion, with the tails hanging down outside his pyjamas, and as my name was emblazoned on these extremities, I continually felt the same pride that fills the Mayor of Little Peddlington, who, in erecting a statue in his market-place to the Queen, has added his own name beneath that of Her Gracious Majesty.

We slept soundly that night in spite of the extreme cold, which froze the milk we had brought up into a solid mass, and which covered the ground with glistening hoar-frost; but it was a long time before the servants thawed enough to start their usual occupations next morning.

Natives are frequently abused for their inability to stand cold, but often little allowance is made for the very scanty provision of warm clothing that they possess. A woollen tunic and a woollen pair of pyjamas, with a single blanket, are considered ample for a servant, when the master is glad of all the thick clothes he possesses, with the addition of his warm bedding at night. The kulis after all had the best of it, for they had all retired to a shepherd's cave in the rocks below for the night, the entrance to which they closed by a huge fire, which, if it did nothing else, must have covered them with a layer of smoke sufficient to keep out any possible cold.

We left the camp standing that day, while Jakhi took us for

an expedition up a ridge which stood out against the sky-line above us. It was with great difficulty that we could make our way up in places, for the ground was at a very steep angle, and the fresh-fallen snow had thawed during the day only to freeze again into a smooth surface of ice. On such ground as this the "steigeisen," which can at once be fixed on to the heels of one's boots, and which are common in Tirol, would have been invaluable.

The views all round were most extensive and magnificent, every detail, even at an immense distance, being clearly defined in the pure atmosphere. We made rather poor progress over the bad ground, and as we saw no hopes of getting a more extended view by mounting higher, we turned, after reaching a height of 11,800 feet by our aneroid. In descending we took another way, down into a nála, where, in the rhododendron scrub, St.G. had a long shot at a musk-deer. It was a source of continual regret to me not to be on this high ground in the early summer, when all the alpine flowers carpet the ground in such profusion. The rhododendrons here were the large broad-leaved kind, the back of whose leaves are of red-brown velvet. They grow in bushes about as high as one stands, in great masses on the mountain side above the level of the forests, and in the spring-time it must indeed be a splendid sight. Unlike the common rhododendron which grows in England, and which covers the lower Himalayas with forest trees, these bushes that grow on the higher ground have much larger and more single bell-shaped flowers, almost of the consistency of wax. Jakhi told us they grew here both in white and red varieties.

It is difficult to say which time of year would be the best for a tour in the Himalayas. In the spring the weather is very uncertain, snow still falling at times on the higher ground. In early summer all the flowers are to be found, but no distant views are to be seen on account of the great haze which spreads up from the hot plains below and envelops everything. Then come the rainy months of June, July, and August, and it is not until September that the weather settles down to its exquisite and uniform serenity. So that perhaps September and October may be considered the best months; but, alas! the flowers have by this time all gone, and it is then too late for any expeditions which entail any prolonged stay near the higher glaciers.

We got back to camp in the afternoon, and were glad to throw ourselves on our beds and have recourse to art, in the shape of a solitary novel that we had brought with us, after our long day with Nature.

Next morning, as there was nothing further to be done, we ran down through the forest, and were at Pulga again by lunch-time. We had had it in our minds to continue up the uninhabited valley for another march, to an alp called Thakur Tua, at the junction of the Ratti Roni and Panda Sao nálas, which form the head waters of the Párbati where they issue from the glaciers; Jakhi was also anxious to take us for a march up the Tóse nála, which joins the Párbati opposite Pulga, to a grazing ground called Samsi, at the foot of the Tóse Nál glacier, where he promised us ibex. But while we were pondering over these alternatives, a message arrived which altered all our plans, as it entailed St.G.'s presence, in connection with his work, in the Kulu valley. There was no help for it, so after settling with the neghi about kulis to take us back to Manikarn on the morrow, we strolled down to look round the village.

It needed only a single look to be struck by the well-to-do comfort of these highlanders. Well-built stone and wood houses, constructed of the splendid timber growing in the forest at their very doors, granaries full to overflowing with the harvest, ample yards into which the cattle are driven in the evening on their return from the day's grazing, were to be seen everywhere. Well-dressed, bonny-looking women leant over their balconies, or stopped their heavy labour of thrashing the grain to crack a joke with us, while their husbands passed in, carrying great loads of grass on their backs from the hills above. Children played about everywhere, or rather followed us in idle curiosity, in no way unlike their Western contemporaries. Everything betokened such ease and plenty in this lovely surrounding, with its fine climate, that we came to the conclusion that many worse places were to be found in the world than Pulga, the highest village in the Manikarn valley.

We had a delightful walk down the valley next day, only varied by an exciting hunt after a troop of tutriálas, or pine martens, that we observed drinking in the torrent below. The rapidity with which these little creatures can make their way uphill, leaping from rock to rock, is surprising. Their fur in winter is a beautiful black-brown on the back, with yellow verging to white under the belly, and if a sufficient quantity could be got, a very handsome rug might be formed by sewing them together. It is difficult to shoot them, however, in any great numbers, for, like all these animals, they roam more frequently at night; but there is no great difficulty in catching a sufficient quantity if traps are systematically set for the purpose.

That night I slept again in the steamy little rooms of the Manikarn bungalow, and next morning St.G. and I parted, he riding away down the valley, taking with him most of the servants and baggage and my pony, while I stayed behind, for I had made up my mind to cross the Rashól and Malauna Passes, and so descend into the Upper Kulu valley.

The day was spent in getting my things into a more portable shape, for two high passes had to be crossed, and my object was to have as little to carry as possible. My party consisted of myself, Nainu, and Madho, Badúlla to cook, and Anandi the Gurhwali chaprassi, whom St.G. kindly lent to me, and who was invaluable in superintending everything on the march. Carrying a tent for myself and a small one for the servants, I found I could not do with less than ten kulis, especially as their loads had to be considerably lightened for these hard marches. The neghi promised to send a man on to Rashól that afternoon, to warn them there

CRICKET AT MANIKARN

that men would be wanted to take me on to Malauna on the following day.

In the Manikarn bungalow there is a small brick-lined pit forming the bath-room, into which, by damming a little channel outside by means of some sods, the boiling stream can be conducted. That night I cleansed myself bodily and spiritually by descending into this Pool of Siloam, which Nainu had filled for me during the day. The water was still almost unbearably hot, and the whole proceeding was rather suggestive of snakes and toads as, by the dim light of a candle, I groped my way down the dark steps into the steamy, slimy pit. However, there is no doubt that, with the help of Hindu Providence and a good cake of soap, the Manikarn water is very efficacious in relieving one of superfluities of all kinds.

My surprise was unbounded in the course of my afternoon's stroll, when, on turning the corner of a chalet in this alpine village, I came upon a game of cricket in full swing! I could hardly believe my eyes. Yet there it was, with bats roughly cut from an old plank, the regulation three stumps of rather unorthodox lengths, and a ball made up of a hard lump of rag. It was the Manikarn school (I won't say "eleven," for I don't suppose there was that number of boys in the school altogether) spending their half-holiday in the enjoyment of the noble game. The ground, it is true, was not large, for the cliffs rose steep on one side and the torrent roared fiercely on the other; but a few square yards of level ground had been squeezed in between two chalets, and there the game proceeded with much vigour, one of the fielders spending most of his time on the shingle roofs, that always afforded a safe run from a well-placed hit. The game had, no doubt, been taught by some Assistant Commissioner to the teacher, and he, in coming up here to this out-of-the-way village, had brought it with him, to the great delight of the boys.

It is pleasant to notice the care that is given to stimulate such rational amusements for young India. In no country in the world do the boys stand more in need of the open manliness that is fostered by honourable competition in outdoor games, and I could not help wishing that the young Englishman who, at some time or other, started the game in Kulu, had been present; he would have been amply rewarded for the time and trouble he had given in sowing the seed, in the sight of it growing and flourishing up in this odd distant corner of the world.

Having found the sporting element of Manikarn thus gathered together, we extemporised a "gymkhana," and spent the remainder of the afternoon in races, long jumps, high jumps, with two-anna pieces as prizes. The hundred yards course was indeed not quite level, for it consisted of a race to bring me a leaf off a bush that grew some sixty yards up the steep cliff; but at the word "Jao!" they were all off. Grown men, lads, and urchins—up they went in less time than it takes me to write it, leaping from rock to rock like a herd of chamois, as nimble as cats; and as for their descent, there seemed only a cloud of dust and a shower of stones down the mountain side, out of which the eager winner darted forward and thrust the leaf into my hands amidst the shouts of the excited villagers.

I made an easy start next morning, for the march to Rashól village was no great one. The kulis were already off under Anandi's care when the servants and I started on the little path that leads down the narrow valley on the right bank of the Párbati to the village of Chilaul. Thus far it is a delightful walk of a couple of hours with varied ups and downs; now passing along terraced fields and again descending to the torrent's bank, from which we disturbed a fine otter in passing. I pulled up at Chilaul, and while eating my sandwiches, and resting preparatory to tackling the steep ascent to Rashól, which lies some 2500 feet straight above, Nainu brought word that a covey of grey partridges were feeding on one of the terraces near, so, taking my gun, I sent the men round to drive them towards where I posted myself, and soon the cliffs around were echoing with loud reports, which somewhat startled the village maidens, who had been unaware of my approach. The birds scattered, and I was lucky enough to get one out of the drive and to pick up another which happened to pitch in the ravine up which the path to Rashól took us.

Game was very plentiful here, for my toil up the steep and stony path was frequently interrupted by excursions after the black kallidge pheasant. There were evidently no village shikaris about here, since the birds, when pursued actively enough to make them rise at all, simply fluttered up into a bush out of arm's reach, and from there complacently surveyed the excited sportsman, as much as to say, "Look here, old fellow, play the game; you surely are not going to be such a cad as to touch me if I don't choose to run." With a good spaniel to flush the birds, an excellent day's sport might be got here, for there was plenty of game, and that without going any distance off the path to look for it.

After shooting a couple of brace for the pot, the servants seemed to think they had enough to carry, so we struggled on for another hour, until suddenly the little village appeared just above us, and in another fifteen minutes I was standing on a narrow terraced platform in front of two picturesquely carved wooden chalet temples. The good people had swept it clean for me, and soon had my tents pitched, and then I had time to look round.

As I had been coming up the steep climb with my face to the hill all the way, I had not taken much notice of what was behind me, but now as I stood on the little terrace in front of my tent, one step from which would have landed me far down into the ravine below, I could see far, far down beneath me a strip of the Párbati valley almost lost in the soft blue haze of the evening light; to the right was the bold wooded bluff that shut in the view on this side, while across the deep abyss rose a beautiful great mountain, the snow on which was growing pink and the shadows opal-coloured in the setting sun.

But it was not a time to admire scenery, for from every rock almost in the neighbourhood came the "chuck-chck-chck" of the cock chikór partridge, shouting defiance to his rival; so, stuffing my pockets full of cartridges and calling Nainu to bring the gun, I was soon scrambling up the steep mountain side in full pursuit of the many coveys. In spite of the exhaustion caused by steeplechasing over narrow terraced fields which cover the hillside here in six-foot steps, I had the best half-hour's sport with the chikór that I had anywhere in the Himalayas. The birds were plentiful and flew to no great distance, and all too soon the short twilight made us turn our steps back to the picturesque brown cluster of houses clinging to the steep hillside, where the lights of the evening fires had already begun to twinkle.

The neghi came to salám and to tell me that he would now return to Manikarn, as this was the end of his beat; and he introduced the lumbadár, who declared that the kulis would be ready next morning without fail, and that grass, milk, and wood were all at my service in plenty. The villagers in this quaint little place were especially civil and considerate, and I heard no objection made even to the servants, who, finding the god was spending a night out, had taken possession of one of his temples behind me, where they made themselves exceedingly at home with the large bundles of hay they found in the loft.

I knew I had a long day's work before me next day, but beyond the fact that I had first to go over the Rashól Pass and then down to the Malauna torrent and from there up to the village of that name, I could gather nothing from the lumbadár—who, however, confessed that the path was in rather a bad state, but declared that, hearing the day before that I was coming, he had sent a man at once to put it in order!

With a long march ahead of you, you can never make a mistake in starting too early, but, in spite of every effort, I found it impossible to get everything packed and started before half-past eight next morning. The tents are still wet with dew; breakfast has to be cooked, and the pots and pans litter the ground up to the last moment; the bed has to be taken to pieces, and that receptacle for all forgotten articles, the bedding-roll, has to be made up. All these things combine, and each adds its little delay, so that it was later than I wished when Anandi started with the kulis, and we followed them out of the little village of pleasant recollections. The lovely fresh morning put good heart into the men as they breasted the hill straight away, but I noticed that before half an hour was passed, all joking had ceased and they reserved their breath for the more serious work of getting their loads to the top of the pass. Indeed, the track was of the steepest; in places rough steps in the rock took us in a bee-line upwards, and in others, where it was too steep even for this, we had recourse to little zigzags, so short as to make one almost giddy with the continual turning. In this way we continued up the bare mountain side for two hours, until we got on to a little ridge which ran down from the pass itself, and where we halted a little to allow the kulis to come up. Anandi was having no light work in getting them along, for they could not pass a single projecting rock without giving way to the temptation of resting their back load upon it. From here we had another 1500 feet of the same steep angle, up which we made but slow progress.

It was now eleven o'clock, and the sun was streaming down in all its heat on our backs, not a particle of wind stirred the thin air, and, though we were still lower than 10,000 feet, I began to feel the effects of the rarefied atmosphere very much. Every few minutes I had to halt with beating heart, and gasp for breath. As long as no exertion was made no inconvenience whatever was felt, but the inability to continue any effort was very distressing. Judging by my own experience, this question of rarefied air does not depend altogether on the altitude but rather on the atmospheric conditions at the time being. The distress seems to be mostly occasioned by the absolute stillness and want of circulation in the attenuated air one breathes, combined with the intense fierceness of the sun, which meets with little resistance in the dryness of the atmosphere through which it passes. On the Malauna Pass, on the following day, where we were more than 2000 feet higher, we experienced no discomfort whatever, and I attributed this entirely to the strong fresh breeze that blew all that day in our faces.

There is no doubt that the difficulties arising out of the heat of the sun, combined with the extreme dryness and stillness of the air, will always have to be reckoned with in any ascents in the Higher Himalayas.

At last, however, in spite of the many halts, we reached the little gap in the sharp ridge which forms the pass at the height of 10,670 feet, and looked over into the deep Malauna valley into which we were going to descend. The view was limited by the high rocks of the ridge on which we stood, but looking back we could get an idea of the immense depth in the drop down into the Párbati valley from which we had come, while away above it stood the beautiful group of Pulga snows, sharp and clear, forming a long and jagged ridge opposite to us. I stayed only long enough to take some photographs, and then ran down after the kulis through the snow which lay thick on the ground on the farther and shady side of the mountain.

Some little way down we got our first view of the solitary Malauna village, which stands here cut off from all the world, and which is approachable only by the way we had come, or by descending from the summit of the Malauna Pass, that hangs 4000 feet almost perpendicularly above the clustering chalets. From where we stood we looked with interest at the great wall up which we would have to go on the morrow; and though the path itself cannot be seen in the photograph, it zigzags straight up the ravine, which may be observed lying in the shadow just to the right of the village, the pass itself being at the very top of the gully.

The kulis found it easier going down than up, and with the start they got while I was taking my photograph, kept well ahead of me as I ran down the little path through the pine forest, which,

MALAUNA VILLAGE FROM THE RASHÓL PASS

in 2500 feet of fall, brought us to a somewhat rickety wooden bridge that was here thrown across the torrent; seven hundred feet of steady rise then took us up to the village of Malauna itself.

I had been warned that I should find the Malauna folk quarrelsome, and as soon as I arrived, several individuals, one of whom turned out to be the neghi of the place himself, approached and addressed us in loud rough voices, in a language that none of us could understand, but by their gestures we made out that they did not wish us to enter their village, so to avoid trouble we followed their directions and endeavoured to find a level piece of ground large enough to pitch the tents on, above the houses.

There is something mysterious about this lonely little colony of human beings, for they know not themselves from whence they came, but buried here in this narrow valley, they keep themselves entirely aloof from their neighbours over the mountains. Though they dress much as do the other inhabitants of Kulu, they have quite a different type of face, somewhat Jewish in appearance, with a prominent nose and weak, narrow chin. Their language also is totally distinct, which is a proof of their almost complete isolation for some centuries, since it is inconceivable that they could have come from anywhere but from the plains below. They have, indeed, a tradition of the Emperor Akbár's kindness to them; but beyond this it is most difficult to learn anything of them, for they are most densely ignorant and incapable of giving information. They don't seem, however, to lack of this world's goods, for the houses are well built and there is an air of prosperity about the whole village and its surroundings.

Seeing that we had not come to give him any trouble, the somewhat evil-looking neghi became less surly, although our conversation was limited to shouts on his part and gesticulations on mine, and I went down with him to see the lower village, in which is an open space, surrounded by curiously carved chalet temples. In this square sat a crowd of men spinning wool with their hands, and shouting at each other with loud rough voices, which gave one the impression of ceaseless quarrelling. They would not let me go into the temples, and seemed to consider the whole of the square rather sacred, so I sent Nainu for the "picture box" and explained to the neghi as well as I could, by means of arm-waving, that I wished to immortalise him. He must have got some inkling as to my meaning, for he took up a position in the middle of the square in as stiff and unnatural a posture as the most ardent photographer could have wished for.

The temples were picturesque in design and covered with rough carving and pendent ornaments. It seems strange that so little is known of these queer people who have thus for so long lived out of the world.

I had told the servants to make no difficulties, but, except for the noisy shouting in the village which was kept up nearly all night, the people gave us no trouble and the night passed without any disturbance. I lay awake for a long time listening to a solitary jackal who wandered restlessly about uttering his mournful "pi-a-o" (for all the world like the mewing of a large cat); while the inevitable accompaniment of all these alpine villages could be heard in the ceaseless roar of the torrent far below, rising up through the still night air.

It was nearly nine o'clock next morning before the things were packed ready for the kulis, but we got away at last and soon settled down to a monotonous ascent of 4000 feet. Some idea of the scale on which everything is made in this country may be gathered from the fact that this 4000 feet was up one single straight ravine, which appeared from the Rashól Pass opposite simply to be a little scratch in the mountain side! Our progress was again slow, for the little stony track mounted as steep almost as the stones would lie, and even the kulis sat down frequently to rest. We pushed on steadily, however, and after the third hour had passed we knew we must be getting near the top of the nála. A cold wind swirled round us in a somewhat threatening manner, giving us the unusual feeling of unsettled weather; but on the whole we

THE VILLAGE TEMPLES AT MALAUNA

welcomed it, for it fanned our lungs, and took away a great deal of the breathlessness from which we had previously suffered.

Two or three snow slopes brought us at last to the top of the ridge, where, with great satisfaction at having accomplished our mounting, we halted to look round. No words can give an idea of the vastness of the panorama. It is so big that the individual mountains look dwarfed, and one longs for a little concentration. I put up the camera with the inevitable disappointment at the poorness of the result, for where the eye fails to take in a panorama there is but little chance of success for the lens.

Over the edge of the snow in front of us was the deep cleft at the bottom of which the Malauna torrent flowed 5000 feet below. Straight opposite, looking as if you could reach it with your arm, stood the immense buttress of Papidarm, over which we had come yesterday,[1] and beyond which lay the deep trench of the Párbati valley, with the Pulga snows in the far distance. Nearer, and to the left, are the jagged peaks of Papidarm itself (18,000 feet); while at the head of the Malauna valley lies the Malauna glacier, descending from a circle of snowy cones. Looking along the broken and rocky ridge on which we stood, we could see the great snowy domes of Deotiba, a giant who raises his head over 20,000 feet above the sea; while farther to the left, facing N.W., rose the innumerable snowy peaks of Bara Baghal, over which some ominous storm-clouds were collecting. The Kulu valley, between us and the Baghal Mountains, we could not see, for it lies some distance off, deeply embedded in the pine forests, which cover the hills below us on this side in a dense mass.

Standing here at this height of 12,200 feet, on what seemed but a little ridge in the surrounding hills, it was difficult to believe that we were not much below the height of the summit of the Jungfrau, and that if that beautiful mountain could have

[1] The Rashól Pass is the right-hand of the two little gaps in the middle ridge seen in the photograph from the Malauna Pass.

been dropped down here, it would scarcely have commanded notice in the vastness of the surrounding panorama.

The gusty wind was bitterly cold, and I packed up my photo kit in haste to follow the kulis, who had got a good start of us. I believe there is an easier track to the left along the ridge, but as it is somewhat longer, it is needless to say the kulis avoided it, and went straight down the mountain side. We had an extremely disagreeable hour until we got into the forest, for this northern side of the mountain was deep in snow, which, having melted somewhat in the hot sun, had again frozen into smooth sheets of ice, so that in places we were at a loss almost how to proceed. Not expecting ice, I had only my leather sandals on, which afforded little or no foothold on the slippery surface. How the kulis got down is to this day a marvel to me, for we never caught them up; but their grass-covered feet must have held well to the ice, for not one single man fell, in spite of the top-heavy burdens with which their backs were loaded.

I was in some anxiety about my precious camera, for old Madho, in spite of many years' wanderings in these mountains,[1] on several occasions involuntarily descended some of the slopes in a sitting position, much to the detriment of his only pair of nether garments. Nainu was really invaluable; he took off his shoes to give himself a better foothold, planted himself firmly at the worst places, and was able to give me a hand in crossing every awkward slope, or with the help of his alpenstock to lower me into a place of safety. We made our way into the head of a ravine where the rocks projected through the ice, and down which we were able to make somewhat better progress,[2] and I was not at all sorry to

[1] Madho was the only member of our party who had been on this ground before, having previously crossed this pass in company with Colonel Tanner of the Survey of India.

[2] Though I experienced no especial pain at the time, the roughness of this piece of the march must have been considerable, for my feet, which were hard with much walking, were much knocked about, and I subsequently lost the nails of both great toes.

FROM THE SUMMIT OF THE MALAUNA PASS. 12.200 Ft

step at last on to the hard frozen ground, where we could relieve our cramped limbs by stepping out briskly.

We found a little track down the nála, and were soon following the stream in its descent through the forest. Nainu whiled away the long march of some nine miles down to Nagar with endless stories of the difficulties he had encountered on the Baspa Pass and the wonders of the Nilung valley near Gangutri, the source of the Ganges, whither he had once been sent in search of butterflies. The mind of a hill man is an extremely undeveloped article, but one cannot help being struck by Nature's eternal law of the fitness of things, and the suitability of these simple children of hers to the peaceful though limited conditions under which they are born and bred.

Pulig village was the first sign of life we came to, and then another long tramp down through the forest brought us to the wooden chalets of Ramsu, where for the first time we began to see the wide Kulu valley opening below us. We could not wait here long, however, for it was already five o'clock, and we had still a good hour's walk before we got down to Nagar. Evening closed in apace, and it was quite dark by the time we groped our way down the stony path on to the little terrace above the pointed temple, where I found camp already pitched.

"Salám, Sahib; it is well that the Sahib has arrived," came a soft voice out of the dark. "O Anandi, is it you? How long have you been here?" "It is half an hour since the Presence's servants arrived. All things have come without loss, and the kulis are ready, Sahib." And while Anandi held the lantern, I walked along the line of shaggy-haired kulis, and presented each with the hardly earned eight annas, which sent him away happy after his nine hours' march over a pass 12,200 feet high.

I was too tired to do anything but pull off my clothes and my chapplis, and tumble into the bed I found ready in my tent, from which point of vantage I reflected on the happiness of having accomplished a long tramp, and the pleasing prospect of again sitting on the White Rat's back, until good Badúlla brought in his savoury messes, and best of all a bundle of letters which Tuarsu, the sais, had brought up the valley from the post-office for me.

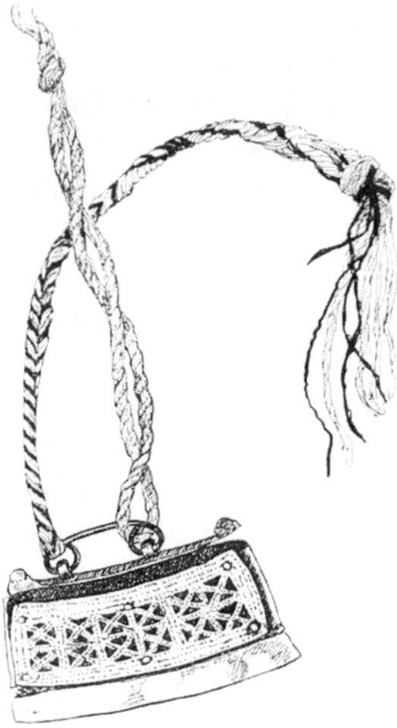

KULU CHAKMAK OR STRIKE-LIGHT

Nagar Castle

THE UPPER KULU VALLEY AT NAGAR

# CHAPTER IV

The Upper Beás valley, into which we had now descended, and which is known as Kulu proper, is at Nagar perhaps a mile wide; and seen from the village, which stands at a fair height up on the hillside, the beautiful cultivated slopes stretch in great profusion as far as the eye can reach, both up and down the valley. Pretty villages are dotted here and there amidst these fields, and the dark pine-woods sweep in long lines down the steep mountain sides, forming bays and promontories in this sea of plenty.

It is indeed a land flowing with milk and honey, and it looked none the less inviting to us after our stay in the wilder mountains. Nagar itself, as well as its surroundings, bears the stamp of prosperity, and its situation at the foot of the pine-woods, overlooking the valley below, shows at any rate great taste on the part of the old Rajas who used it as their capital some three hundred years ago. At present it is but one of the many prosperous villages of the valley, the study of which always presents a scene of homely peace and comfort.

The Kulu zamindár's house is generally solidly built of grey dressed stone in the shape of a square, and is strengthened as well as relieved in colour by the brown wooden beams that tie every few courses together. A wooden balcony, running sometimes completely round the upper story, projects most picturesquely from the stone walls, and is often the subject of much skill and attention in its ornamentation, especially where in the better houses it is arched in by columns and panelled with elaborately designed wood-carving. It is here that the bright colours of the women's dresses are to be seen passing to and fro, as with a laugh they only half hide themselves from the stare of a stranger who stops to admire the scene. Great flat stones cover the roof, on which may be seen the golden heaps of drying corn, or a profusion of millet almost smothering the whole in its warm embrace. Every available shelter is piled up with the fruits of the year, while the bees fly in and out of the holes left for them in the walls with a busy hum.

Nor are the inhabitants of the house themselves less occupied. The men have gone out in the morning, in charge of the little black oxen, and are cultivating the terraced fields on the upland above their home, with the primitive wooden plough that they have carried up upon their shoulders. On the flat terrace beside the house two laughing girls, half-smothered in the mass of straw, are pounding with heavy pole the hard-grained rice, to the accompaniment of a crooning song; while alongside their brother follows the patient bullocks, who circle round a rude mill, formed by an L-shaped beam, the short end of which revolves laboriously in a large hollow stone, expressing the oil from the kernels of the peaches and apricots which he from time to time throws in. Children, the same all the world over, play about, getting in every one's way, until recalled by their mother, who stops her household work on the balcony above to lean over and rebuke them.

As the day draws on, the other members of the household return, driving, perhaps, the cattle from the alps above, or returning from the dark forest with loads of firewood piled in kiltas[1] on their backs, a task which the strong, well-built girls are fully able to share with the men. The whole is as bright and prosperous a scene of peasant life as one could wish to see, and though no doubt he too, like most of us, is troubled with the cares of life, yet we could not help

[1] These kiltas are in shape exactly like the baskets carried by the Swiss on their backs.

A ZAMINDÁR'S HOUSE AT NAGAR

thinking that, outwardly at any rate, the Kulu zamindár must be reckoned as one whom the gods delight to please.

The spot where my camp was pitched was on the little terrace in front of the conical-roofed temple, round which, forming a sort of amphitheatre, the terraced ground rose in steep steps to the fine deodar forest which surrounded us. To-day the place was cheerless enough, for the Bara Baghal storm had burst upon us during the night, driving in wintry gusts the mist-laden atmosphere up from the valley below, and saturating our tents with the pitiless rain.

It is on this very spot, however, that quite a different scene is enacted on a May morning, when the sound of the distant drumming, accompanied by ear-piercing trumpet blasts, announces the approach of the village gods to take part in the Nagar mela, or fair; for to-day is a Kulu holiday, and every one in the neighbourhood, from hill above and vale beneath, must don their best clothes and hie together to the festival. On every path are to be met brightly dressed groups of women in all colours, and men gaily adorned with flowers, hastening to the rendezvous, for the mela is dear to the Kulu heart. As the morning wears on the crowd increases about the little temple, for religion is mixed up with their pleasure, and it is a field-day for the Brahmins, who sit at the receipt of custom, impressing with no great difficulty the ignorant peasants with their sanctity and virtue. Suddenly amidst the hubbub is heard a renewed tomtoming as, headed by several men blowing discordant blasts upon great curved trumpets, another village contingent arrives, escorting its deity. The latter arrangement consists in a sort of chair carried on the shoulders of two men by long poles. The chair is covered with trappings of all sorts, on which are arranged many silver masks of rough workmanship, the whole being much bedecked with flowers. There is apparently a fashion in gods as well as in most things, for there is little variety to be seen in the appearance of any of these village patrons, except that a richer village may perhaps afford a gold mask or two, and express its religious fervour by an additional clamour of trumpets and drums.

The god, having been carried round through the admiring crowd, is then unceremoniously relegated to a back seat, and deposited in the row of fellow-deities who have also come here to grace the day with their presence, but who now command but little reverence or respect.

By midday the scene is most brilliant, and the noise of the drumming and piping deafening. The little arena is crowded with men standing in long lines dancing a sort of slow shuffle to the encouraging strains of the musicians. Aimlessly and without any seeming purpose, like all native dances, they keep it up by the hour—to the great interest, however, of the thronging bystanders. A booth or two have been run up, and cover the stalls of sweetmeats, which find eager buyers in the women and children. Even the Rai of Kulu himself has come up from Sultánpur, and under his immense umbrella sits hour after hour, a willing spectator.

But by far the greatest attraction are the rows upon rows of women who sit round upon the terraces, filling the little amphitheatre with a blaze of bright colouring, right up even to the dark shade of the pine forests above. Dressed in all colours, they wear the soft woollen blanket dress, in which white and red, grey and brown, with a great fondness for checks, largely predominate. Bright-coloured handkerchiefs are tightly tied round their heads, for to-day every one has put on her cleanest and her best, and fully intends to captivate all those who come within her reach. The amount of jewelry worn is simply amazing, and is no small proof of the very easy circumstances in which these peasants must live. Scarcely a single woman is to be seen without her silver necklace and her large hooped earrings; while the olive-brown skins and handsome faces of most of them are almost hidden under the heavy weight of silver, with which are mingled strings of red coral and frequently a green turquoise or two. Taken as a whole, the women are very good-looking, with clean-cut features and large eyes, and when seen thus dressed out in their holiday attire, the close-fitting blanket dress well setting off their finely-shaped figures, no brighter picture could be desired.

NAGAR FAIR.

A little native dancing goes a long way with us Westerns, and one cannot but wonder at the idle way the women sit still the whole day long, looking down upon the monotonous evolutions of the men below. But they see and are seen, and the consciousness of the part they play in contributing to so pretty a picture, no doubt makes the day a happy one to them.

After all they are but intensely ignorant children, and having no idea of any intellectual pleasures, the mela is the only form of social gathering that relieves them from the daily drudgery in the fields, or the dull routine of work at home, and as such it is welcome to all.

It would be well, however, if the melas ended at sundown, for by this time the frequent drafts of *lugri,* a wretched spirit which is distilled from rice, have inflamed the passions of the men, and with the increasing excitement, the fun grows boisterous. Torches are lit, and by their glare the revel is continued far into the night, with all the evil consequences of free intercourse of the sexes under such circumstances. Dazzled by the light, the noise, the music, it can cause but little surprise that the women, with no home ties as we know them to bind them, wander off with their lovers into the dark forest, where, in the warm night, the tall deodars spread their sheltering branches over them.

Much has been said in condemnation of these gatherings, and rightly so, for the evil results that arise from their abuse are as bad for the men as for the women; but it is difficult to see where the remedy is to come from as long as the present ignorance and weakness of moral restraint continue to exist in the valley, the causes of which no doubt lie in the want of consideration given to the marriage tie.

Boys and girls are sometimes betrothed in their youth, but as a rule it is not until he is grown up that a man begins to look round in search of a wife. He is not then troubled by any romantic feelings in his choice, but goes straight to where he considers he can get the best article for the money, and offers the father of the fair one a sum to compensate him for the loss of the labour of his daughter; most likely the girl's consent is not asked, but she no doubt views the case philosophically, seeing that she must work for somebody; a few presents are given by the bridegroom to the bride's relations, and the affair is then completed by the girl following her husband to his cottage.

Of course in cases of this kind married happiness must be a lottery, and it is indeed not looked for, for the remedies are always at hand. The man knows that he can carry on his intrigues with any other woman he prefers, without any loss to himself; and his wife, brought up in a home with the example of her parents' infidelity constantly before her eyes, sees little harm in choosing a lover from the many that offer, knowing full well that the last person to object will be her husband, for should she leave him, he would only be obliged to spend some thirty rupees in buying another wife to supply her place, while she, on the other hand, would be welcomed back by her family, as an additional worker in the ancestral fields.

In Kuram, as will be seen later, they manage these things better, for there they supplement women's fidelity by a lock and key, and conjugal rights are insisted upon at the point of the sword; but here in Kulu, it must be admitted, things are rather at a deadlock, for in the absence of education and any moral fibre, they have not even the courage to fight for the possession of their wives—a form of virile energy which was considered legitimate and praiseworthy even in England, before the emancipation of women taught us the error of our ways.

I was lucky indeed to get over the Malauna Pass on the day I did, for the weather broke with the heavy storm, and I might have been imprisoned at Malauna by the deep snow that now fell on all the mountains round, the cold from which made us realise that we were still nearly 6000 feet above the sea.

The days, however, were passed pleasantly enough in exploring the fertile valley of the Beás, where the busy winter cultivation was

A KULU LADY

in full swing. Fruits of all kind grow here to such perfection that several Europeans who have settled in the valley have seriously turned their attention to growing it for the Simla market. Apples, pears, peaches, apricots, quinces, all thrive and grow in a way that could not be believed had not one seen the trees; but in spite of this abundance of Nature, the cost of transport of the fruit on men's backs over the ten marches to Simla is almost prohibitive, especially as owing to the perishable nature of the crop it has all to be packed in double kiltas or baskets, between which hay is wedged in order to soften the blows that it receives at the hands of the rough kulis. A few tea gardens are still in existence, but for some reason or other they have not had the success that has attended the neighbouring Kangra plantations, and the area is not extending.

Nagar Castle, the residence of the Assistant Commissioner, which looks down upon this prosperous valley, is an interesting old block of grey stone buildings, quite unfortified, and having the appearance rather of a large, rambling, English country-house. It was probably built about the middle of the seventeenth century, and was used as the palace of the Rajas of that day, until they moved the capital to Sultánpur, when it fell, as most native buildings do, into disuse and disrepair. Now again it has become the seat of government (in a country where one man represents that authority), and its fine rooms have been modernised by the addition of glass windows and balconies.

It is an interesting old place, though of no great architectural pretensions, and its commanding situation overlooking the valley gives it a more imposing appearance than it perhaps deserves. I wandered through the old courtyards, now silent, wondering what it could have been like in the former days of the native court, when dark eyes looked down from the windows above, and the serai was crowded by the Raja's motley retinue. The glories of the East were, no doubt, never at any time to be found up here in the mountains, for they are only bred in the heavy air of the sun-stricken plains below, where the heat has dried up all effort, and where the weary eye is attracted only by a wanton blaze of colour.

The weather now became so wet and cold that I turned my steps down the valley and rode some twelve miles down to Sultánpur, the White Rat being a pleasant change after Shank's mare. It is a beautiful bit of road the whole way, passing through the rich cultivation that fills the wide bed of the open valley. About half-way the road crosses the Beás and continues along the flat river-bed beneath the shade of some of the finest alders I have ever seen, which quite equalled English elms in size. The villages lie mostly on the slopes of the hills above, so that comparatively few are seen in the day's march, but numerous colonies of Ladakhis are met with, encamped in their brown tents on the flat ground beside the river. These people come over the Rotang Pass in the autumn to trade, bringing borax and salt, and evidently find the banks of the Beás a more comfortable winter abode than their own lofty and inhospitable valleys.

As you ride up to a cluster of the dark widely-spreading tents, you are greeted by the loud barking of numerous sheep-dogs, whose evil looks and shaggy coats give them more the appearance of half-bred wolves. The noise brings the inhabitants to the doors of the tents, and you are welcomed with a smile that but scarcely conceals the unmitigated hideousness of its owner. The type is distinctly Chinese; the small sloping eyes peer out above the prominent cheek-bones, the thick lips, especially in the older women, hang in a coarse repulsive way, while the narrow chin gives the whole face a weak and irresolute appearance. But they are an easy-going, good-natured people, and manage very well to conceal their roughness under a certain instinct of hospitality which is not often found amongst natives who perhaps outwardly are more inviting. Some of the men wear their hair in pig-tails, but the straight black locks of the women, very much of the quality of horse hair, hang in an unkempt fashion over their greasy shoulders, a suggestive harbour for creeping things innumerable. They never wash: what more need be said?

There is no accounting for tastes, however, for on our approaching a moon-faced damsel whose features were so small as to be scarcely discernible in the dirt on her cheeks, Nainu was smitten with love at first sight, and whispered to me, "Sahib, these women are more beautiful than any we have yet seen, and this one is surely the fairest of all,"—from which I gathered the comforting assurance that Nainu and I at any rate would never be rivals.

NAINU'S FANCY

The only interesting thing that I could see about them was a red flush on the girls' cheeks, which showed even through the superimposed layer of mother earth, and the rough but artistic necklaces which some of the women wore. These consisted of strings of coral beads along which, at intervals of a couple of inches, were strung alternate lumps of amber and green turquoise of a size equal to a large walnut. Even at the risk of getting more than I bargained for, I tried to buy a necklace of this kind off one of Nainu's beauties; but no, she would not sell it, no, not for many rupees. When asked why, she also said that she could not replace the coral if she parted with this; so it would be well next time that one comes up here to bring a string or two in one's pocket wherewith to satisfy these dusky ladies.

The men, seeing there was money to be made, with a far keener eye to business than the Kulu folk, produced little bags of turquoises, very few of which, however, were without large flaws. In size they varied from one's little finger nail to somewhat larger than one's thumb nail, and being of a greeny blue in colour, they appeared to me far more beautiful than the sky-blue ones so common in Europe. I do not know where these turquoises come from, but evidently they must find them in the country north of the Himalayas, for few Ladakhi and Thibetan women are without them, wearing, as they do, on their heads a broad leather strap closely studded with them. The price asked for these stones seemed to me considerable, but possibly this was because the Sahib bought in person.

It was quite a new sensation to find myself nearing a town again, if indeed Sultánpur is big enough to bear the weight of so great a name; but as it is the capital of a country, and has a Raja, a palace, a paved alley and a bazár, I suppose we must give it its due. It is well situated on a spur of the hill between the Beás and the Sivbari stream which here joins in from the right, and is compactly built, though not surrounded by any walls. We rode up from the river-bed into the town, and passed down the narrow "High Street," which was lined with the little shops one sees all over India, and peopled by the enterprising Punjábi merchants, in whose hands all the trade of the valley lies. The paving was clean and well swept, though of course in the absence of all wheeled traffic the streets were extremely narrow. Once through the town, the wide bed of the Sivbari has to be crossed, and the farther bank mounted, on the top of which is a large, flat, grass-covered space known as the maidán or plain.

There is nothing these hill men admire so much as a maidán. They go to see it as we go to see a mountain, and loud were the servants' expressions of joy at the unusual sight of a quarter of a mile of flat grass. We put up at the comfortable Dâk Bungalow, ordered dinner, walked to the post-office, bought stamps, and in general treated ourselves to all the luxuries of civilisation that Sultánpur could afford.

The palace of the Rai of Kulu is at the lower end of the town, and though large and rambling, has not many architectural features worth noticing. The Rai is now only the titular ruler of the country, but is still looked up to by the people as their lord and master.

STREET IN SULTÁNPUR

Great mourning was still hanging over Sultánpur, for a couple of years before the dread cholera had swept through the valley, carrying off hundreds of victims, including even one of the few Europeans that reside here. Terror reigned supreme, every one who could escape fled, and to make the disorganisation more complete, just about this time the Rai himself—an excellent and much-respected man—was carried off by small-pox.

I heard that the scene in the palace was most distressing as the poor man lay dying, for on these occasions the Brahmins exert to the full the power they have over their superstitious flock, and they seized the occasion to extract from the poor heart-broken Rani a fresh supply of gifts and donations to appease the angry god. After the Rai's death an event occurred which illustrates the dark sides of Oriental life. Among the Rai's household was an extremely pretty slave-girl of the Rani's, a child of only twelve, very gentle and modest by nature, who, being one of the younger ones of the household, always kept behind the Rani on all occasions. One morning she was found in one of the rooms lying dead, with her throat cut. It was given out that she had killed herself to do honour to her dead lord and master. Whether this was so or not will never be known, but it seems unlikely that so young a child should have committed such an act. It is much more probable that she was murdered by the Brahmins' orders, who hoped thereby to fan the religious devotion for self-immolation on the part of widows.

There is no doubt that the Government would not hesitate to hang any Brahmin if found guilty, to the first tree, but in cases of this kind it would be quite impossible to get evidence; the influence and power held by the priestly caste is so great, and the superstitious belief in their virtue so strong, that few natives could ever be got to believe a Brahmin guilty of such a crime, even though they saw it with their own eyes, much less would they accuse him of it openly, in a court of law.

The Government has quite enough to do without embarking on

such fruitless chases as these, and, wisely perhaps, abstains from the attempt, for stories from time to time come out in the courts of law which give an extraordinary picture of a native's capacity for bearing witness, a fact that he himself admirably expresses in his proverb: "Great is the justice of the white man—greater the power of a lie."

The Rai of Kulu, though not a ruler, holds a sort of hereditary dukedom, and with it as much of a court and appanage as his somewhat slender means will allow. He can only marry a girl with "royal" blood in her veins, and should he wish to do so he receives a proposal from the girl's father offering his daughter in marriage. In the case of a rich girl the father can command the Rai to come to his house with as many followers and attendants as he considers due to his daughter's position. On the Rai's approach with some two or three hundred followers he is received in great state, presents are exchanged, and the marriage is completed by a curious ceremony in which the bridegroom walks seven times round the bride.

It is the custom then for the Rani to be accompanied to her new home by a suite of several girls, the daughters of any villagers whom her father has influence enough to impress, though in some instances, if they are beautiful, he has to pay for them! These girls become a part of the Rai's household, and are from time to time supplemented by new purchases of the Rani's, whom she presents to her lord and master.

The late Rai had two Ranis, the elder and the younger, and some sixteen of these girls, and being a most kind and enlightened man, they were very well treated by him, often accompanying their lord (in closed conveyances) on the occasions of his visits to the Ganges, to bathe in the sacred water.

The Rani has a room of her own and her food is cooked for her by a Brahmin, while the girls all live happily together in a big upper room with glass windows on all sides, where they sleep at night on mattresses placed in rows along the walls, each being covered with a clean white durri on which the occupant's name is carefully embroidered! In the daytime the mattresses are rolled up and put away, and each girl cooks her own food in little rooms set aside for the purpose. The Rai's bed stands in the middle of the room, and he spends his time partly here and partly with the Ranis, without apparently exciting any jealousy in this well-ordered household.

The simplicity of the whole arrangement may be gathered from the fact that these "ladies-in-waiting" receive as pay each eighty pounds of grain a month, two pieces of homespun, and two pairs of shoes a year, while one anna (about a penny) is given her a month as pocket-money! The girls always dress in the homespun cloth of the country, the Ranis alone wearing the richer coloured muslins.

No doubt some people would urge that the position of these girls is nothing more nor less than slavery, but slavery is such a wide word and covers so many varied conditions of life, that it may be said to include almost every phase, since no one is quite his own master. In spite of the horror that this name implies to the average Briton, as a matter of fact in the East, domestic slavery only becomes an evil when those in subjection begin to desire to change their life, which they very rarely wish to do, for they accept dependence and subjection with no different feelings from those of a Western girl in a humble state of life, who is obliged to earn her living by service.

In considering the position of these girls who belong to the household of a Raja, it must be remembered that they acquire a status that has been held in honour ever since the days of Solomon. Their life of ease and comfort, with ample provision of food and clothing, their freedom from all care under the protection of an indulgent master, must be contrasted with the alternative offered to them by remaining at home. In the latter case they would make a *mariage de convenance*—in other words, be sold by their father for a few rupees to some young peasant. A life of toil and drudgery would then commence, in which "home life" as we know it, would most probably be embittered by the infidelity of the husband and by her own intrigues, with an old age of neglect and want as a consummation. Of the two, the latter picture presents quite as many features of slavery as the former, with the addition also of hard labour for life.

During my stay at Sultánpur I was anxious to get some of the silver jewelry worn by the women, and went frequently to the dark alleys in the town where the silversmiths sit in their little open shops at their work. As is the custom of the country, they had nothing ready made, in spite of the fact that almost every man,

SILVER PINS OF THE KULU DRESS (½ natural size)

let alone woman, in the streets wore a silver necklace of some sort. They had no specimens, and simply told me that if I left the rupees, they would make them into anything I desired. As no man or woman will sell the jewelry they possess, not even for double its value, having no need of money, it was impossible to get it otherwise than by having it made.

After some difficulty I was able to persuade a woman to lend me a pair of pretty earrings she was wearing, and having borrowed one of the rough enamelled necklaces of a man, I had these copied in the bazár; and by great good fortune one of the silversmiths happened to be making a chain ornament for some damsel's head, and this he willingly also repeated for me. Almost the best silver work I obtained, was that made for me by the carpenter in one of the villages; it showed great taste as well as fine execution, which

SULTÁNPUR FROM THE MAIDÁN

is somewhat rare in Kulu, for the best silversmiths are said to come from the neighbouring Kangra.

The chief fair, or mela, in Kulu is held annually on the Sultánpur maidán in October, and is the cause of assembly of a great number of people from the valley; and though it is a semi-religious holiday, at which over one hundred village gods have been known to be present, yet it is in a great measure the chief market of Kulu, the maidán being covered with booths, while large flocks of sheep are brought down from the mountain sides and find a ready sale to buyers, who drive them down to the plains for killing. But at this season of the year the great maidán is empty, save for the presence of a curious little temple on wheels which is used as the chariot of the god at the fairs, and is untenanted except by a stray bullock or pony, to whom it affords but a scanty grazing.

After a few days at Sultánpur, I started again and marched down the pleasant valley some ten miles to Bajáora, where I hoped to meet my brother again. The road follows the right bank of the Beás through the same cultivation as above the capital, though as we get lower down the flat valley-bed loses all its mountain character, and the greater heat is shown in the different appearance of the villages. The wooden chalets have disappeared, and the little thatched mud houses have replaced them, while a high screen of reeds surrounds each little compound, affording shade and privacy to the inmates. As we rode along through the fertile valley the regular beating of the tomtom and the minor wail of a pipe near a little hamlet drew us away from the path, and we came upon the autumn signs of plenty.

On a flat, clean-swept piece of ground lay a great heap of orange maize cobs, which were being thrashed by the vigorous strokes of four strong men in time to the strains afforded by some strolling musicians, who, in return for a few handfuls of grain, had come to encourage by voice and sound the labour of the day. The yellow crop stood close at hand, and was being cut down by some, others lopping off the cobs, while two old crones paced backwards and forwards carrying the severed heads to the ever-increasing heap. The little hamlet half buried in the heaps of straw, the rich valley stretching away to the uplands in the blaze of morning light, the golden grain, the measured beat in time to the wild strains of the musicians, whose red turbans threw in a dash of colour—all made up a picture of a harvest-home which needed no additional decoration.

These lucky peasants get two crops off their land a year, at the cost of but little manure; for the soil is good, and with the hot sun, tempered by frequent irrigation, there is little to check the promise of an abundant growth. The wheat is off the ground by June, but the soil is given no rest. Immediately the ploughing begins again, in preparation for the summer rice crop. The ground is made quite level, no rollers being used, but a rough flat board, on which a man stands to add his weight, is drawn by bullocks across the little field. When all is prepared, the water is let in upon the soft ground, which it thoroughly saturates, until it lies to a depth of about six inches on the top.

In the meantime the rice seed has been sown in little nurseries, and has quickly shot up, and is ready for transplanting. Thus far the men have done the work. Now is the women's turn.

The neighbours all are summoned and cheerfully come to render the annual service of mutual assistance, for which no pay is taken, though the owner provides them with their homely meals. Musicians are got together, and soon the rows of laughing girls with kilted skirts are standing up to their knees in mud and water, planting the bright green shoots in the soft ground at their feet. It must be hard labour, this stooping all day long in the hot sun, but the work goes on merrily to the weird sound of the music and the drum. The singers chant of love, always however in the minor key, to the running commentary of the light-hearted girls, who emphasise each point with many a joke upon their comely neighbours, while the bystanders lose no opportunity of throwing in a rough jest to raise the colour in the cheeks of the girls before them. Captain Harcourt in his Government report has given such a

HARVEST IN KULU. THRASHING MAIZE

picturesque, as well as exact, account of this scene that I cannot do better than conclude with his own words:—"Towards evening, when the workers are pretty well wet through, and one would think the toil (and very severe toil it is) would result in fatigue, the spirits of the party rise and the more playful members of the fair sex commence slyly throwing water on those near; this is returned, but usually in the wrong direction, and soon all are busily engaged in pelting each other, till struggles for supremacy occur, and, with a shout of laughter, the weakest go bodily into the water. Sometimes a more than usually audacious damsel advances to the bank, and before the spectators can be aware of her intentions, one of them, possibly the owner of the field, is dragged from his place of safety and water is poured down his neck, to the delight of the bystanders, who, however, have to be careful that their turn does not come next."

As I rode into Bajáora I met St.G., who had finished his work, and we were soon comfortably sitting on the verandah of the little bungalow discussing our past adventures and future plans. He told me that he was obliged to go back to Simla, and that he intended to return a different way from which we had come; that by crossing the Dolchi Pass into Mandi and going from thence to Bilaspur we should march through the lower hills, and so avoid the cold that was beginning to make itself felt. This route would take us back to Simla in ten marches, and, as it was new ground to me, I decided to accompany him.

We spent a fortnight at Bajáora, passing our time mostly in the pursuit of the black partridge, that at one time were to be found here in good numbers, but which are now rather shot out owing to the persistent harrying they have received from some of the residents in the valley.

Our preparations for our new march were soon made, and, having obtained some mules from Sultánpur, we started one morning, in rather uncertain weather, up the road that leads up the nála behind Bajáora.

The Englishman's hand had again been at work here, for while our kulis followed the bed of the ravine straight up to the pass, we spent some hours winding in and out of valleys and spurs on a gradient so gentle that even a well-laden four-wheeler might have trotted up it with ease. By degrees we rose and obtained a last look down into the Kulu valley, as we got into the rhododendron forest at Kandi, the top of the pass.

The rhododendrons here are some of the best in the Himalayas, and among the glorious blaze of crimson are also to be found many white ones. No more beautiful sight can be imagined than one of these rhododendron forests in April and May. The trees, some twenty-five to thirty feet high, when seen from above, are one mass of large crimson flower-balls, which, contrasted with the dark-green foliage, give the mountain side the appearance of one vast flower-bed. I looked in vain to see if I could find anything especial in the soil which made these trees grow to so fine a size, but in general the ground seemed rather poor in quality, and there was no trace of the sandy peat that we associate with these trees in our gardens.

We slept the night at the bungalow on the top of the pass—a cold and somewhat dreary night after the late rains. A few steps along the path next morning took us to the little gap which forms the Dolchi Pass, at the height of 6700 feet. A last glimpse is obtained here over the forest, of the Kulu valley lying far down below, above which rose up some fine snow-peaks, now wreathed in the clouds of a winter storm.

Looking forwards over Mandi, a most curious sight is seen in the endless, herring-boned, bare, red ridges, which rise in lines one above the other. As all these slopes face south-east, scarcely a tree is to be seen upon them, and the appearance of this sea of brown hills is truly monotonous. There was nothing to keep us here, so we ran down the long and winding road that took us to Kataula.

I can never pass a tomtom without an inclination to go and see what "devilment" is up, and as we descended to the low ground, the monotonous thud of the drums enticed me down to a hamlet,

VILLAGE GOD, KATAULA

where I found no one less than the village god himself out for an airing. The erection consisted of a sort of small round table surrounded by an orange and white striped drapery. Over the table was an umbrella-shaped canopy of red and white lappets, while on the table itself, embedded in many orange and white flowers of the jessamine kind, lay the silver mask of the deity with several other silver charms and tokens; a silver stick stood beside the table, and in front of it a little brasier with smoking incense. There is something maddening in the beating of these tomtoms, for the noise is always redoubled on the approach of any Sahib, as if to stir the god himself up to the realisation of the fact of the white man's arrival. Probably in this case some one had been ill in the cottage, and the visitation was made to drive out the evil one, for the Brahmin sat immovable (except for the instant that the lens cap was taken off!) beside the door, while the peasants squatted in a circle in simple adoration.

We got into Kataula somewhat early, and only regretted that we had not loitered on the way, for the bungalow that was to be our home for the night was, without exception, the most uninviting construction we had yet come across, and its situation on a bare, treeless flat is in keeping with its architectural beauties. Any boy of ten with a blunt axe and a wooden spade would, I am sure, have had no difficulty in turning out a more suitable human habitation.

Next day we continued down the stream we were on, until it reaches the Úl river, a large tributary of the Beás, which we crossed on a fine iron suspension bridge that the Raja of Mandi has had built.

The march is not an interesting one, but for variety we could not help being amused at the antics of an immense crowd of monkeys, who were being scared from the fields on the hillside across the river by the shouts of the angry villagers. Skipping down the steep bank, stopping now and again to watch if the pursuer was in real earnest, they escaped across the torrent below us, leaping from boulder to boulder in some magnificent bounds. The monkey is a spoilt child, for his semi-sacred character in the eyes of the natives causes his ravages amongst the crops to be patiently borne, while in towns where he cannot help himself, an excellent system of outdoor relief causes him to be supplied with the necessaries of life; and when in his abundance he becomes unbearably impertinent, the municipality of the great Government itself undertakes a raid upon the offenders and, catching them in numbers, deports them in a special train, personally conducted, to the jungles, where they are set free.

This troop, having escaped the shouts and the stones of the villagers by crossing the stream, sat down to amuse themselves, conscious that they were out of harm's way. They are quaint beasts. As we watched them, one old fellow, as if proud of his agility, ran up to the very top of a sapling and there, just like a child, swung himself backwards and forwards as if on a trapeze, while the crowd below gazed up at him in wondering admiration, encouraging him with ceaseless chatter. As soon as he got down, another, jealous of the applause, flew up the tree and repeated the performance, with even greater success, until a bullet from my little rifle flying just over his head caused him to spring at one bound into the arms of the astonished crowd below, and in a minute they had all disappeared up the rocks into the scrub.

From the Úl river a good path leads up a steep ridge, from the top of which a fine view is obtained of the Beás valley below in which the town of Mandi lies, our evening's camp. The whole country about here is very much like the Apennines, and has, I fancy, much the same climate. Everything has a dry and burnt-up look; the trees are poor, the hillsides being covered with a good deal of scrub, but there is a fair amount of field cultivation in the valley bottoms. Such country needs the morning and evening light to make it attractive, for any beauty of tint or colour is lost in the strong midday glare.

As we approached Mandi, plenty of evidence that we had left British territory and entered a native state was to hand in the well-cared-for roadside temples, and the well-built stone platforms at the base of the spreading pepul trees, those resting-places so dear to the

MANDI

native heart. Each spring by the roadside was carefully walled in, affording clear cool water to the passers-by, while in a niche above the water sat the hideous, fat-bellied, elephant-headed Ganésh giving his blessing to the thirsty traveller.

This sort of rule appeals to the native, I imagine, much more than does the cold justice of the English *régime.* Their native Raja oppresses them, no doubt, at times very hardly, but when he is in a good humour he appeals to their hearts by spoiling them a little; and if he neglects the more useful ways of spending the money of the state, he atones for it in their eyes, by lavishing it now and again upon some popular fancy. The English Ráj, on the other hand, cannot go in for fancies, but keeps all its money for roads and railways, irrigation and education, and such-like prosaic works, which, however useful in the long-run, do little to bring personal comfort to Rám Buksh as he plods, at a very gentle pace, along the path of life.

Mandi is a wonderfully pretty little town, built just where the Sukéti river joins the Beás in a deep green pool. A fine iron suspension bridge (the Raja's "Victoria Jubilee" offering) joins the banks of the Beás, while a row of pointed-roofed Hindu temples, with steep broad flights of steps down to the river, adds to the picturesque appearance of the place as you come in from the north. When this bridge was being built by Captain Hoskyns, R.E., who was lent to the Raja for the purpose, it caused a great sensation in the neighbourhood, the natives declaring that it would be impossible to build a bridge from bank to bank. After some little delay, however, a couple of light wire ropes were stretched across, high above the river, from which a few single planks were slung, in order to facilitate the passing across of the suspension cables which were to form the bridge. Captain Hoskyns, having to absent himself for a few days just at this time, returned to find the hill men making full use of this light and airy structure, imagining that the Sahib's work was done; their only complaint to him being that they could not get their sheep to cross it!

The little streets of the town were well paved and well swept, though their narrowness reminded us again that we were still in a wheel-less country. We passed through a rather picturesque open market-place, well thronged with people, one side of which is overshadowed by the Raja of Mandi's palace, the older part of which is rather a tumble-down native erection, to which has been added a newer building of very doubtful European architecture, adorned with much painting and colour. The Raja is by all accounts a most enlightened little man, as well as terribly orthodox, for the East is a country of strong contrasts, and while standing on the iron "Victoria Jubilee" Bridge you can gaze into the deep green pool below and see the great mahseer swimming lazily along which bears the soul of the Raja's late lamented grandfather in his capacious bosom.

Civilisation has certainly extended to the Mandi bungalow, which actually numbers amongst its attractions curtains to the windows. Here we met Lieutenant Ryder, R.E., who was surveying in the neighbourhood, and who came in to see St.G. about his work. He was the third European we had seen since we left Simla more than two months before, and on these occasions one morally embraces the new-comer as a man and a brother; the fatted calf was killed in the shape of our last tin of salmon, and we dined merrily in the somewhat gloomy magnificence of the Mandi bungalow. St.G. got away early next morning, while I went back through the town to take a photograph of the river with the bathing ghats. On crossing the bridge I met a Ladakhi, who was wearing one of the curious necklaces of large turquoises, blocks of amber, and coral beads roughly strung together. I urged him to sell it to me, but as he asked the absurd sum of forty rupees for it I passed on, hoping that when I returned from taking my photographs, I might find him in a more reasonable frame of mind. However, with the characteristic disregard for money of the natives, he had not waited the quarter of an hour that I was away, and in spite of a lengthened search he was nowhere to be found. I mention this to show the extreme difficulty of making any purchase in India, unless one is staying for a lengthened time in a place and can devote the time necessary for a "deal."

Our road was now to take us from Mandi on the Beás over the low watershed to Bilaspur on the Sutlej, with a night at Sukét and one at Díhr on the way. I had rather a long march to catch up St.G., and as soon as I had got through the town again, I mounted the White Rat and, leaving Nainu to follow with the sais, cantered along the excellent path leading almost on a level up the narrow Sukéti valley. Numbers of huge mahseer lay basking in the clear pools of the stream below the road, for they are all unmolested owing to the presence among them of the Raja's lamented relative. I could not help, however, somewhat irreverently dropping a stone on to the back of one huge monster, much to his astonishment and indignation.

After a few miles of this narrow valley, the road runs out into a wide flat basin with hills some 3000 feet above us all round. It is a sudden change to all the characteristics of the low country. Open flat fields, thatched villages clustering under the tall clumps of waving bamboos, groves of bananas, and the inevitable sugar-mill, round which two pairs of oxen wander sleepily to the tune of the creaking wooden wheels, until the driver infuses new life into the machine by a twist of the bullocks' tails. It is a primitive affair, the sugar-cane being pressed between two wooden rollers while the clear liquid is caught in a pot beneath. This is then boiled until the heavy brown sugar is left at the bottom. I took a photograph of the mill at work, and gladdened Nainu's and Madho's hearts by buying, for four annas, a huge cannon-ball of the black sugar for them, which certainly weighed as heavy as lead.

I overtook St.G., and found him eating his lunch in the shade of a clump of bamboos, while the smoke of the pipe of peace curled up from the group of servants hard by. It is from here that a road branches off to the west to Unúh, passing by the Rewalsír

Lakes, which are the goal of so many pilgrims. These are small sheets of water lying in the hollows of the mountains, and are fed by the rain that falls into the little basin, the most curious feature about them being the celebrated floating islands, which are worked by the Brahmins in attendance to the advantage of their pockets as well as to the wonder of the pilgrims. As far as we could see they were really floating, and probably consisted of a mass of wooden débris on which enough soil had collected to grow grass and a few sedgy plants. The Brahmins had stuck sticks into them, from which red streamers hung and fluttered in the wind as the little islands slowly drifted about with the passing breezes. We tried to see if the Brahmins controlled these movements by means of strings, and also whether they had made the islands artificially themselves, but apparently neither was the case; still no doubt whenever he gets the chance the good Brahmin does his best to assist Nature in sustaining what must be to him a fine source of income. Some Thibetans who were here on a pilgrimage, were going through a strange performance. They made the circuit of the entire lake by measuring their lengths upon the ground in repeated prostrations; standing where their heads had reached, they threw themselves flat on their faces, only to repeat the process again and again. If the path to their heaven is a difficult one, surely these good gentlemen must almost have reached the goal by this time, for I can imagine no sort of progression more wearisome and disheartening than this.

It was late in the afternoon when we rode up to the bungalow at Bhójpur, another forlorn tumble-down building standing in the middle of a bare piece of ground.

One is constantly coming across traces in India of bygone pretensions reduced to a most sorry plight. Possibly they are the old-fashioned luxuries that served the Jos Sedleys of former days, which have indeed been kept alive, though lamentably fallen from their high estate. In this case we groped our way into the musty, dilapidated rooms, disturbing a family of rats that seemed the only tenants, and threw ourselves into a couple of chairs, most magnificent as to their backs of green and gold, but alas! totally wanting in seats, the cane bottoms having long since disappeared.

We were now in the little native state of Sukét, a fact of which we were reminded by the announcement of the arrival of the Kotwál, a sort of Lord Mayor of the village. He comes riding up on his white horse—which, judging by his uneasiness, he has evidently mounted for the first time in our honour—accompanied by a retinue of some half a dozen followers and some servants carrying baskets. The whole turn-out is very oriental, without any of the magnificence.

He dismounts respectfully at a distance, marshals his underlings, and approaches, bending low. "Salám Sahib, Sahib salám." "Salám, Kotwálji. How is His Highness the Raja?" "The Raja Sahib sends his saláms, O Protector of the Poor, and places everything at the Presence's feet." A pause ensues, in which the Kotwál shifts uneasily from foot to foot, while "the Presence" thinks of a suitable answer, and turns over a couple of rupees in his pocket, wondering whether they will satisfy the great man. The Kotwál, however, breaks the embarrassing silence by beckoning to the scantily clad servants, who approach and lay at our feet some four or five baskets, containing a few pounds of rice, flour, a pot of ghee (clarified butter), a ball of sugar, a couple of chickens, and some vegetables. "The Raja Sahib has gone out hunting, O Protector of the Poor; but sends these poor offerings to the Presence. The Sahib will be pleased to accept them?"

The well-known rule in India is, that no Government official is allowed to take anything from a native; but in these out-of-the-way parts one cannot well refuse these customary *dalis*, or presents of fruit, without giving offence; so the sad-faced jemadár, who has been watching attentively in anticipation of a free meal, is called, and the baskets are handed over to him for the use of the men.

The conversation then becomes more easy, and the Kotwál relates a long-winded story in which it appears, while hunting in the hills near, that had it not been for *his* prowess and *his* cleverness in shooting at the critical moment, the Raja's life might have been in danger, owing to the attack of a great, great boar, so immense a one never having before been seen! At last the good man retires, the jemadár announces that everything is "thík," which is the native for "all right," and we sit down after our long march to the cook's most excellent dinner, on the gold-backed, bottomless chairs.

It is again a somewhat monotonous march, down a long narrow valley enclosed by low hills, from Bhójpur to Díhr on the Sutlej, though the change to the lowland vegetation is interesting. Bananas, bamboos, and wide-spreading mangos tell of the heat in summer, for one is here only some 1800 feet above the sea. Our march was only enlivened by some excursions off the road after black partridge, to whose presence the dogs now and then called our attention; and after some four hours we came to the summit of a low ridge and saw before us the wide flat valley of the Sutlej, backed up by the hills opposite.

We were soon down at the new Díhr bungalow, which had only just been built on a low cliff overlooking the wide shingle bed of the great river. Water always has an immense attraction for me, and I at once made my way down over the quarter of a mile of rough shingle which separated me from the ferry that here plies backwards and forwards over the dark-green swirling stream.

The great boat lay idly moored to the bank, and the old ferryman squatted before his little reed house, conversing with his fellows, and enjoying his evening pipe after the day's work, for the sun was sinking and no more travellers would come to cross that day. Only an old fisherman stood at the water's edge casting his net in the time-immemorial way of the East. A flat circular net some eight feet across, loaded with iron weights all round the edge, and held from the centre by a light rope, is gracefully whirled

FERRY ACROSS THE SUTLEJ AT DIHR

round the head and cast over the shallow water in a great flat disc. There it falls with a splash over any unsuspecting fish that may be lying sunning themselves, and entangles them in their efforts to escape.

Needless to say, though we watched him for some time in the evening light, he was not successful in landing any. There ought to be a proverb, "The watched fisherman catches nothing."

We turned to the old ferryman and asked him about the possibility of floating down the river on senais to Bilaspur, our next march, as an alternative to toiling along the dusty road. He stopped drawing at his hubble-bubble, and stood up with an effort to his thin old limbs. "It is as the Sahib pleases. I have no bed whereon the Sahib may sit, but I will send to the village, if perchance one may be found. Senais we have, and this man who is my brother, and another, will go with the Sahib, so that there be not trouble. Yes, Sahib, at this season of the year, because there is little rain, the water in the great river is low, and there will be danger in passing the rapids where the water is broken. The Presence will then be pleased to land and go on foot until the water is good again. But in the rainy season, as the Sahib can see, when the water is up over all these stones, there is no difficulty, and Bilaspur can be reached before the sun begins to fall in the heavens."

Next morning we were down at the ferry in good time, and while they were getting the senais ready, we watched the huge flat-bottomed ferry-boat being brought across. St.G. said that he would go on, as he doubted the possibility of my making much progress down the river, and, getting into the boat with our horses, was soon swept across to the other side, while I sat down to wait.

The great ferry-boat had time leisurely to go and return, and then was made fast to the bank. Some peasants with a buffalo and donkey, who had been patiently basking in the sun on the bank awaiting their turn, now summoned up courage, and scrambled headlong into the boat. No sooner had they settled themselves comfortably, than over the wide shingle bed in a cloud of dust came the long line of the Sahib's mules, the cooking-pots rattling noisily on their backs as they jogged over the rough stones. They were headed by the tall Anandi, who was in charge of the baggage this day. His first proceeding was to jump into the boat and with voice and arm bodily to remove the animals and the bewildered peasants, while our mules congregated in a great circle on the bank above, lost in admiration at the stubbornness of the donkey who for a long time resisted all Anandi's efforts. The peasants, seeing their animals put ashore, followed philosophically, and squatted down quite happily on the bank again, taking it all as a matter of course.

What matter indeed to them? They were journeying from one village to another, and the Sutlej was a great river to cross. They had waited patiently for some hours, until those boatmen who were so wonderfully skilled in taking the huge ship across, were ready, and a pipe of tobacco as they sat on the bank contemplating the river was but a natural solace. At last all is ready, and they make up their minds to embark, and think, no doubt, with satisfaction that the curtain has dropped on the first act. But no: a long string of mules, which must belong to some great man, appears in sight, headed by a well-dressed, brass-badged officer, whose commands must be obeyed. Who are they, poor peasants, to stand in the way of a Sahib's retinue? And so out they bundle and sit down complacently to wait for another start as they watch with wonder the vigorous efforts of the men, who with force and abuse pack the great boat full of mules. Then, when all is ready, the grass rope is cast ashore and the heavy boat is towed by three men slowly up the stream in the back eddies for some fifty yards, when with a jump the boatmen board her, seize the big oar, and, to the melody of the boatman's song, sweep the lumbering craft out into the rapid stream, where, after a few minutes' struggle in the boiling water, it drifts peacefully into a sandy haven on the farther side, and is again made fast.

While I lazily watched these proceedings, the senais were

being brought down to the bank—those wonderful skins, which for all the world resemble some antediluvian animals, but which are nothing more than the hides of the harmless buffalo, removed from the body without cutting, which have been inflated through one of the hind legs, and which are universally used in the East as a means of crossing the rivers. In using them the men themselves simply balance their bodies by lying across the inflated skin, using a paddle in their hands and propelling themselves along sideways with their feet; but for the Sahib, who is unaccustomed to such acrobatics, a bed is laid across two skins, whereon he sits, the whole being guided by two men, who, each floating on his own senai, grasp the bed legs at each end, steering and paddling with their feet.

How old this method is, may be seen by these tracings from an ancient Assyrian relief at Khorsabad, where the men are observed blowing out the skins, and then steering a raft by floating on them, exactly as they do at the present day.

The motion as one dashes down the rapids is most exhilarating, not to say exciting, for as the raft draws only some three inches of water, the great black boulders, which are plainly seen in the clear water, and over which one flies at lightning speed, are literally only a few inches beneath one. It is a series of mad rushes, with intervals of peaceful floating down the long deep pools, in which the stillness around is broken only by the gentle splashing of the men's feet as they paddle swiftly forward.

In the quieter reaches of the river I had a few shots at some duck and teal, which seemed not to notice my approach in this silent manner; and then, owing to a succession of wearisome "portages" across the rough shingle beds to avoid some bad rapids, I dismissed the men after floating about half-way to Bilaspur, and scrambling up on to the path above, continued on foot with Nainu.

Bilaspur, the capital of the little native state of that name, lies almost hidden in the trees on the high bank of the Sutlej, where it takes a sharp bend. The small white-washed houses are so scattered about in the dark-green foliage that no idea is obtained of the size of the little town, and we marched through it on to the big open maidán almost without realising its presence. This is indeed not a country of industries which gather men into crowded spots, but here, where every one lives by the produce of the land, the hamlet is found a more convenient unit than the town.

We were sorry that the Raja, a boy of fifteen, was away shooting, for he is a nice little fellow and a most keen lawn-tennis player. He has been brought up under English influence more or less, and shows it in the active life he leads, and in his love of games. There are two great attractions in Bilaspur. One is the flat piece of ground known as the maidán, and the other is a carriage and pair in which the Raja drives round and round it, to the great admiration of the inhabitants of his wheel-less realm. This great honour was paid to us too at the Raja's request, so St.G. and I were driven solemnly round and round this enlarged circus, drawn by a prancing overfed pair of horses, until our souls sighed for paper hoops and the crack of the ring-man's whip.

The Raja's palace is an imposing great stucco building of arches and domes, and for the accommodation of travellers he has built a very nice little two-storied bungalow on the high bank above the river, the upper rooms of which have been devoted to his studies. The lower rooms we found very comfortably arranged, and as soon as it was dark, the smell of Badúlla's excellent roast mutton saved Abdurrahmán the trouble of announcing that our evening meal was ready.

SENAIS ON THE SUTLEJ

In India one dines *à la Russe*, and as the cook-house is always at a distance, and side-boards not always plentiful, our roast leg was deposited upon the floor of the verandah outside our door; hence, by the light of a candle, Abdurrahmán brought St.G. some luscious slices, upon which after our long day's march my gaze rested in fond anticipation. There was, however, a vast slip between the mutton and the lip on this occasion, for in the man's momentary absence a wretched pariah dog, which no doubt had been lying in wait, pounced upon it out of the darkness, and with one bound carried off Badúlla's *chef-d'œuvre* into the black night! It was but poor satisfaction to me to hear the thieves quarrelling for hours long behind the bungalow, and I can only trust that the severe stomach-aches which these half-starved beasts must have had after this surfeit of solid meat, were a warning to them not to meddle with other people's dinners in future.

Next morning we continued our march, and leaving the low Sutlej valley behind us, began our long climb up on to the higher ground again. The absence of forest makes the country here very ugly, the bare hillsides being at the best but clothed with scrubby bushes and hideous cactus-like euphorbias, from which oozed a white sticky milk at every thrust of our alpenstocks.

It is a long six hours' pull up the four thousand feet of rise to the little Namóli bungalow, which stands on a sharp ridge overlooking an immense depth on both sides. The architect must evidently have appreciated the situation, for the opposite ends of the empty room were all glazed with windows, and through the numerous chinks in these the chilly evening wind now blew in gusts, as we sat impatiently waiting for the arrival of the mules, with our few comforts of civilisation on their backs. The sun had long set behind the distant ranges, and the short twilight had turned to dark, before the usual clatter of the pots and pans told that the belated ones had arrived.

The path next day continued along this high level, rising slightly in the course of some seven miles to cross the ridge on to the head waters of another river. The views to our left were very pretty at starting, looking across a deep, wide, broken valley, the spurs of the hills being richly cultivated in many cases, while the little white hamlets dotted about here and there caught the early rays of the morning sun. To our surprise, near the top of the ridge, after sundry alarums and excursions, the dogs flushed out of some thick scrub a couple of large birds, one of which St.G. bagged, and which turned out to be a peahen, whose presence was quite unexpected at this height of over four thousand feet.

It is a long tramp of some seven miles more from the top of the watershed down to the little town of Erki, whose Raja's big castle on a spur above his capital has more pretensions to picturesque architecture than almost any place we had yet seen. As we sat in the verandah of the bungalow, overlooking the houses, and watching the Raja's two elephants being solemnly exercised up and down the open square, they brought to us a poor boy whose leg had been very badly bitten and torn by a dog some days before. It was little wonder that the wound had made no progress in healing, for besides the infallible remedy of rubbing the palm of his hand with a round stone, the wise man of the village had smeared the boy's leg with some clotted mess which looked for all the world like curry powder. We had the wound well washed in warm water, and then applied that unfailing remedy boracic acid ointment on a piece of clean linen, giving the boy a fresh supply wrapped in a leaf, to be applied a few days later under the same conditions.

The natives, with unbounded faith, expect every white man they meet to cure them of all ills, real and imaginary; it is therefore very advisable to carry with one a good supply of simple remedies which can be given in all cases without harm, and which, when swallowed with an unlimited amount of faith, often work wonders.[1] It is customary to say that natives have no idea of the meaning of the word gratitude, so it is worth mentioning that this

[1] See Appendix D.

FROM NAMÓL

boy's father, hearing a fortnight after this that some travellers were passing Erki on their way to Simla, came and begged them to take a grateful message of thanks to the unknown Sahibs at Simla, to announce that the wound was quite healed again. By a curious coincidence these travellers stayed with us on their arrival, and in relating the story, unconsciously delivered the message to us.

From Erki to Simla is a double march of some seventeen or eighteen miles, which entails difficulties with the kulis, unless arrangements are made for a new supply at Sukrár, a place about half-way; so we decided to camp at that spot, in a somewhat desolate little nála, where we slept rather uneasily in our tents, on account of the presence in the jungle a little higher up the ravine of one of the Raja of Dhámin's elephants. This animal, in the somewhat inconsequent way that elephants do, had got off his balance, killed his mahout the day before, and retired to the jungle solitude, where he defied all comers. He was good enough, however, to leave us undisturbed, and after a long toil uphill, we next day marched into the Jutóg bazár, where the familiar sound of the artillery bugles on the hill above disagreeably recalled to us the facts that our clothes were torn and dusty and that our boots sadly needed polishing if we wished to hold up our heads again in this civilised region.

Four miles more took us to Simla, where the world of fashion had been happily consoling themselves during our absence, and where the yoke of civilisation sat somewhat heavily on us after our delightfully free life in the mountains.

Nothing can come up to the pleasure of such a march through the Himalayas. Healthy for mind and body, there is food in abundance for varied interests; while the continued life in the open air at these high elevations brings with it an exhilarating feeling of the greatness of God's world, which is almost lost sight of in the pressure of our narrow and confined struggle for existence in this nineteenth century.

# INTERMEZZO

# THE SUB-HIMALAYAS

# INTERMEZZO

A few weeks' stay was more than enough at Simla, for a summer resort in the winter season loses much of its *raison d'être.* During most of the time I was busy developing and repacking my photographs and making preparations for my journey to the the N.W. frontier; but as I was not due there for another month, I determined to march through the hills from Simla to Dehra Dún, where by the kindness of Messrs. Mackinnon I had been promised some shooting. There are two ways from Simla to Dehra—the one, which may be called the upper road, *viâ* Fágu and Mudhaul, which wanders up and down the high ground; and the other or lower road, skirting the hills through the native state of Sirmúr, which passes through the Kyárda Dún into Dehra Dún. I had received an invitation from the Raja of Sirmúr, whom I had previously met in Simla, to visit him at his capital, Náhan; and as I hoped to have St.G.'s company during his inspection of his men, who were working among the low hills in this direction, I chose the lower road, and our preparations were soon made.

In order to be able to part whenever his work compelled St.G. to leave me, we each made our separate arrangements, and I sold myself body and soul to a cook who contracted to keep me alive (tinned provisions excepted!) for the modest sum of Rs. 1.8 a day. St.G. kindly lent me Abdurrahmán, who with Nainu, my sais, and a camera-carrier made up my retinue. Four mules, engaged at Simla for twelve annas (1s.) each a day, made me independent as to transport.

K

Our servants and baggage therefore having been sent on three days ahead, St.G. and I, one morning early, walked up to the Simla Tonga office, and there climbed into the two ekhas that we had engaged to run us down the forty miles of the fine Kalka road to Dagshai, at which point we were to overtake our men, and leaving the high-road, were to strike off to the eastward across the hills. We chose native ekhas as a means of conveyance instead of the more lordly post-tongas partly for economy's sake, for a tonga can only be engaged for the whole distance to Kalka, while we wished to stop some seventeen miles short of it, and partly because on a beautiful bit of road like this, all downhill, a swift-trotting ekha pony does his best to make one forget the absence of springs to the vehicle and the somewhat uncomfortable seat upon which one is perched.

It was amusing to notice the change of behaviour of the natives towards us owing to our having adopted this humble means of conveyance, for on this much frequented high-road it is expected of the Sahib that he should confine himself to the tonga; so mistaking us for "waláyati kulis," as they call Tommy Atkins,[1] they treated us accordingly. No one we met on the road made the usual pretence of getting out of the way for us, and we were contemptuously scowled at by the drivers of the lumbering native carts, who almost pushed us off the road; and it was only by the forcible application of my fist to the driver's back, as he sat on the shaft just in front of me, that I could convince him of the necessity of using the usual third personal pronoun, instead of the disrespectful "thou" with which he invariably addressed me.

It will be a long time before the native fully understands the fine distinctions of modern civilisation; at present he still pays more respect to the coat than to its wearer.

We rattled down the fine road, which in its many windings has much in common with the Swiss Alpine highways, to Sólan, where

[1] Mr. Atkins is the only European member of the genus non-Sahib with whom the native is acquainted.

we stopped an hour for lunch in the excellent Dâk Bungalow in order to rest the ponies. A long rise, which rather told on the speed of the little animals, took us then to the top of the ridge, and after another speedy descent we pulled up at five o'clock by the way-side, and found our ponies waiting for us, to take us up the steep half-hour's climb to Dagshai, where the long, low barracks of the cantonment lined the crest of the bare ridge against the evening sky.

After a night in the Military Works bungalow, we shook off the dust of civilisation from our feet once more, and struck out in a south-easterly direction along the little stony path which, as usual in the Himalayas, clings where it is possible to the crests of the ridges. We marched for two days along this ground at a level of about 5000 feet above the sea, now over the bare brown hillside and now through scrubby forest of pines, rhododendrons, and ever-green oaks, stopping only to scour any likely-looking glen for the kallidge pheasant, which is to be found here in abundance, and which consequently figured so frequently in our daily menu, that for variety's sake we were driven to adopt the fashion of Continental hotels and christen the homely bird with the fine-sounding names of *poulet*, *poularde*, *pintade*, *faisan*, *dindon*, and *dindonneau*.

At a place called Sarhán we left the high ground and plunged down into the deep narrow valley of the Jalár, down which we marched for three days more to Satibágh.

The track led down the enclosed valley, where the wretched mules suffered much. At one time the stony track would scramble up the steep hillside, through scrub and tangled thorn bushes, only to drop again as steeply into some deep nála which here joined the main stream. In crossing this the mules would frequently fall amongst the slippery boulders and lie helplessly in the water, until all hands had relieved them and carried the soaking loads across to the farther bank. To add to our discomforts, the rain now began to descend with a force that precluded any feeble attempts on our part to keep it out. Everything seemed awash, from the running water-course under our feet to the dripping leaves overhead, which poured shoots of water down our backs as we passed underneath them. Progress was very slow, for the men had continually to put down their loads to help on the mules.

Just before reaching Mypur village on the second day, we forded the Jalár, the water of which was now up to our ponies' bellies. As we plunged into the rushing torrent the rain came down in sheets, until the water fairly leapt and hissed around us; while opposite, under a rock, we overtook a number of our unfortunate men who were vainly endeavouring to keep under cover. A diversion to their misery, however, was created by the stumbling of one of the mules, whereby my cook's large bundle was deposited in the stream, to the intense delight of the other servants; for on the previous day this somewhat lordly individual had had the laugh on his side as he accompanied us to carry our lunch, the others walking alone having missed the path and gone some miles out of their way.

The wretchedness of encamping on wet ground under wet tents with wet baggage need not be gone into; and it was after twelve o'clock next day before we could collect the dripping things together again and find the necessary kulis to carry them on to Satibágh. It was no use our waiting, however, so we pushed on down the valley with a few necessaries, leaving the tents to come on as soon as possible under Anandi's charge. At Mypur there were two fine waterfalls, no doubt somewhat swollen by the rains, but still forming at any time a series of fine cascades over some cliffs. They were all the more noticeable as they were the only waterfalls that we came across in all our wanderings in the Himalayas. The absence of cliffs and the drier atmosphere no doubt account for their being so rarely met with. It was late that evening when we descended to the junction of the Jalár with the Giri river, at which point, under a grove of magnificent mango trees which spread their dark branches over the little ruined shrine, lies the encamping ground of Satibágh. We were glad to sit round a fire which the men at once made, and warm ourselves, for the rain had made the air feel very chilly and it was a long wait

DRYING CAMP AFTER THE RAIN. SATIBAGH

in the dark until the baggage arrived. But the longest lane has a turning, and at last the encouraging shouts of the mule-drivers, "Shabásh, bahádur!" ("Well done, my conqueror!"), to the stumbling mules, and the tinkle of the bells, told us they were not far off, and soon they emerged out of the black darkness into the fitful glare of our fire. Lamps were lit at once, and in a short time all were busy pitching tents, until a late dinner at 9.30 sent us to bed tired but satisfied.

It was a most delightful rest next day to wake up and find all the glories of an Indian winter morning before us—the wonderful stillness of the air, fresh and crisp though warmed by a blaze of morning sun, the sense of budding Nature all around after the late rains; even the fine Giri, in his wide shingle bed just below our tents, seemed to sparkle with the enjoyment of it all; while the blue smoke of the little village on the farther bank curled up from amongst the thatched cottages as lazily as befits this indolent East.

We took advantage of this change in the weather to turn camp inside out, and soon the whole of our worldly possessions might have been seen hanging out to dry, while Nainu and Raganathu busied themselves baling the superfluous water from out of our gun-barrels. St.G. took his rod and started off to try for mahseer in the pools of the river, I being reduced to that somewhat common form of employment in camp, the sewing on of buttons.

Buttons certainly belong to a higher state of civilisation than befits camp life, for they are awkward things for the uninitiated to begin upon. There is no doubt that the fact that a button has more than one hole is a distinct deterrent from a state of celibacy. The proceeding commences as the needle goes down through the hole with wonderful ease, but nothing will persuade it to come up again in the proper place. In vain you try, it will come up and bump against the button; more readily still it will come up and prick the finger that you imagined was miles away; and at last, when it is good enough to find a hole to come up through at all, lo and behold it is the same hole down which the wretched thing went! The man who invents a practical shirt button with only one hole in it, will deserve a gold medal and the thanks of all bachelors on vellum.

I was still employed at this miniature game of tilting at the ring, when St.G. came back and said that it was no good fishing, for the worthy natives had seized the opportunity of the flood water to float down timber in such quantities that it was impossible to throw a line; so we took our guns instead, and wandered off through the thick Bér jungles, whose thorny bushes cover a great part of the flat river-bed.

The red jungle-fowl (*Gallus ferrugineus*) abounds in these dense thickets, which are just to his liking, and though it is difficult to get this beautiful little game-cock out of his hiding-place in the middle of the day, yet in the mornings and evenings he may be met with wandering about outside, picking and scratching the ground in search of food. We spent four happy days in this delightful spot, pursuing the inhabitants of the jungles about, until our hands and clothes were nearly torn to pieces by the thorny trees that grow everywhere in this warm climate, for Satibágh is not more than 2000 feet above the sea. We considered a peacock, three or four jungle-fowl, a pheasant or two, and a hare a fair bag for a long day's sport, for in these rough countries one has to work hard for one's shots.

We paid a visit also to the sacred lakes of Ranka, which lie in a secluded little valley about a mile from the farther side of the Giri. These small sheets of water, buried in semi-tropical vegetation, are visited in the summer by thousands of pilgrims, who, if they have eyes for anything else but the holiness of the spot, must assuredly be struck by the extreme beauty of the placid waters, which reflect the overhanging branches and here and there a stately palm on their mirror-like surface, that is only broken by the splashing of the numerous wild-fowl of all sorts which here find a safe haven of refuge. Mallard and teal, pintail and pochard, sheldrake and shovellers, and many others whose names we did not know, swam about tamely before us, conscious of the security afforded them by the sacredness of the place. There is no village at the lakes themselves, but a temple with some bathing-steps, and the small court-house of the tehsildár, stand by the water's edge. The insanitary state of the ground, however, where the pilgrims camp on approaching this sacred spot, is another reminder that it is "only man that is vile" amid a scene of such exquisite natural beauty.

We could have spent another week at Satibágh very happily, but St.G. had to go off to see some of his men's work; so we reluctantly gave the order to load the mules, who also must have been sorry to quit this spot of ease and plenty.

Crossing the Jalár river again, we climbed the hillside opposite, up a rugged path that brought us up the 2000 feet to the top of the ridge. These sub-Himalayan hills are covered with a thick vegetation of the scrubby order, which in winter is not very interesting, but when we passed through them again a few months later, in April, a glorious mass of colouring was to be seen everywhere. On the higher slopes the crimson rhododendrons carried all before them, lighting up the sombre forests with their blaze, while down below, in the hot valley bottoms, the magnificent scarlet sprays of the numerous pomegranate trees seemed all the more brilliant in contrast to the glossy dark-green of their leaves.

We camped that night at the top of the ridge, from which a fine view is obtained of the low country towards the plains, and next day marched a few miles along the ridge till we reached the white-washed little temple of Jínta, which forms such a striking landmark to the country all around. Here to our sorrow my brother and I had to part at last, with many vows of meeting again in these valleys a few months later, when we hoped the rivers would be in better order for fishing. St.G. and his men continued along the ridge back towards Simla, while I with regret made my way alone, with my small following, down the rough path towards the little town of Náhan, which was prettily situated in the broken ground some 1100 feet below. I approached the little capital of the Sirmúr state in some uncertainty where to camp, and as I walked up through the hilly streets, which contained some large white offices well shaded with trees, I asked the passers-by the way to the bungalow which I had been told was here. On arriving there I found the Raja's gorgeous scarlet-clothed chaprassi, a jemadár or officer of his forces, and a clerk who salámed low, all of whom on the Raja's behalf placed themselves at my disposal and informed me that I was to consider myself His Highness's guest. It was rather embarrassing suddenly to have this greatness thrust upon one, for I was not accustomed to be waited upon by such splendid creations in scarlet and gold; but I made the best of it—to the delight of my servants at any rate, who saw in the arrangement a few days of idleness and free rations—and was ushered into the spacious bungalow, which was an excellent one in all respects save that the mud roof had fallen in only a week or two previously, and after the manner of the country was still lying where it fell, giving the floors of some of the rooms the appearance of a ploughed field.

It is a great thing in the East to be punctilious about etiquette, so I got rid of one of the scarlet gentlemen, who shadowed my movements everywhere, by sending him with my saláms to the Raja to ask His Highness when it would please him to see me; and on the following morning, attended by Nainu in his Sunday best —now alas! sadly tattered and torn by our wanderings—I walked out to the Raja's handsome Italian villa, which stands on a small hill about half a mile from the town. It is a well-built house, standing in a pretty garden in which is a fine fountain that does not play, with large flights of stone steps somewhat overgrown with weeds leading up to the entrances. I was kindly received by the Raja without any state, in one of the rooms which was comfortably furnished in European style, and spent an hour very pleasantly with him alone. He is a middle-aged man of the good and quiet type, well educated but rather heavy, though perhaps in this respect he was handicapped by the English, which he spoke in a somewhat slow and measured way. As rulers go, he is one of

A HILL MAIDEN

the better kind, for he at any rate spends his money on estimable, even if rather unpractical objects, and has erected quite a large foundry and several workshops in Náhan, which are managed for him by an English engineer—the only remunerative product of which, however, seemed to be a small iron sugar-mill to crush the cane, thereby displacing the cumbrous and antiquated wooden arrangements everywhere in use by the natives.

Rajas often, in their initiation into Western civilisation, show an extraordinary variety of tastes in their development of the disease. One, after his country has been carefully nursed for him during his long minority by the British Government, will, on succeeding to his patrimony, become a jockey, associate with grooms, and squander the money of his state in extravagant horse-racing. Another, preferring the bottle, will consume all the fire-water within his reach, until he is reduced in his mountain home to cheering his flagging spirits with Worcestershire Sauce. A third will develop the sporting mania, and surpass the most up-to-date subaltern in the loudness of his checks, in the smartness of his slang, and the swiftness of his polo ponies. All of which things point not so much to an inherent vice in the native character, as to the difficulty they have in the East of assimilating Western ideas in due proportion.

The good Raja of Sirmúr's tastes, however, lie in the more orthodox direction of government by means of forms, tables, and returns; and when on leaving he asked me if he could do anything for me, and I begged for permission to shoot in his State, he graciously accorded this to me in the shape of a large printed "Game License," on which all the animals, both feathered and furred, that the bearer was permitted to shoot in His Highness's territory, were classified in columns in such an exact and scientific way, that I trembled to think that for the last ten days we had been shooting away at them, quite regardless of the existence of this great legal sanction.

I stayed three days at Náhan, on one of which I watched a

game of football played on the maidán. The game has been started by the Raja's energetic English doctor, who is one of the three Englishmen resident in the place, and was played with great eagerness, even the Raja's two grown-up sons—the elder of whom is Lord Chief Justice, and the younger Commander-in-Chief of the state—joining in, in a way that made one admire the native's extraordinary capacity for rolling democracy and the feudal system into one. Only the other day I saw a man throw himself on the ground at St.G.'s feet, craving pardon for some trivial offence; and here just such another tumbles his Commander-in-Chief, his Raja's own son, over, in the all-levelling game of football.

From the Náhan bungalow, which is on the brow of the hill, one gets a lovely view to the south over the flat plains of India, stretching far away to the distant horizon. These had been freshened up by the late rain, that even now threatened to descend again from the black clouds above. The Kyárda Dún is a broad valley lying about a thousand feet below Náhan, between the low Siwálik range and the Himalayas, and into this new country we now marched, leaving the hills behind us. It was a great change to find ourselves amongst the wide stretches of cultivation, now brilliantly green with the young wheat, or yellow with the plentiful crop of mustard. Alternating with this cultivated ground are large patches of forest, mostly of sál trees—a valuable wood, whose broad leaves afford a dense shade to the thick jungle-growth beneath them. The road is a wide earthen track leading through this pretty, homely country; hamlets of little mud, grass-thatched huts are dotted about, giving an air of peace and abundance to the scene.

This was a most unusually wet winter, for the rain came on again in torrents, making our camp at Kólar a wet one, and causing us to delay a day at Májra, where we took shelter in the large, rambling, pretentious bungalow, which turned out to be truly a forlorn abode. The rooms were extensive and lofty, and a noble colonnade supported the front verandah; but the glory had long since departed, for the columns were bent and cracked with age, and scarcely supported the thatched roof, through the rents in which the rain streamed pitilessly down on to the mud floors of the rooms. I pitched my tent in the main room, to keep out the wet, and the servants, by lighting wood fires on all the hearths, endeavoured to dry off some of the damp and musty smell that pervaded the place.

But winter rains in India are not persistent, and next morning, as if to apologise for its late remissness, the sun shone out with renewed brilliancy, causing the whole landscape to sparkle in the delicious freshness. While our wet tents were drying, Nainu and I, armed with gun and rifle, not to mention the Raja's great game license, sallied forth for a walk through the jungle, and soon came across the black francolin partridge in the tall brown grass, and some peacocks picking up their food near the edges of the cultivation.

Before we got home I had a snap shot at a cheetal stag (*Axis maculata*), and bagged a smaller hog deer (*Axis porcinus*); but in order to shoot successfully in this kind of country, one needs to be elevated above the surrounding cover on an elephant's back, for the grassy jungle is so high that on foot one can see but little. I think it is not at all unlikely also that wild animals are very sensitive through their feet to the vibrations of the earth caused by man's tread, for no matter how noiselessly one walks in the jungle, its inhabitants will mostly move off at man's approach long before he comes into sight, whereas they will bear the close approach of an elephant, whose footsteps they know, undismayed.

A traveller gets philosophical about time in India, where the methods of delay are reduced to a fine art, but unless one has become quite deadened as to its loss, it must be admitted that one is often exasperated beyond endurance. I had a long march from Májra, and wished to get well across the Jumna before evening, with an hour or two's rest in the heat of the day, so orders were given to Nainu that we were to start next morning at six, which orders were duly passed on to the mule-drivers.

Now the Punjábi mule-driver is a champion waster of time, even in this country of procrastination. I awake, then, at seven, after a night's rest in all the forlorn magnificence of the Májra bungalow, and stand upon the verandah. No one is moving, only a pair of pretty little grey-striped squirrels are gambolling on the grass in the morning sun, while the inevitable crow lazily caws in the tree overhead. "Abdurrahmán." No answer. Louder, "Abdurrahmán." A sleepy answer from the recesses of the little cook-house across the lawn, "Your Highness." "Bring tea." "Very well, your Highness": and half an hour later, when I am dressed, tea is brought.

At eight o'clock Nainu begins to roll up the tents, and my things are packed into the mule-trunks.

By the time I have breakfasted nine o'clock has arrived. Losing patience, I send for the mule-men, whose answer is that they "are just coming."

9.15. The mule-men are to be seen aimlessly wandering about near the picketed mules, each carrying a bit of rope or a salíta—the blanket in which they sew up the load.

9.20. Boiling over, I rush out to them with a stick. "Why are you not ready, O sons of pigs?" "All is now prepared, Sahib, we are ready to start." The mules look on unblushingly at these barefaced lies: they have heard them before. However, my presence, and a harmless torrent of English expletives, has an enlivening effect, and they move a trifle faster, and carry two ropes instead of one. I walk back to the bungalow hopelessly, where Nainu is carrying out the boxes on to the verandah.

The mule-men now leave the mules, and come to arrange the loads, which have to be wrapped and sewn up in the salítas before they can be thrown over the beasts' backs. Although this is the twelfth day out, you would imagine that the mule-men had never seen the loads before: each in turn is lifted, weighed, and put down

Madho Nainu The White Rat

[illegible]MATIS [illegible]RSONÆ

again; and at 9.45 scarcely any progress has been made,—until, convinced of the futility of leaning any longer upon such broken reeds, I send Nainu, who is looked upon as a marvel of energy, to do their work for them, and they gladly leave the matter to him.

At last, with the help of Abdurrahmán and Abdúlla, the cook, the loads are got ready by about ten, and with much mutual encouragement the mule-men shoulder their long poles, and file off after their charges, and in the end reach their destination without further mishap,—unless, indeed, the mules fall upon some bad piece of road, or get frightened, as they did on this day, and kick off their loads at the sight of the Raja's long string of elephants, that they met returning from the river Jumna.

I rode off after them through this pretty flat Kyárda Dún, upon which the crops of this bountiful wet season promised an abundance for the villagers, whose life in their little grass huts has nothing in common with that of the hill men, but is completely that of the peaceful agriculturist of the plains.

At Páonta I picked up a few new kulis that the tehsildár had kindly got for me, and then marched three miles up the Jumna to the ferry at Rajghat, which took me across into the British territory of Dehra Dún.

The change from the native state could at once be seen in the engineer's hand on the roads and in the neat and tidy forest-officers' bungalows about. I camped that evening near the Public Works Department bungalow, and looked out over the pretty country towards the Asan river, where I had spent some very happy days ten years previously. The same jagged points of the Siwáliks, the same sál forests, and the same rushing torrent in which we had fished, seemed but little changed in the years that had passed.

Next day I pushed on to Rajawalla, to which place the Mackinnons had most kindly sent their two elephants for my use, and where I met many old friends, among whom was the faithful old Bíru, now grown grey, and the shikari Nathú, whom I had a year or two before escorted over Woolwich Arsenal under very different conditions, on his visit to England.

Sapri, Mónu, and others whom I remembered as little black pot-bellied urchins, who used to excel with their pellet bows, had now grown into lithe young men, Sapri having even taken unto himself a wife, and reproduced his former self in miniature. I was made warmly welcome by them all, and as Nainu was amongst his "brothers" again, I felt as if it was quite a "home-coming."

I intended spending a week here, awaiting the arrival of a shooting-party that the Mackinnons had got up, so on the following morning, Nathú having come to tell me that the elephants were ready, I sallied out and found the two huge beasts resting under a tall clump of bamboos, where they stood philosophically munching the grass, which they plucked with their trunks from time to time from the ground at their feet. The larger had a howdah on her back, from which I was to shoot, while the smaller animal carried only a mattress pad, upon which the game was to be strapped when shot. At the command of her mahout, the big one, with the slow deliberation that characterises every movement of an elephant, spreads her legs out forwards and kneels down, and while Nainu holds her tail up for a stirrup, I scramble up with difficulty over her hind-quarters and climb into the howdah; gun and rifles are handed up, Nathú and Nainu join me, and then after being violently thrown backwards and forwards as the elephant rises, I find myself standing in the howdah with my head some fifteen feet above the ground, looking down on the scene that seems an immense distance below. Sapri has scrambled up on to the pad elephant, and we move off with that slow and swaying motion down the path which leads through the green cultivation about the little hamlet, to the wide jungle-covered bed of the Soarna. Pea-fowls rise in numbers all around, the long tails of the cock birds trailing gracefully after them as they fly away. These beautiful birds are to be found here in numbers both morning and evening, when they come out to scratch about among the villagers' crops, and I have counted as many as sixty at a time in the flat cultivated fields below the bungalow.

The whole of this part of the Dún, except where there are patches of cultivation, is what is called forest country in India. This consists here in stretches of sál trees—a straight-growing tree pole with few horizontal branches, but whose broad round leaves give a density to the growth. All through this forest country, wherever a break in the trees allows of it, the tall pampas-like grass, now brown with the winter's dryness, has grown up, often to a height of ten or twelve feet, forming large fields of dense cover for the game that shelters in it.

It can easily be imagined that one can do but little shooting on foot in such a country as this, and an elephant is as much a necessity as a comfort for a day's sport here. The general flat lie of the ground is broken frequently by gullies or water-courses, quite dry at this time of year, which are known by the universal name of *nálas,* and which, being mostly full of a tangled mass of grass and bushes, afford an excellent place of retirement to the larger game during the heat of the day.

We filed in silence down the steep bank into the broad bed of the now waterless Soarna river, whose shingly course is almost lost amidst the wide islands of tall grass, on which the thorny Bér trees and acacias grow in a thick scrub. Into this tangled jungle we plunge, the pad elephant taking a course parallel to us, some eighty yards on our left, where from time to time she is visible as she emerges out of the thick into the open. Not a sound is heard but the continued swish, swish, as with slow and steady steps the elephant ploughs her way through this sea of grass, twisting and turning hither and thither, now to avoid a group of trees, now to tread out an especially thick clump of grass which reaches almost above her head.

If a camel is the "ship of the Desert," surely an elephant may be well described as the "ship of the Jungle"!

As I stand leaning over the howdah with nothing in front of

me, for the mahout is well below and the elephant's neck is short, I feel as if I was looking over the bows of a ship at sea—the wide expanse before me, the slow swaying motion, the deep look down, the hissing noise of the dry grass rustling against the elephant's feet, increasing almost to a surge as she ploughs into the thick waving stalks, and then the silent calm of her measured tread in the open, while all the time, never increasing her pace, never stopping, she moves ahead with that effortless deliberation that seems to render her progress irresistible.

The elephant is a fascinating animal to observe, for his small and expressionless eye gives not the slightest clue to what is passing within his brain, while all his movements betray an intelligence and docility that constantly appeal to one's admiration. No one ever heard of an elephant stumbling, for he gives you the impression of moving with only one leg at a time while he holds on with the other three! With regular and well-considered steps he will make his way over any imaginable ground, now lowering himself steadily down an almost precipitous bank, only to climb with equal deliberation up the opposite one. Again he picks his careful way through the great boulders that strew the river-bed, and then forces his way through the densest forest on the other side, pausing only to wrench off with his trunk an overhanging bough, or to break down a tree as thick as one's thigh, by placing his foot against it, and bearing slowly on it with his weight, until with a crash it gives way and leaves a path clear for the passage.

All these things and many others he seems to do out of his own intelligence, but as a matter of fact, though nothing is said, every movement is directed by the mahout as he sits astride of the short neck; for with his knees concealed under the elephant's huge ears, he conveys by pressure all his wishes and directions to the docile beast.

The interest is intense as one is thus silently carried into the very home of the wild animals, as any step may reveal the expected game. Every eye is strained to catch sight of the looked-for forms.

Then as the elephant brushes through the tall grass, or parts the sál saplings in his way, suddenly Nathú behind me whispers "Dutt, dutt"; and as Bhagan the mahout silently stops the elephant, he points through the trees, where with much difficulty I make out the heads of some alarmed cheetal standing for a moment. "Madín" (females), adds Nathú, as they bound away showing their graceful forms in their headlong flight over the tufted grass. Again and again this happens, for it is quite remarkable what a number of hinds one sees for every stag. The noble stag at home, indeed, treats his female relatives to very scant protection, being always the first to disappear and the last to venture when there is danger about.

On we go in our search, now wading into an especially thick clump of grass, when a headlong rush from under his very feet causes the elephant to give a shrill trumpet of alarm, and I get half a glimpse of something black which tells me that a drove of pig are flashing through the grass at lightning speed. A snap shot at these, or maybe at a single hog deer (so called from the pig-like way he bolts through the grass), is all one gets. Following the direction the cheetal have gone, the whirr of a black partridge getting up just in front makes me hastily put down my rifle and seize my gun. Another quarter of a mile through the thick trees as we circle round to try and head the deer we had noticed, when "Dutt, dutt" again stops the elephant, and I get in a shot through the thick trees at the place where I see the horns of a stag above the cover.

One has to get used to shooting from an elephant's back, for though seeming to stand still yet he is always moving, gently swaying to and fro.

"Lugga, Sahib! Mail, mail, Bhagan jaldi" ("Hit, Sahib! Hurry on, Bhagan"), calls Nathú as the elephant, urged on by Bhagan, crashes at a shuffling pace through the trees in the direction of the wounded deer. The pad elephant, attracted by the shot, has approached, and Sapri has already slipped to the ground, is walking before us parting the long grass with his hands and picking up the traces of blood in a most marvellous way. A hundred yards farther on we find the panting stag, and Bhagan, slipping down from his perch, rushes forward just in time to perform the Mohammedan ceremony of Halál, by cutting the animal's throat as he utters the words "Bis millah" ("In the name of God"); for meat is not fit food for the follower of the Prophet unless the life is taken in this way.

The pad elephant is now brought up and with some difficulty

coaxed near, for in spite of their stanch courage many are timid at the sight of blood; but at last the deer is slung upon its back and tied with ropes, and off we go again, halting only in the middle of the day when the sun is hot, to eat our lunch of cold meat and chapattis under the shade of a big tree, while the men squat on the ground in a circle round the few burning sticks they have kindled, and pass the consoling pipe of tobacco from hand to hand.

Perhaps the whole afternoon may be spent in looking for a

stag in vain, and though tigers' footprints are continually seen on the little sandy forest paths, we looked without success for that prince of beasts himself. So we turn our steps homewards, beating through the brown grass beside the stony bed of the Soarna, where the peacocks fly up from their evening stroll, affording pretty shots. An old bird is dry and tough, but the young ones are well-flavoured and excellent eating.

I get home about five o'clock, and am glad to stretch my legs after standing all day in the howdah, when the insatiable Sapri approaches and begs me to come while he beats the bank along the edge of the river-bed for jungle-fowl; and in a few minutes I am running on ahead, looking up at the steep jungle-covered bank, while Sapri, Nainu, Mónu, and all the little black imps of the place are making the air hideous with shouts and stones as they drive the pea-fowl and jungle-fowl out of the sheltering bushes.

Of an evening I stroll out and watch the homely life of these simple people,—the little boys exercising their hunting instincts in shooting at small birds with their pellet bows with marvellous skill; while the mahout's children, little mites whose long black elf-locks formed almost their sole clothing, made always a pretty picture as they played fearlessly with the huge elephants, one little girl sitting in the curved trunk of the great beast as he good-naturedly swung her backwards and forwards in answer to her shrill demands.

A week of this pleasant and interesting life passed all too quickly, and I hurried into Dehra to join my friends the Mackinnons, who with true Indian hospitality had taken the great trouble to collect a number of elephants together for a week's shooting in the Eastern Dún.

The amount of organisation and care required to get up a successful shooting camp is often little realised by those who are asked to share in the sport. It is not easy to get together even fifteen elephants, for the owners of these useful animals are few and far apart, and it is difficult to get the loan of them all at the same time. Sufficient camp equipage has to be got together; provision of food has to be made both for the shooters and for the army of followers; the camp has to be pitched where there is fodder and water for the elephants; and if the spot is out of the way, a post has to be established to get letters and necessaries from head-quarters. All these things and a thousand others entail an amount of care and trouble that no one who has not been behind the scenes can realise; but in India such trouble is lightly undertaken by those who unselfishly delight in giving pleasure to others; and to this fact, no doubt, is due the happy recollections that every one has, whose good fortune it has been to journey thither in search of sport.

Our camp was first pitched at Raiwala on the Ganges, a few miles above Hardwár; and those of the party who did not fish were out every day in the jungles of the Eastern Dún, where our long line of thirteen elephants swept over a large strip of country at each beat. Amongst our party was the Raja Ranbír Singh, whose father was one of the chiefs of the Punjáb when we conquered it, and who, on our taking over the country, was pensioned. The Raja now lives in Delhra, and is known everywhere as one of the best sportsmen as well as one of the most courteous and unassuming gentlemen of the district. He has all the pleasant manner and disposition that is so characteristic of the Sikhs; and though on the whole, owing to bad weather setting in, we were not very fortunate in our sport, yet it was a pleasure I often enjoyed, in being on the elephant next to the Raja, to see the sportsmanlike way he brought down his game.

We shot towards Kans Rao, and though the Raja, who knows every inch of the ground, took us to all the most likely places for tiger, yet we were not fortunate enough to come across one.[1]

[1] That there are tigers about here was proved in a sad way only a few months after our visit to the neighbourhood. The Raja and an English friend of his, who had many years been resident in the Dún, were staying at Kans Rao, and one morning the Englishman, who was an old and well-tried hunter, taking with him only a single native, started off early and made his way to the high ground of the Siwálik range in the hopes of stalking a stag sambur at daybreak. Being unsuccessful, he was retracing his steps, when he heard at no great distance the loud purring of a

FROM THE TIGER'S POINT OF VIEW

Still we had fair sport among the pig and the cheetal and the partridge, while our bags sometimes included such curiosities as porcupines, and once a low grey-backed animal looking like a cross between a badger and a sloth, whose proper place in natural history none of us knew.

The shooting and the fishing went on for ten days, when the party broke up, and after a flying visit to Mussoorie, I had to think about starting for the frontier, for in such pleasant company time was slipping by.

I got rid of all my men except Nainu, who happily had little idea of the journey that was before him; and after the usual preparation of condensing my baggage to a minimum, I said good-bye to my kind friends, and started off on our forty-five miles' drive to Saharunpur to catch the train that was to carry us off to new scenes and new faces, to a country which, though in the same province of the Punjáb, was as different from that in which I had been spending the last four months as one could find in the world.

tiger, and on cautiously approaching the spot he found a male and female tiger playing together in the open, and so occupied were they with each other that he was able to approach within fifteen yards of them unnoticed. He could not resist the temptation of so easy a shot and fired. One tiger moved off, but the other, apparently unwounded, turned sharply round, and springing upon the unfortunate man, seized him by the thigh and carried him off into the thick cover, where it proceeded to maul him. His native attendant's account was that he found his master after a short search in a dying condition, and was asked by him to go at once to the Raja for help. This the man did, finding the Raja fishing near Kans Rao. The Raja very wisely at once ordered his elephant to be got ready, and accompanied by the man, went up to the scene of the accident, where, however, they had some difficulty in finding the exact spot. While searching about, the tiger, which had evidently been watching them for some time, to their intense surprise, sprang suddenly out of a thicket on to the elephant's hindquarters. The Raja was unable to fire owing to his nearly being thrown out of the howdah by the violent struggles which the elephant made in its endeavour to free itself from the brute that was clawing it. At last the plucky animal succeeded in shaking off the tiger, and then stood firm for a moment, while the Raja sent a bullet through it, which killed it on the spot. Not far off, the body of the unfortunate Englishman was found. The tiger had apparently not returned to him after killing him.

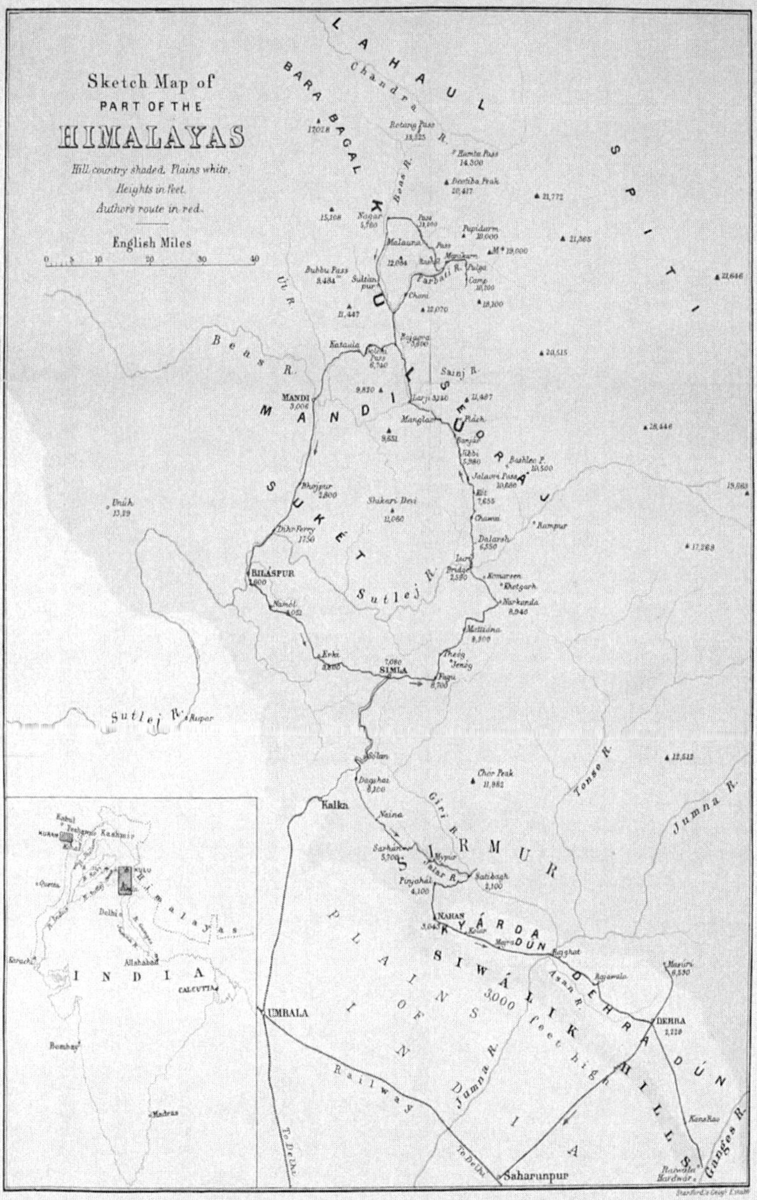


London: John Murray.

# PART II.—KURAM

## CHAPTER I

THE green plains of India are left far behind, the cities embowered in trees and teeming with hot life have disappeared from off the surface of the earth, while all the morning we have been passing through a most extraordinary broken and barren stony desert of low hills, cut up by deep ravines; and now all heads crane out of the windows as the train slowly crawls into the little wayside station of Attock. Even the hot midday sun cannot lull the excitement which one feels at reaching the Indus at last, and stepping across that great natural boundary between India and Central Asia.

The train pulls up at the unpretentious platform just at the commencement of the great bridge, and we dash out with quite unnecessary haste, for, as the good-natured guard reminds us, we are still in the East, and Indian trains are in no hurry to start again without ample warning.

We run down the steep rough path to the strip of sand on the river's edge, and there before us flows the Indus in great brown swirls, looking very sullen and deep, as if in no pleasant humour at being confined between these narrow cliffs after wantonly spreading at its ease over the flat country above. A noble river even at this time of the year when it is at its lowest. And there, hanging high above our heads, in fine contrast too, is the great iron railway bridge, which, regardless of the river's temper or power, stands firmly astride of it, a striking if peaceful emblem of

England's hold upon India. The bridge itself is of the ordinary straight-girder type, on high latticed iron columns, starting from a masonry foundation. The whole of the difficulty in the construction of this great work, the main artery, so to speak, of the N.W. frontier traffic, must have been in these foundations, for they have to withstand a rise of some sixty feet of water during the rains, when the river comes boiling down with an almost immeasurable force.

One gets a good view also of the bridge after the train has slowly rumbled across, and has run up the opposite bank until abreast of the old Attock ferry with Akbár's picturesque fort commanding it. There is always plenty of ancient history attaching to a ford or ferry, and Attock has been for centuries one of the gates of India. The still more ancient road, however, from Afghanistan to India crossed the Indus some twenty-five miles below Attock, at Níláb, and it was probably at this place that Alexander and his army were ferried over. Possibly also a testimony to the former greatness of Níláb—the words mean "blue water"—lies in the fact that to this day all the profession of boatmen on the Kabul river and the Indus are called Níláhbis.

The train loiters along slowly enough for one to get an admirable view of the country, it being even on record that the sporting subaltern lets his fox-terrier out for a run at one station and picks him up at the next, for happily the iron horse has suited his temper to his surroundings, and has adopted a gentle trot in the place of the bustling gallop that we Westerns are so accustomed to in railway travelling.

The Valley of Peshawur now opens out in a large basin, some thirty miles across, and the view is typical of this part of the world. High rugged mountains surround the flat basin, brown in middle distance and blue in the far-off ranges of Bunér and Swát, with the snow-capped peaks of the Chitrál country away to the north, almost fading into the opal haze of the Indian sky. The valley looks barren enough—stones and dry earth in abundance, with scarcely a tree; for here we have to deal with a country where water does not come to the land by nature and art has to be resorted to to supply the want, the average annual rainfall being only some fifteen inches (about half that of England), while the heat in summer is intense. About once every five or six years, however, the heavens are bountiful, and an abundant winter rain sends every man out to plough the moistened ground and throw in his wheat and barley seed. The whole valley then is transformed suddenly into one bright sheet of green, and "the desert blossoms abundantly as the rose."

The train dawdles leisurely along the flat open country, the only incongruous feature in the landscape being the neat and tidy railway stations at which we pull up every ten minutes. Here we learn from the orthodox white board with the orthodox black letters that this part of Central Asia is called Jehangira Road, the next Naoshéra, and then Pabbi. Strangely out of place also on the neat conventional platform is the surging, hurrying crowd, that always is to be seen at an Indian railway station. Where they are going to and why, as the Afghan himself would say, Allah 'álim (God alone knows). But here they are in masses—old men in tattered garments with heavy bundles on their shoulders, the burly peasant wrapped in his dirty postín or sheepskin coat, timid women dragging children after them and vainly endeavouring to keep up with their hurrying lords. Here come two strapping young fellows six feet high at least, elbowing their way through the crowd, evidently young Pathan sepoys from the regiment near. They wear no uniform off duty, but their loose white cotton trousers, like full skirts, are spotlessly clean. A dark cloth tightly-fitting tunic covers their lithe bodies, and a wonderful turban, with one long end behind falling to the waist, sets off their round chubby boyish faces. A finishing touch of swagger to these young bloods is the black curl or love-lock, which they wear carefully plastered against their cheeks just in front of their ears.

The crowd surges to and fro up and down the platform, vainly seeking room in the already crowded train; now tumbling in their confusion into a first-class carriage, only to be pulled out by the hind leg again by the angry guard. Truly the train is no respecter of persons, and at last they are all bundled in somewhere and somehow, and on we go to have the scene repeated ten minutes later at the next station. It is like a scene in a play, only the game is in earnest to the bewildered Oriental.

Soon the irrigated green fields and the fine clumps of trees tell us that we are nearing Peshawur, and in the evening light we catch glimpses of the dusty red mud walls of the big fort and the confused mass of houses of the city. The crowds swarm out of the train only to be lost in the greater crowd on the platform, and the train, now empty except for two or three Sahibs and their attendants, steams slowly on to the Peshawur cantonment, the end of all things and the last railway station on the line towards the unknown future.

As all the world knows, we hold India ultimately by the sword, though some are ignorant enough for their own purposes to blink at the fact; and though we live in the cantonment at some distance, surrounded by well-swept roads, gardens, racket courts, perambulators, and other signs of civilisation, yet almost within hail of us lies the great seething city of Peshawur, which probably contains a greater number of blackguards per square inch than any other town of its size. But, in the pride of your white face, quite forgetting the regiments drilling on the burning parade-ground in the cantonments, or, for the matter of that, the lives of such men as Mackeson, Fulford, and Adams (the latter cut down on this very spot), you walk as carelessly through the Kabul Gate as you would through Bond Street, and satisfy your curiosity by wandering idly through the crowded bazárs and narrow alleys of the city at your will.

And what a crowd it is—sombre and dark in colour, but with a bewildering number of types: Jewish-looking Afghans, black-haired Khattaks from the Indus, sleepy-looking Persian merchants, here and there the face of a Tartar, who has come from Bokhára

with his camels laden with carpets; Afrídis from the Khyber, Yusuffzais from the valley, and a host of others. But how unlike "India" here! One instinctively feels that all are men, and there is no saláming, but one has to draw oneself up an inch or two taller as in passing by they take your measure in their bold, straight stare. Happily they know, better than the innocent traveller does, that if they touched a hair of his head the arm of the Sirkár (as wielded by the Deputy and Police Commissioners) would fall swiftly and heavily on the whole street.

The inhabitants of the city have evidently always been of a class who have needed a strong hand. The kindly relations of the governors and the governed, even in the time of the Mogul Empire in the 17th century, are expressed in the well-known lines that Kipling has noticed:

> Pa sabab da Zalimáno Hakimáno,
> Pekhor, wa gor, wa or,
> Drewarah yau dí.

(On account of the tyrannous governors, Peshawur, the grave, and hell-fire, all three are one.)

Then the Sikhs conquered the city and had their turn. Avitabile, a Neapolitan in the Sikh service, who was governor of Peshawur for some years, found it necessary to hang his criminals from the walls of the Gór Katri in the face of the whole city. And now, as the idle traveller leans over those very parapets, nothing looks more peaceful than the brown mass of house-tops spread out before him; here the white domes of a small mosque peeping out, there the dusty red walls of the Fort showing between the trees. In the foreground some women and children are spending their day upon the flat house-tops below, and in the background, across the twelve-mile stretch of flat desert, rise the brown hills of Afghanistan and the Khyber.

The city, like most in the East, is intensely interesting; and though there is no architecture worthy of the name, there are many picturesque corners, notably under one huge tree in the bazár, where the money-changers sit with piles of coins spread out before them—coins of all sorts, from Greco-Bactrian silver pieces which still survive the long gone dynasties, to the new rupees from the Kabul mint.

The eye, however, is delighted with the thronging mass of picturesque life, the strings of camels and donkeys. Here a heated bargain between a buyer and seller attracts as idle a crowd as does a fallen cab-horse in Piccadilly; there a crowd of Salvation Army proportions follows some wildly posturing Hindu dancers to the rhythm of strange music and clashing cymbals; while to and fro flows the endless stream of passers-by of all sorts, from the swaggering young Pathans, walking boldly hand in hand, to the timid Government babu, with now and then the figure of a woman wrapped from head to foot in her white linen búrka.

No one who has been in India can go away without having experienced the graceful hospitality of the country; and after an uncomfortable night in a so-called hotel, I found myself established in the delightful bungalow of the General commanding, Sir Henry Collett, to whose kindness I, as well as many others, owe many pleasant reminiscences.

Of course no one can go to Peshawur without having a look at the Khyber. It is a matter easily arranged, for on Tuesdays and Fridays the pass is, in official parlance, "open." The dog-cart is ordered, and a pleasant drive of twelve miles in the crisp dry morning air, over a flat stony desert, brings us to Jamrúd Fort, at the edge of the plain and at the mouth of the Khyber. These frontier forts are just such as children delight to make out of mud, and I looked on this one with envious eyes. Their smooth mud walls have a round tower at each corner, and the keep rises in tiers above the outer wall, with the conventional flagstaff on the highest point, from which the dear old Union Jack hangs lazily down in the still air. Here at last we are really on the frontier, and one step will take us across it. Groups of wild-looking men of the Khyber Rifles stand about in their long black military greatcoats, with Snider rifles in their hands, and the

JAMRÚD AT THE MOUTH OF THE KHYBER

escort that has been provided for us of a couple of sowárs of a native cavalry regiment stand by their horses. Colonel Warburton, who has charge of the pass, welcomes us with the assurance that he is only too glad to see as many visitors to his pass as can come, for, as he says, the more the Afrídis get used to seeing people coming and going the better. The fact is that the old system of leaving these wild tribes to their own devices has been given up as a failure. We used to wait until they had accumulated a sufficient number of murders and robberies and raids on the more peaceful dwellers in the valley, to exhaust the patience of the long-suffering authorities. Then an expedition was ordered; with great difficulty troops were marched up into the stony mountains; a few long shots were exchanged, a village or two burnt; and as nothing was to be seen of the inhabitants, we retired; medals were then handed round, and the bill came to many lacs of rupees. Now a wise Government says to the tribes, "Look here, my friends, we will pay you *first* on condition that you are good *afterwards;* but understand, should you misbehave in any way, we won't trouble ourselves to ask who has done it, but we simply stop the allowance of the tribe in whose district the outrage is committed, as a fine."

Now an Afrídi, at any rate in his own estimation, as much as any other man, must live. His country grows only stones, and his precarious existence is eked out by selling in Peshawur, in the winter, scanty bundles of firewood collected off his barren hills. So their chief occupation has come to be thieving and robbing. Captain James in his interesting report says of them: "Expertness in thieving is the sole characteristic which leads to distinction among the Zakha Khel Afrídis on the south entrance to the Khyber Pass. It is a virtue which maidens seek in their future husbands, and mothers fondly look to for their new-born babes. Every male child is consecrated, as it were, at his birth to crime; a hole is dug in the wall similar to those made by burglars, and the infant is passed backwards and forwards through it with the words, 'Ghal shah, ghal shah, ghal shah,' 'Be a thief, be a thief, be a thief.'

They are the principal enactors of the daring crimes formerly perpetrated in the Peshawur cantonments, but by no means confine themselves to these, but rob the Bangashes of Kohat as well as the Khulils on the Peshawur-Attock road, and no other tribe is safe from their depredations. It is also related of this tribe that, being without a ziárat, or place of pilgrimage, in their own borders, and being thus compelled to resort to the territories of their more fortunate neighbours, they seized and killed the first worshipful subject who came in their way. The unlucky man was a Khattak, and as he answered all requirements he was slain. Stones were heaped over him, and in a few days the Zakha Khel were proudly paying their devotions at the grave of 'their own' Pír, or Spiritual Lord!"

It will easily be understood that it would be an expensive business to pay such men as these to be quiet every day of the week; so the arrangement has been come to, that for such and such sum paid to them by the Government they are to behave like Christians on Tuesdays and Fridays. They therefore do their throat-cutting, pillaging, robbing on five days of the week (Sundays included), but on the remaining two sit quietly on the hill-tops, no doubt with watering mouths watching the rich caravans of laden camels, and now and then the British tourist, passing to and fro in the narrow valley below. If a shot is fired, that part of the tribe in whose division of the road the shot was fired, gets Rs. 1000 stopped out of its allowance next quarter-day—500 of which go to Government, and 500 to the lucky man fired at.

This arrangement is business-like, and with the help of the Khyber Rifles—a useful body enlisted from the tribes themselves and ably commanded by Mahomed Aslam Khan, who garrison Ali Masjíd and other forts in the pass—it works well.

It will thus be seen that a ride through the dreaded Khyber is under present arrangements an easy and interesting, as well as a possibly lucrative, way of spending a day.

A very well laid out, though stony, road leads from Jamrúd over

ALI MASJID FORT FROM THE KHYBER PASS

a ridge, and then drops down into the Khyber valley just before reaching Ali Masjíd Fort, which stands well on the top of a hill, in the centre of the pass, just where it is most closed in. I certainly had imagined, and I think it is a common impression, that the celebrated Khyber Pass is a romantic "gorge" shut in by "cliffs" on both sides rising to stupendous heights, but the photograph on the opposite page will give a better idea of this the narrowest part of the valley. There is no "gorge," nor are there "cliffs" here. It is rather, as the photograph shows, a narrow, barren valley, with steep stony mountains on either side—the whole devoid of vegetation, except for a small evergreen bush that grows between the stones. Still it is very impressive, as being the only gate into India that is at all practicable on this part of the frontier, and the romance of its past associations with the disastrous retreat in 1841 still clings to it.[1]

The mountains are very sparsely inhabited; not more than one or two villages are seen in the six miles' drive from Jamrúd to Ali Masjíd, and the only living things that catch your eye are the two sentries of the Khyber Rifles, who occupy every hill-top over the road, and present arms to the white faces passing below. It is a wild and rugged scene, inhospitable to the last degree as a human habitation, and one would need an Afrídi's lungs to be able to do any good on such hills as these.

Ali Masjíd, which derives its name from the little white mosque that was built some 600 years ago at the foot of the steep hill on which the fort stands, probably by some Túrki invaders, was once a famous and powerful stronghold, but has had to bow its head before the long-range cannon and far-shooting rifle of modern times; and its walls still bear the marks of the shot from the guns of the

[1] Curiously enough the massacre of our troops in this retreat has no real connection with the Khyber Pass. It took place in the Khúrd Kabul and Lataband Passes, the last stand being at Gandamak, some sixty miles from the western end of the Khyber Pass itself, the sole survivor reaching Jalalabad, which itself is forty miles beyond the Khyber.

British battery that forced the pass in the war of 1878. Now it is but a post of the Khyber Rifles, and a goal for the British tourist to visit, from the walls of which he can conveniently solve the whole of the "Afghan question" to his own satisfaction.

A fine caravan of some 200 camels, on its way to Kabul, slowly straggled along the road below us, as we sat on the walls of Ali Masjíd; and were it not for the heavy tolls exacted by the Amír, a fine trade might be done with Afghanistan by this route. As it is, the light tolls levied by the English on passing goods almost cover the cost of the Khyber Rifles.

While at Peshawur the colonel commanding the 28th Punjáb Infantry was kind enough to get up a "Khattak dance" of the Khattaks in his regiment. They are a tribe that live on the west bank of the Indus no great distance from Kohat, and are celebrated, like other highlanders, for their sword dances. A huge bonfire was made on an open plain, and after dinner we all walked there through the starry night, and found a tent pitched and chairs put for us to sit on, for like most Eastern dances it is a long business. A great crowd of natives and Sepoys, the latter not in uniform, stood round in an enormous circle, their faces lit up by the flare of the fire and their big turbans and flowing trousers made more picturesque by the weird light. Then began the inevitable tomtom, drummed with the palms of the drummers' hands, a dull thud to the shrill but monotonous melody of a reed-pipe such as the Italian *pifferari* use. Following the music, in a long single-file procession, marching with slow and hesitating step in exact time to the drum, came the Khattak Sepoys, dressed in their white skirt-like trousers to the ankles, with bare feet, a dark tunic of some sort fitting closely to their active forms. Their big dark pagris, one end of which hangs down their backs, made them look all the taller, big men though they were.

After circling the fire in a wide ring, for there were some sixty dancers, the measure increased in time, and the steps became quicker, as they stooped first to one side and then with a sudden twist again to the other, gesticulating with their arms and clapping their hands together now and again, in time to the music. Gradually the music warms up, the drums beat faster, and the pipes become wilder, while the men answer with leaps and cries. Suddenly a rush is made for the swords which lie in a heap on the ground, each man seizes one in his hand, and the long procession again slowly circles the fire with spasmodic jerky step, twisting and turning and stamping the ground in strict time to the music; a sort of "engaging the enemy" first on one side and then on the other, until the air is full of twisting men, their skirts flying out, their swords flashing wonderfully in every direction, the music gradually working them up to the quickest step.

Then out of the line came flying first one and then another, executing a very graceful *pas seul*. Skimming over the ground with invisibly small steps, waving a sword in each hand round their heads, they pirouetted and executed feats of agility, no doubt to show off their fighting activities, feats which were applauded by the ever-increasing wild cries of their companions, until in the climax of excitement they finally threw themselves down before the maddened musicians, their heads being surrounded by a sort of halo of flashing swords lit up by the glare of the fire, the flames of which leapt high into the sky owing to the plentiful libations of Baku petroleum, lavishly poured on by the enthusiastic attendants.

A strange wild sight indeed, which gives one an idea how close one is to the edge of civilisation as one sits there comfortably in an arm-chair in one's dress clothes and patent leather shoes.

While at Peshawur I was fortunate enough to get the Government's permission to join the Kuram force, where my friend Merk was at that moment engaged in extending the British Empire, and I called on Mr. Hastings, the chief of the Peshawur Police, who was kind enough to give me the help that is always so willingly extended in India.

My arrangements were soon made, for instead of going back by train to Rawal Pindi, and returning thence by train and road to Kohat, a zigzag journey, I wanted to ride from Peshawur through the Kohat Pass, direct to Kohat, and so accomplish a long-wished-for journey through that point of the enemy's country between the Peshawur and Kohat districts that I have so often contemplated on maps, sticking out obstinately as it does into British territory.

I was told that the road was bad, but that a lightly-loaded ekha *could* get through. So on the evening of the 5th of March I called Nainu, whose ideas of the greatness as well as the wickedness of this world were increasing in proportion to the distance he travelled from his beloved Himalayas, and gave him my final instructions that my luggage was to be put on three ekhas, and that he was to start with it at six o'clock next morning, punctually, in order to get it through the forty miles to Kohat in the day. He seemed about as cheerful as a country child would be on being told to find its way alone across London, but I comforted him by telling him that I should be coming along the same road a few hours later, and would pay the necessary funeral obsequies to his corpse. Poor Nainu, the mild Hindu pahari, I expect, often had some wild nightmares in this rough Mohammedan country.

Next morning at nine, owing to Mr. Hastings' kind arrangements, Syud Mahomed Amír, the dapper commandant of the Border Military Police, drove up to the bungalow in his dog-cart, and after a cordial God-speed from the General, I started on the twenty-miles' level drive to Aimul Chabútra. A heavy fog and drizzling rain, which seemed strangely out of place in this dry country, made the earthen roads very bad going, and I soon began to have my doubts as to the progress of Nainu and the baggage, for even our pony was only able to pull us a great part of the way at a walk. Long before the fog lifted we had left Peshawur and its green cultivation far behind, as the Mír Sahib and I whiled away the time, he telling me stories about the country, and I endeavouring

AT THE GATE OF ALI MASJID FORT

to enlighten him as to the difference between the East and the West; but it is rather trying to one's Hindustani to be suddenly thrown into conversation with a native gentleman, in which "áps" and the third personal pronoun predominate to an extraordinary degree; but by dint of filling up every pause in the conversation with them, I trust he did not think I was disrespectful enough to wish to *tutoyer* him.

All too soon the expected sight of the three black specks on the broad open plain was seen, and before long we were up to Nainu and the three struggling ekhas. The wretched ponies looked dead beat, the wheels were clogged with mud, Nainu was walking with his shoes in one hand, pushing the ekha with the other, while the wild-looking driver on the other side adjured the pony with voice and arm to make another effort. The end of the "made road" was some four miles farther on; time, midday; and still twenty-four miles to Kohat. Inwardly my mind went back to my schoolboy days. If an ekha takes six hours to travel sixteen miles along a "made road," how many hours would the same take to do twenty-four miles over the Kohat hills? Multiply the answer by the number of ekhas, three, and the product gives the time when I expected to see my baggage again.

However, sympathy with misfortune is in many cases direct discouragement, so I waved my hand in a friendly way to Nainu, and called to him that he would find the guard ready to take him through the pass a few miles farther on, and drove away.

Aimul Chabútra, the Resting-place of Aimul (though why he chose such a place to rest in "God alone knows"), is a little mud fort standing alone, just at the base of the hills where a narrow valley comes out. It is surrounded on all sides by stones and sun, and, from its appearance, looks as if it had never known the meaning of such words as water and shade.

It is one of the posts of that excellent force, the Border Military Police, to whose care is confided the peace of the actual frontier. Some half a dozen of them turned out and stood at attention as their commandant drove up, and a native bedstead was brought out for me to sit on while I partook of some very sugary and milky tea, that was however very refreshing in the scorching sun. After eating my bread and meat and bidding the courteous Mír Sahib good-bye, I got on a horse belonging to one of the police, and, accompanied by a mounted trooper, rode across the frontier, that invisible line which is always coloured so prettily on the maps.

The road lies up the bed of a river, which in this case was not much more stony than the surrounding hills. The valley is quite narrow and flat-bottomed, absolutely barren except in some corners near the widely scattered villages, where a field or two is irrigated with water from some invisible source.

The Kohat Pass has lost its value since the railway has been made from Rawal Pindi to Khúshalgarh on the banks of the Indus. Pindi has thus replaced Peshawur as the base of Kohat, and the pass is now only occasionally used by travellers as a means of communication between the two districts. Much the same style of affairs exists on this road as on the Khyber. The Jowákis and Adam Khels loot, rob, and murder all round, but, as they put it, "*Sarak ziárat dai*"—the road is a sanctuary—and they are left to their own devices as long as nothing happens to disturb its inviolability. The usual promenades have been made from time to time over their detestable hills, a few villages burnt and towers blown up, in poor satisfaction for their accumulated sins, and then things settle down for another spell of quietness.

It is perhaps too hard to judge these wild Afrídis by Western standards. Their country is so poor that they cannot live at peace and multiply. Their scanty sustenance is eked out by what they can loot from the traveller or from a neighbour a trifle better off than themselves, and this, instead of being a crime in their eyes, is to them an honourable and, indeed, almost the only profession open to them. The morality of it, after all, is quite as high as that of the successful stock-jobber who picks the pocket of his less wide-awake

LOOKING DOWN THE KHYBER PASS FROM ALI MASJID

opponent, for the Afrídi is at any rate prepared to risk his life in the process. These Pathans have their good qualities, too, as well as their bad. They are hospitable to a degree, and are a cheerful and happy people whose lot is, as the world goes, a hard enough one.

One meets but few human beings as one rides along over the rough stones at a walking pace, and the miles grow longer and longer under the burning midday sun, which is here shut in by the steep and stony hills. The villages, being built of the rough round boulders which are scattered everywhere over the country, would scarcely be noticed were it not for the towers which ornament as well as defend them; and it was with great pleasure that I came upon Kháni Ghari, the "half-way house," where I changed my guard for another. The people of the village, wild, dirty-looking ruffians, came out and hospitably offered me shelter and milk, but my conversation with them was limited, as they understood no Hindustani and their Pushtú was worse than Greek to me. It is impossible to look at these tribes without thinking of their alleged Jewish connection. An interesting story tells that the Afghans themselves trace their descent from Sarúl (Saul), the son of Kais (Kish), of the tribe Ibn Yamín (Benjamin). Their accounts of Sarúl's doings are very much what we know of Saul from the Bible. Such stories as his search for his father's asses, his visit to the witch at Endor, occur in their ancient books. According to their account Sarúl had two sons, Barakiah and Iramia (Jeremiah), both of whom were born in the same hour of different mothers, but both of the tribe of Lawi (Levi). After Sárúl's death on the battle-field, Barakiah and Iramia succeeded to high honours under Daud (David). Barakiah had a son named Assaf, and Iramia one called Afghana, and these two flourished during the reign of Sulemán (Solomon). It was Afghana who superintended the building of the Bait-ul-Mukadas, or Temple of Jerusalem; and when the latter was sacked by Bakhtún-nasr (Nebuchadnezzar), the numerous tribe of Afghana was driven from Shám (Palestine), took refuge in Kohistan, and centuries later spread eastward over Afghanistan.

It is supposed also that the tribes about the Khyber were the last to resist the spread of Mohammedanism from the west, for a well-known Afghan couplet, after extolling the virtues of Umr, Osmán, and Ali, concludes with the words: "Whoever denies one of these is much worse than the bear, the pig, and the Jew of the Khyber."[1]

The physical appearance of these people, too, strangely accords with our Jewish type as found in Galicia. They have also many old customs that the Jews had, notably the sending away of a scapegoat or calf in times of severe pestilence into the desert after the mullahs have laid their hands on its head.[2] Also the customs of punishment by death from stoning, dividing land by lot, the necessity of the younger brother marrying the widow of his elder brother, prevail among them.

It is more probable, however, that after the Captivity the ten tribes were planted by their conquerors as far away on the eastern borders of Persia as possible, and that here they came into contact with the Duránis, who are the pure Afghans, and who were, at that time, nomads. Possibly the aristocracy of these nomads intermarried with the Jews, and so derived their traditions, for physically the type of the Duráni most nearly resembles the Jew as found in Palestine at the present day. The Pushtú language, again, bears no trace of any Semitic dialect whatever, and there is no doubt that many of the customs of these Pathan tribes are strongly defined as purely Aryan. So that whatever the composition of their blood may be, it without doubt contains a large proportion of Aryan element.

The sun was beginning to get low before any change came to my trooper and myself as we rode alone along this stony winding valley, and my chief food for reflection at any unusually large boulder was, "I wonder how Nainu will get past *that*." At last the road suddenly leaves the river-bed, and turning sharp to the left, zigzags up a short steep rise to the top of the pass, from where, immediately below, the basin of Kohat is seen, the small

[1] Dr. Bellew. [2] James' Report.

station planted in the middle, nestling prettily in its bower of green trees. A steep winding path down and a quick gallop a couple of miles over the flat, to stretch my stiffened legs, brought me into the straggling little station, where the bugles of the Punjáb Infantry there quartered gave a friendly welcome, and that excellent institution, the Government Dâk Bungalow, soon sheltered my weary person from a storm that now swept down from the hills.

I had time to stroll out to make my arrangements for the morrow by going to the civil officer of the station, who delegated my needs to his chaprassi, who passed them on to the ekha chaudri, who ordered two ekhas to take me to Hangu the next day. Truly this is a country of middlemen.

Hangu, I learnt, was twenty-six miles off, so the two ekhas were to stay the night with me at the Dâk Bungalow there, and take me on the thirty-eight miles farther to Thull next day. A good meal of "muttin charp and kárhi báth" brought a long day to an end, and just as I was getting into bed at ten o'clock, I heard, to my surprise, shouting and the jingling of ekhas outside. "Ohé Nainuá, is that you?" and as I looked out into the dark night, there actually were my three ekhas! How they got there, to this day I do not know. Nainu told me that all the ekhas had to be unloaded four times, and the baggage carried on the men's backs, in order to get them over the worst places; and as he remarked, "O Protector of the Poor, the roads in this country are very bad," I did not venture to contradict him, but gave him a cake of tobacco and told him to get to sleep, which I fancy he speedily did, with true Eastern philosophy.

The ekhas for this journey of sixteen hours over the worst imaginable road, or rather track, got 6 rupees 4 annas (about 7 shillings) each, and the drivers went away happy.

Next morning I was away early, for I heard that the lieutenant-governor was about to arrive, and when the gods come down upon earth, we poor mortals are apt to fare badly. So it was with a light heart that I escaped from Kohat with a jingling ekha under me, to the sound of the booming of guns which announced the great man's entry at the other end of the station.

When on the frontier one does so much ekha-driving, that a few of the merits and demerits of this wonderful production of the East may here find a place. First, then, the only merit it has is, that it cannot come to grief—for the reason that it is entirely made of pieces of wood, tied together with rope and string, and any breakage only requires a fresh piece of string to tie it together again. It is difficult to know which demerit to begin with, for as the miles pass by they seem to multiply so rapidly. At the start you don't notice that there are no springs, for the sweeper has just been along the mall, and has carefully swept off every pebble. It is true that it strikes you as rather a poor arrangement to have to stretch out your legs flat along the bamboo shaft beside the driver, who occupies rather a prominent position almost in your lap, but there is no help for it, unless native-wise you like to sit on them. Also the inordinate number of pillows and supports that are required to prop up your back are certainly rather a trouble to arrange, but after all they keep their place as long as you sit still. So we fly out of the station exhilarated by the quick trotting and in the happiest frame of mind. But the lazy sweeper, confound him! has not continued his efforts to any great distance, and the rude bump over the first stone reminds you that there are no springs to the cart, the second, immediately after, disturbs the carefully arranged pillows, while a third causes the back of the ekha inconsiderately to knock your helmet over your eyes. However it is as well to be good-humoured, and the difficulty is easily remedied by taking off your helmet and putting on a cap. The pillows then being rearranged, a fresh start is made. After a few minutes you begin to realise that you have been sitting for half an hour on a flat seat with your legs stretched straight out on a level. You draw them up and sit with your knees in your mouth, but in doing so the pillows become loosened, and again show a wish to fall out of the ekha. After carefully rearranging these as well as the bumping and jolting ekha will allow, the brilliant sun begins to beat down on your head, and you think of putting on your helmet again, but find that in this position there is no room for it under the covering of the ekha; and so you move to readjust yourself, and one of the pillows falls out on to the dusty road, and has to be recovered by the driver, while there is a pause for bad language.

A FRONTIER JOURNEY

About midday you begin to cease to take any interest in your surroundings, and your attention is fixed on clutching the pillows, water-bottle, revolver, helmet, and other accessories of travel, while you are tossed about in the ekha box like a schoolboy in a blanket; and just as you are beginning to grow used even to this pleasing motion, an extra big stone bumps you up in the air again, and your head comes into violent contact with the wooden bars of the ekha covering!

And yet one survives it all and drives into Hangu alive,

though not perhaps in love and charity with all men, least of all the man who invented ekhas.

The road was along the frontier up a pretty cultivated valley now green with patches of wheat, irrigated from the stream. The big, brown, stony Samána Range is close by on your right, and low, but equally stony, hills shut in the left, but there is nothing especially remarkable in the monotonous drive except that the road is fairly good. Hangu has derived some fictitious interest by having been the base of operations in the last Samána-Miranzai expedition. When not serving for this useful purpose, it consists of a Dâk Bungalow, a tidy little square stone battlemented and loop-holed fort, inside of which is the treasury, the jail khana full of villainous-looking marauders, and the Assistant Commissioner's office; for Hangu is the summer residence of that official, whose winters are spent in a still more exciting place called Thull.

One cannot but feel struck again by the work done by these young Assistant Commissioners. Young boys straight from an English public school, with only the stamp of the Indian Civil Service examination upon them to distinguish them from their fellows, are sent out to India, and after but a few years' experience, find themselves on the frontier, in some such place as Hangu or Thull. Here they practically have the burden of the Empire on their backs, for they are responsible, in the first instance, for the peace and welfare of perhaps the most inflammable border of the whole of the Queen's dominions.

It is true that some sixty miles off this solitary boy can fall back upon his Deputy Commissioner, but in practice the peace and order, progress and advancement of an area perhaps as large as Yorkshire, depend upon the energy and ability, the tact and *savoir faire* of this boy. In a great measure his word is law. Taking his line from his chief, the Deputy Commissioner, he carries out his ideas with a freedom and power that no other profession can offer. He combines in himself all the lower administrative and judicial functions, except where the cases are too serious; these he refers to his chief. He is in practice engineer-in-chief, road-maker, educational inspector, policeman and Minister for Foreign Affairs. He is a small emperor, in fact, whose subjects are a wild and but half-tamed lot, and whose neighbours across the border are ever on the watch to catch him tripping. But by his tact, and above all his personality, this boy makes his influence everywhere felt, and spreads the light that, one is proud to feel, can shine out of an Englishman's face.

His solitary life can hardly be pictured. For two or three years he will be alone at Thull and Hangu, amidst a waste of barren stones, which are baked to fire heat by the summer sun, and chilled by winter frosts. Scarcely ever does he see a white face, except for a day or two's run to Kohat, a small garrison town some sixty miles off, which to him is a reminder that "England, home and beauty" do still exist, somewhere in the far-off distance.

It is his work, however, and above all, the responsibility that makes him feel a pride in the visible success of his work, that keep him going; and the consciousness that he is the only white face among all his darker surroundings gives him a standard below which he feels he cannot afford to fall.

It is to the credit of the English name that, among the many boys who are sent out to India to fight our battles of peace there, so few fall below what is expected of them. That India is the brightest jewel in our Queen's crown is surely in a great measure due to her 1100 Indian Civil Servants, who control the welfare and destinies of her 260,000,000 dusky subjects.

And yet we are told that all men are equal! I could only wish for the exponent of this plausible doctrine a year's residence in Thull, where his surroundings would speedily convince him that Superiority and Inferiority are the upper and nether millstones between which his Equality would soon be ground to powder.

Away again next morning from Hangu—for twelve hours at Hangu is enough for us who are not Assistant Commissioners—and along the wide, open, treeless valley; the same features as yesterday, only with less cultivation. Not more than three or four villages are seen in the whole of the thirty-eight miles' drive, and the passers-by on the road are few and far between. Now and again a rough-looking peasant is seen scratching the ground with his primitive wooden plough, drawn by a pair of small and stunted black bullocks; but otherwise there is little of interest and little to be seen.

At one little walled village on the road we stopped to feed the ponies, and I was soon surrounded by a crowd of village urchins and urchinesses, who were made supremely happy by some handfuls of Huntley and Palmer's mixed biscuits, a tin of which I had open in the ekha; while the empty tin itself, with its coloured label, no doubt now adorns the "drawing-room mantelpiece," as a work of beauty and art, in the mud house of the headman of Surozai village.

Thull appeared to retreat as fast as we advanced, and the journey seemed endless and the bumps infinite over the stony track, until at last we were rattling down a long straight clearing on the stony and scrubby slope, which the driver told me was the avenue approach to Thull. At last the little mud fort came into sight, and though it figures always in such beautiful big print on the maps of India, the whole of it could be conveniently put into a corner of Trafalgar Square without in any way inconveniencing the traffic. However, these were gala days for Thull; for our relations with our neighbours being strained, a whole company of native infantry was encamped at its gate, so that there was much coming and going. The fort inside is not more imposing than outside; a line of little huts for some 100 men of a native infantry regiment, and an office or two and small detached quarters for the Assistant Commissioner when there, filled the whole area. One or two wretched saplings ill requited the care spent upon them in trying to make them grow; and the native sentry at the gate stood apathetically on guard over this important piece of Government property.

Thull evidently owes its greatness not to itself but to its position. Though we nominally took over this country after the

Sikh wars in 1848, yet we never administered it in any way until 1878, when during the last Afghan war a road was made from Kohat to Thull. Since then, lying as it does just at the mouth of the Kuram valley, Thull has had an importance thrust upon it; for though you scarcely notice it, across the wide stony river-bed from the fort an unusual collection of stones indicates the presence of the city of Thull, the county town of the Kuram Turis. This poor-looking village is one of the chief Turi towns, for being at the mouth of their valley, all their communications with the outer world must pass through it.

At the fort I found an orderly and some ponies waiting for me, with a message from Merk to tell me to come on a further four miles down the main valley to Bilandkhel camp. Accordingly after getting directions from the orderly—whom I left to bring on Nainu and my baggage, whose ekha had lagged behind—I mounted and rode down alone to the ford across the Kuram river, which here flows out of the Kuram valley, a rapid, tumbling mountain stream some forty yards across at the ford.

Following a track down the open valley, which is sparsely covered with thorny bushes, I soon came to a straight and cleared track, at the end of which I could see the long white line of the tents of the camp.

The sun was getting low as I cantered towards the camp, and on meeting Merk and Colonel Brownlow of the 1st Punjáb Infantry, who were walking towards me, I was greeted with the truly British welcome of "What the devil are you doing here without a guard?" from my anxious friend, who was responsible for my safety! The fact was that I had left British territory behind in crossing the Kuram river, and as a Havildár of the mountain battery had been cut up a few evenings previously on this bit of road, strict orders had been given that no one was to leave camp without a guard. I was, however, soon forgiven my sins in the kindly welcome I received from all, and was duly installed again in the comforts of a "Kabul tent."

Darkness falls apace in this country of no twilight, and as I stood quietly at my tent door that evening, the charm of the novelty and the poetry of the surroundings stole over me. The stars shine brilliantly down on the camp out of the black sky overhead. The cavalry trumpets sound out clear in the still night air. The bagpipes of the 1st Punjáb Infantry are playing before the mess tent. The rows of cavalry horses and transport mules are munching away at their grass. The fires of the pickets on the hill above shine down their protection upon us; while nearer the sentries' tramp is heard steadily pacing up and down the thorn hedge, which surrounds the whole camp. Far away up the valley the signal lamp on Thull fort is flashing its messages through the darkness to us, almost as quickly as one could speak, and forming a thread, as it were, in our communications with India, with Europe, with England, and with home, along which one's thoughts fly from out of this strange new world to those one cares for so far away.

## CHAPTER II

THE presence of the camp at Bilandkhel was due to one of those moves in the political game of chess that is continually being played upon the frontier. Moves and countermoves are carried out with such skill on both sides that an intimate knowledge of the methods of the game is necessary to the onlooker, if he wishes to follow the process with any degree of intelligence. It is far beyond the scope of these pages to enter into such considerations. Suffice it to say, that the lane from Kohat to the top of the Kuram valley is a long and narrow one, in which there is a sharp turning just where Thull is situated.

The mud village of Bilandkhel, which lies a few miles off just at this spot, though outwardly innocent and unpretending, is locally somewhat important as the gathering-place of the many discordant elements in the neighbourhood, and on this occasion, owing no doubt to the thunder in the air, it began to fester. Those turbulent rascals the Wazírs, encouraged secretly by their more powerful friends at a distance, pushed themselves forward to such a degree, that it was found necessary on our side to apply a poultice to the spot in the shape of a small force of all arms, to soothe the inflammation. That the political officer in charge was a Hakím as well as a Hákim, was proved by the success of the treatment; for after sitting quietly there for three months, the camp eventually withdrew, with no further complications than a few shots fired and the loss of the doctor's bottle of ink, which was stolen by one of the marauders of the country.

Even this insult was avenged by the exaction of a fine of Rs. 70 from the offender's family; and as the thief, imagining a bottle stolen from the doctor's tent must be medicine, had drunk it to ward off future illnesses, he was considered to have sufficiently expiated his crime.

It is a new experience for a civilian to find himself in a camp on active service, and there is a seriousness about it that gives a *raison d'être* to the order and precision that reign everywhere. The even rows of white tents, the straight lines of picketed horses, the wide, level, cleared roads, all give you the impression that within everything is in its place, ready to be utilised any moment it may be required. The thick thorn hedge that has been piled up round the camp, at the openings in which the sentries pace up and down, gives a secure as well as a tidy look to the whole; while the pickets on the hills round form an outer fringe of protection which afford you, as it were, a little breathing space, and take away the confined feeling that a small camp is apt to convey.

The force at Bilandkhel was half of the Kuram escort of Mr. W. Merk, C.S.I., chief political officer detailed to Kuram, and consisted of the 1st Punjáb Infantry under Colonel Brownlow, one squadron of the 5th Punjáb Cavalry, and two guns of the Peshawur mountain battery under Captain F. Birch, the whole under the command of Colonel Turner, C.B. These all belong to the celebrated Punjáb Frontier Force—the P.F.F., or "Piffers," as they are called in the vulgar tongue. This force is another reminder of how much bigger "India" used to be before the days of railways, for it is a special force, raised in 1849, of ten infantry, five cavalry regiments, and four mule mountain batteries of six guns each; these, with the small mixed force of "Guides," were detailed under their own general (and until 1886, under the direct orders of the Lieutenant-Governor of the Punjáb) to guard the north-west frontier from Kashmir to Sind. Though the railway has now brought them under the orders of the Commander-in-Chief, they, with the pride of their past distinguished service behind them, are jealous of their

CAMP AT BILANDKHEL

individuality, and are still kept to their special work. Their headquarters are dotted at even distances all down the frontier from north to south—Abbottabad, Hoti Murdán, Kohat, Bannu, Dera Ismail Khan, Dera Ghazi Khan, and Rajanpur; while the very frontier itself, which as a rule runs along the foot of the hills, is watched by outposts from these headquarters, generally some fifty men under a native officer. The native officers by this means acquire the necessary self-reliance by being put in these independent commands, where they have to use their own judgment and tact. Each regiment is complete with its own transport, and is ready to move, literally at a moment's notice, either to meet a border raid of the tribes, or to go on active service across the frontier.

The Punjáb Frontier Force is in a way a picked force, whose readiness and elasticity make them specially fitted for the rough work of all sorts that falls to their lot, as their long and brilliant record of service testifies. At the same time their work is hard and trying. Excepting Abbottabad, which is a small sub-hill-station, the other headquarters are mostly dry and dreary spots enough, long distances away in a wild, lonely, and barren country, where the heat in summer burns with a fire that almost makes the stones red-hot, and where life is interesting chiefly from its hard work and freedom, in a country which is far more like Central Asia than the India of our imagination.

I was most kindly received by the officers in camp, and soon fell into the routine of camp life. Every one was busy all the morning at their work. The cavalry were out raising the dust on a piece of open ground on one side of the camp, while the long line of infantry went through their evolutions on the other. Inside camp one could roam about as one pleased through the long lines of tents, and I mostly spent my mornings taking photographs of some of the men—fine, big, strapping sepoys, who were as eager as children to have their pictures taken. Then my wanderings would take me round to our corner of the camp, where Merk, the political officer, sits enthroned on an old camp chair at the door of his tent.

In front of him is spread a large Persian carpet, on which sit, all huddled together in the blazing sun, a number of wild-looking ruffians, maybe a Jirga, an assembly of leading men of one of the tribes, come down from the hills to discuss the future with him.

The principal men sit in front, the less influential crowding round the outskirts; but in truth, to an unaccustomed eye, there is not much to choose between them, either for beauty or squalor, wildness or evil looks. Dressed in sober-coloured cotton and woollen coats with loose trousers, the dirt on which has made them much the colour of the earth they sit on, with aquiline noses and deep-set hawk-like eyes, their unkempt shaggy brown beards set off by their large dull-coloured pagris, any one of them would make as good a villain in the play as no doubt he is in earnest on his native heath. Yet there is a certain dignity of manner about them. One feels they are at any rate men, and that, according to their own lights, there are even certain refinements of blood amongst the front rows.

"Salám, salám aleikum," comes from their guttural voices as they approach the tent door. "Peace to you, Sahib; are you well? are you fresh? is your health good?"

"Be seated, O well-born ones. May you too prosper; you are welcome here." After these polite inquiries business is commenced, both sides as a rule making long speeches and arriving slowly and with dignity at their different points.

"See here now, O Sahib, what can we do? The Sirkár says that we are no longer to levy tolls, as we have ever done on passers up and down the valley. How can we live? We are a poor but free people; what will you do for us?"

"Why should we do anything for you, my friends; how are we beholden to you? You have raided and robbed, and much innocent blood has been shed. You know that the Sirkár will not allow this. Still, if for the future you cease this raiding, I will perhaps ask the Sirkár to give you the same grants they did in compensa-

PEACE OR WAR? . JIRGA OF MASSUZAI ORUKZAI

tion during the last war with the Amír of Kabul. What say you to this, O men of sense?"

"Oh no," shouts some wild blood from the back rows, "what satisfied us then won't content us now; we are free to do as we like and will fight for our rights." And as they all sit there eagerly leaning forward, some thirty or forty of them, each grasping his long rifle in his hand, they look wild and ready enough for mischief.

"All right," answers Merk, laughing, "we are quite ready and will be only too glad to fight you; you see, we have nothing else to do here! There are the regiments, there are the little guns, go and take a good look at them yourselves!" For a few moments their wild eyes flash angrily, and heated words betoken the coming storm, until Merk breaks in.

"Stop now, O greybeards and nobly-born ones, cease this child's talk and be men. See we are both at the bottom of the well together: you cannot get away from us nor we from you. If you want to fight, please yourselves and your blood be upon your heads, but remember that the man who lights a fire against his own walls must not be surprised if his house is burnt down; and you know too your saying that 'it is not well to sit down to eat corn-stalks in company with an elephant.' Be sensible, then, and take what the Sirkár may offer you."

After much talking they rise and troop off to a solitary tree outside the camp, under whose scanty shade from the blazing sun they sit all the afternoon discussing the matter; the young ones of course wishing to run the risks, while the old ones counsel prudence. In the evening they return and the Jirga is resumed. Each man has his say in this open democratic assembly, any one at the back chiming in with what he considers an opportune word. Now the conversation is excited. Now there is a general laugh as Merk chaffs one who has put in his word with more eagerness than logic; for he is fluent enough in their Pushtú language to be quite a match for them in the proverbs and similes they so dearly love.

In the end they agree, and part with expressions of goodwill, the ceremony winding up with a sudden and reverent hush as they bow their heads and mutter a few words in prayer for a blessing on the interview. Then as they all disappear, the chief one, an old fellow with an evil countenance and long black beard, dyed red in places, comes back to the tent and squats on the ground beside Merk's chair. With anxious glances at me, as I sit on the bed, he whispers what he considers his secret remarks about the interview and its probable consequences.

The whole scene is typical of this country where all men are unequal—the wild number of excitable Easterns, each grasping his rifle and ready to spill blood like water; the single Western sitting before them in his cricketing flannels, laughing and smoking his cigarettes, with never a pistol or guard at his side, but quite conscious all the time that he is the better man.

The mess bugle brought us all together again at lunch, the total number, including the colonel commanding and the whole of his "brilliant staff," being fourteen, of whom four, belonging to the cavalry and artillery, had a separate mess, a tent pitched some fifty yards off—an excellent arrangement which enabled you to have the pleasure of "dining out" even at Bilandkhel. There was little to do in the afternoons, for the sun was hot, and it required some of the sportsman's energy to walk down the stony valley followed by a guard of a couple of sepoys, on the chance of getting a stray shot at a chikór partridge as he rose off the barren ground. Our usual occupation was to take a constitutional along the straight cleared path towards Thull, to the picket of four men of the 5th Punjáb Cavalry, who stood picturesquely beside their horses all day long, guarding the road since the killing of the artillery havildár. This promenade of three miles, followed as we were solemnly by our guard, was a truly monotonous proceeding, in which we met and greeted other couples on a like errand, as if we had not seen them for ages.

One afternoon we walked through the village of Bilandkhel. Entering through a hole in the wall under one of the many towers,

we wandered down some dirty lanes only a few feet wide, for wheeled traffic is of course unknown in the country. Shut in by rough walls of mud and stone, one sees little or nothing; occasionally an open door gives one a glimpse into a dirty yard where the ground is pounded into mud by a lean bullock or two. Everything is of the poorest description. The dwelling-rooms are little better than clean-swept mud sheds, and there is a total absence of architecture. Only in one spot did we come across any signs of life, and that was an open space where a few Hindus displayed some articles for sale in several tumble-down-looking sheds. Here the garrison of some fifty men of the 1st Punjáb Infantry who had been detailed to hold the village were to be found, mostly off duty, and consequently without uniforms. We picked our way back through the mud and dirt, and were glad to get out of such unsavoury quarters.

Coming back to camp there was always the football to watch, for the Sikhs are great players, and both at Sangina camp up the valley and here football was played with great zest nearly every afternoon on the parade-ground, both by the younger European officers and by the Sikhs. Surely no better training could be had for faithfulness in a tight corner, in time of need, than the friendly rivalry and tussle between officers and men before a goal. Loud were the cries of "Shabásh, shabásh, chowkidár!" ("Well done, watchman!") from the excited onlookers all round the ground, as the goal-keeper successfully met the rush of the eager subaltern and kicked the ball away.

The Sikhs and Pathans are about equal in numbers in these regiments, and each have their good and bad qualities. Both are fine, tall, well-built men, the Sikh perhaps the more powerful of the two, while the Pathan has greater physical endurance and agility. The Sikhs have very pleasant and handsome faces, rather round in shape, with small well-cut noses. Their custom of never cutting their beards, but twisting them up instead in a neat black roll on either cheek, gives them a smart and soldierly appearance. In character they are often almost bovine in their stupidity.

Being all of the yeoman class and dwellers in the plains, they are full of sturdy self-respect, resolute, obedient, and always under control. Their fighting qualities are too well known to need comment, and arise no doubt from their solid and steady courage and their contempt for death; but they are wanting in the initiative and dash that go to make up a perfect soldier. They have cheerful and agreeable natures, and nothing could have been more pleasant and well-bred than the manners of the Sikh native officers I met, most of whom had been promoted from the ranks. They struck me as being very like Italians in their unselfconscious, respectful bearing, which made one's intercourse with them at once easy and unconstrained. They were like children in their delight at having their photographs taken; and when I met some of them again, some months later, at a railway-station far off in India, they rushed up to me with warm greetings, and were full of regrets that when their pictures were taken in Kuram, owing to their being on active service, they had not with them the smart black-leather, silver-mounted cross-belts which they then wore! Nice, simple, outspoken fellows, as naïve and as vain as children, and as brave as lions in a scrimmage, what better type can one get for a soldier?

The Pathans, on the other hand, are highlanders whose training and traditions have been totally different.

Bred in their wild stony mountains under the fanatical influence of Mohammedanism, they are very impatient of all control from their own people; but when they take service with us they fight well even against their own tribesmen in time of war, though they find it much harder to submit to the bonds of discipline when encamped in peace-time at the foot of their own hills. They are very intelligent as a whole, but are consumed with intense arrogance and vanity, and are bloodthirsty to a degree that often amounts to homicidal mania. Though liable from sudden panics to lose their heads, when excited they are recklessly brave and fight with great *élan*. Against these somewhat numerous bad

NATIVE OFFICERS OF THE 1ST PUNJÁB INFANTRY

qualities must be set their physical and mental energy, their cheerfulness, their great personal loyalty to those to whom they have given their allegiance and friendship. They are excellent marksmen and born skirmishers, and for a successful dash, especially in their own wild mountains, they are almost unequalled.

The Sikh indulges in a hearty contempt for the Pathan—a feeling which the latter as warmly reciprocates; but they get along very well together in their different companies of the regiment, and class quarrels very rarely occur. The comparison of the Sikhs to the Germans and the Pathans to the French is not altogether an ill-suited one, and socially it is much easier for the English officer to mix with the former than the latter. For the Sikhs and ourselves have a common love for games and athletics, whereas the Pathan takes no part in either, and looks upon the Sikhs and Punjábis who appear in a semi-nude condition at these competitions as men utterly without shame and honour.

Our evenings were enlivened by the excellent pipers both of the 1st P.I. and of the mountain battery. Natives take wonderfully kindly to bagpipes, both as performers and listeners. Any Highland regiment might have been proud to possess such excellent performers as the mountain battery had, and it was amusing to see the pride with which these fine fellows strutted up and down to the time of their inspiriting music. Most of the airs they played were Scotch, but now and then the popular frontier march of "Zakhmi" issued somewhat weirdly from the pipes.[1] This Peshawur mountain battery is indeed a credit to its commander, Captain F. Birch, R.A., who is well known for the pride he takes in his men. All huge fellows, mostly Punjábi Mussulmans, it was always an interesting sight to watch them march out to practice. The battery here on active service was turned out as spick-and-

[1] This well-known march is of Pathan origin, and was composed by a celebrated musician named Miro. The words "Zakhmi pa gham kkhenast yam," etc. ("Wounded with grief I sit, pierced by the dagger of love," etc.) convey sentiments that are not confined solely to the East.

span as for a general's inspection. The mules (a relief set always accompany the gun-carriers) are fine big animals, sleek and fat yet in excellent condition for scrambling down the stony ravines and up banks which try severely the wind and limb of their two-legged leaders.

NO. 3 PESHAWUR MOUNTAIN BATTERY

They are armed with the long muzzle-loading gun, which, in order to lessen the load for each mule, is made in two parts that screw together, the wheels, trail, and axles being carried on the backs of three more. At the word of command, in less time than it takes to write it down, with a sudden clatter the mules are relieved of their burdens, the disjointed pieces of the guns and gun-carriages seem to fall together, and the row of long, fierce-looking little pieces are ready to send their shells off with an accuracy that the frontier tribes by experience know only too well. A deputation of one of the tribes even came one day into our camp to beg the loan of a few shots against their enemy, offering 150 rupees for each shot that we would fire for them; while the gunners themselves almost venerate the cannon in their devotion to them, one native officer coming out regularly every morning to salám to them and pat them affectionately as his children as they stood in a row before the guard!

PESHAWAR MOUNTAIN BATTERY IN ACTION. BILANDKHEL

The incidents in a camp in an enemy's country where there are no enemies, are few and far between, and one is grateful for excitement of any kind. One night as we sat at dinner in the mess tent, our eyes dazzled by the brightness of the row of kerosene lamps that stood on the table before us, a noise of galloping horses almost like thunder, mingled with the shouts of men, suddenly broke out, and we all started to our feet. In the momentary pause of expectation one of the youngsters called out "An attack!" and in an incredibly short time we were all outside! Blinded by the glare of light inside the tent, I stood for the first moment in utter darkness, wondering how long it would be before the expected Afghan knife was buried up to its hilt in my unresisting body! I cannot say that I felt like Casabianca, or that any equally noble sentiments crossed my mind; I only thought it was confoundedly dark and wished some one would take the bandage off my eyes! The noise continued for a minute or two more and then quieted down, and we all returned laughing to our dinner on hearing that a sais had carelessly set fire to the grass in the cavalry lines, and that the horses had taken fright. Luckily they did not break loose, and still more luckily the sentries did not fire, or the whole camp would have been under arms, sending volleys into the hard rocks around.

That night later, as I lay in my tent, I was awakened by the sentries firing, and I sat up awhile in bed and waited for the development of events, but as nothing further happened, I turned over and went to sleep again. The firing at night was of somewhat frequent occurrence, but in the darkness few of the marauders or marauders' shadows are ever hit. There was an opening in the thorn hedge close by my tent, at which a sentry was posted, who used to cause me some amusement. "Halt! who go there?" was invariably his sharp challenge. "Friend." "Pass, friend; all's well." Then, falling back on his more voluble Hindustani, he continued, "What manner of man are you? What the devil are you doing here?"

One soon, however, gets used to the noises in camp at night, and sleeps undisturbedly through some and pays little heed to the others.

Though the nights were still cold, yet being already the middle of March, the sun burnt fiercely down during the day out of the cloudless Eastern sky; and the only people who really appreciated his presence were the signallers, who were continually flashing with the heliograph to Gulistán, a post on the Samána range, about thirty miles back towards India. The little mirror on the top of the distant mountain looks like a sparkling diamond, and the native signallers read the messages, repeating the English letters as they come with wonderful rapidity, though of course they don't understand their meaning. A native seems to have no difficulty in learning to imitate anything; where he fails is in originality of resource. The faithful Nainu too, who masked his crass stupidity by the facility with which he learnt what was shown him, mechanically repeating it, exhibited some of his native character here by never moving out of my tent in camp. Not even the bagpipes or a Khattak dance of the sepoys or the cheers of the football players aroused his curiosity. He was quite happy to sit quietly near his food supplies. When remonstrated with, he simply showed that to him at any rate novelty had no charm.

As owing to the course of high politics there appeared no chance of the camp being able to move, Merk and I decided to march up the Kuram valley, where he had business to do, and join the remaining half of his escort, who were encamped at Sangína. Preparations did not take long, for on active service everything is always ready for a move. Our baggage was put upon camels, and my precious photographic plates, which had tried every sort of conveyance in India, experienced a new motion in the slow swing of the "ship of the desert." They marched off ahead of us under a guard of sixteen sepoys, with a native non-commissioned officer, and soon were lost to sight in the scrubby flat stretching up towards Thull.

Later in the day, in the hot sun, Merk and I rode out of camp with a couple of sowárs of the 5th Punjáb Cavalry and a guard of several wild-looking ruffians perched upon their shaggy ponies, who were some day to blossom into mounted Turi militiamen.

## CHAPTER III

A GLANCE at the map at the end of this volume will show the position of the Kuram valley better than words can describe it. Roughly, it is a long narrow valley, some eighty miles from end to end, with a sharp bend to the south about half-way down it at Sadda village. The upper half is a more open basin, some five or six miles across, and has on the north side of it the stupendous line of the Saféd Koh range, which, shutting it in like a wall, rises to a height of nearly 16,000 feet, or 10,000 feet above the valley itself. The south side of this basin is composed of lower, broken, and stony hills. From Sadda down to Thull, where the Kuram river, so to speak, strikes British territory, the valley is much narrower, and for a few miles above Thull is quite shut in by steep and barren mountains, which give the approach to the valley a desolate appearance as well as a dangerous character.

Our interest in the valley was brought about by the fact that it is one of the two roads by which Kabul can be approached from the east. As is well known, it was by this valley that General Roberts advanced on Kabul, and in December 1878 forced the Afghan position at the Peiwar Kotal. After the successful termination of the Afghan War, in spite of our assurances to the Turis to the contrary, the valley was evacuated by British troops, and the Turis were granted the blessings of Home Rule, which was indeed a polite way of getting rid of an obligation that the Government found it inconvenient to carry out.

It needed no great foresight to realise the consequences. In a country of mountains and stones, the possessors of the valley and water are naturally the objects of envy, and the Turis in their valley again became the centre of interest to the wild and hungry tribes in the mountains all round them. Danger is supposed to rally the threatened together, but even this was denied the unhappy Turis, owing to the conditions under which they lived. A bold, reckless, and vigorous race, still conscious of their conquest of Kuram from the Bangashes, they are proud of their position. Like all Pathans, they are intensely democratic. No Turi can bear to see another Turi put in a position of authority over him, and they are eaten up by family, village, and clan feuds and factions.

Now while all the surrounding hill clans—Zaimushts, Mangals, Muqbils, Wazírs, Orukzais—are Sunni Mohammedans, the Turis alone are Shíahs, and as such, hold in particular veneration the Syud families, who are the descendants of the daughter of Mahomet and Ali. Ali thus, to the Shíahs, has a semi-divine character, and owing to this every Syud with the sacred blood in his veins is considered almost to have some of the divine attributes of his ancestor. Each Turi, therefore, considers himself bound to be the Muríd, or disciple, of some Syud or other, whom he looks to as his Pír, or spiritual head. The whole of the valley is, in consequence, split up into two great semi-religious factions—the *Dréwandis,* who follow the lead of the Syuds whose head is Syud Abbás of Ahmedzai, and the *Mián Muríds,* or those whose spiritual lord is Mír Akbár of Shakadarra.

The Dréwandis, though numerically the stronger, are so continually at variance, caballing and quarrelling amongst themselves, that the weaker Mián Muríds are able to hold their own; and while the attention of the spiritual leaders of the Mían Muríds is much concentrated on increasing their personal following, the Dréwandi ideas may be described as rather more liberal and national.

Every Turi is thus under the religious influence of one Syud family or other, and is educated to a partisan life, in which the general good is always subordinated to individual advantage. The Afghan governors, who ruled the country up to 1878, naturally exploited this mass of Pathan and spiritual faction for their own benefit, playing at first with one family and then with another, pitting clan against clan, faction against faction, until the whole of Kuram was a hotbed of intrigue, and the Turis lost all sense of unity in the violence of party spirit.

These were the conditions of life when General Roberts with his army marched through and occupied the valley at the end of 1878; and with this excellent education we left them, a year and a half later, to the delights of self-government.

The inevitable took place: anarchy broke out, and every Turi did what was right in his own eyes. The people split up into a thousand different factions, quarrelled amongst themselves, and the absence of any constituted authority gave full opportunity for the unbridled play of intestine faction.

Upon this interesting scene the spectators on the hills round could not look down long unmoved. It is a moot question whether the Turis first raided uphill or their neighbours obeyed the laws of gravity and swooped down on the valley. At any rate, for ten years the raiding and counter-raiding went on. Probably not many lives were lost, for the Pathan loves a long shot, and his jezails do not carry very far; but life and property were both about as insecure as they could be made, even in this country where might is right. The best men in the valley, who still retained sense enough to look ahead, struggled vainly against the strong current which was sweeping their clan to destruction. This state of affairs soon produced the man able to take advantage of it.

Up in the mountains, on the right-hand side as you go up, there lived a humble person employed as a miller's watchman, a Zaimusht of the Zaimushts, whose broad, thick-set frame betokened him to be a man of great endurance, and whose powerful but evil-looking face proved him to be a man of far greater intelligence than his neighbours. He adopted the most paying as well as the most honourable profession of his country, and became a thief. By the success of his robberies he soon gained a pre-eminence amongst the young bloods of his clan. The proceeds of his robberies gave him wealth, and the daring with which he carried them out soon collected a band of admirers round about him, who were ready under his leadership to augment their scanty incomes at the expense of others. Chikkai—for by this nickname he is universally known—soon made himself useful to those who had grudges against their neighbours, by letting himself out as a hired assassin; and this Rob Roy with his armed following, was always ready to take his share, and more than his share too, in other people's quarrels.

In the Zaimusht hills there is a rich village called Chinárak, which, after the manner of the country, was divided against itself. Chikkai, ever ready to play the part of the disinterested friend, took the part of the weaker side, and helped them to drive out their more powerful rivals. This being done, he had little trouble in soon getting rid of his new friends, and, settling himself in their place, found himself one of the leading gentlemen of the Zaimusht clan, owner of the rich village of Chinárak, with a devoted following of some 80 to 100 well-armed men. As was only natural, the Zaimusht hills soon became too small for him, and he began to fly higher; but though the stage was greater, the play was the same.

On the south side of the Kuram valley lay the Afghan district of Khost, which at this time was also in trouble. Núr Mahomet, a cousin, and enemy, of the Kabul Amír's, was in rebellion, and Chikkai, ever ready to help the oppressed, marched across into Khost, and assisted Núr in driving out the Amír's representative and establishing himself in his place. As soon as this was done, Chikkai turned round and, with equal readiness, helped the Amír's troops to turn out Núr Mahomet and recover their position in Khost, whereby he gained great favour at Kabul, besides spreading his influence as a successful king-maker, and as leader of the Sunni clans round Kuram.

Meanwhile the Turis were fighting amongst themselves, Chikkai keeping the pot boiling by alternately with great impartiality assisting one side and then the other. The Mián Muríd faction, in their jealousy of the Dréwandis, played into Chikkai's hands; and after much fighting, the Sunni Bangashes, Zaimushts, and Wazírs in 1891 drove the Dréwandi Turis out of Lower Kuram, the Mián Muríd Turi villages in that part of the valley looking quietly on. These latter, however, did not gain much by their disloyalty to their Dréwandi brothers, for the Sunnis immediately turned upon them also, and driving them out, became the possessors of the whole of the lower valley from Thull to Sadda. The Turis now saw that their only chance was to rally, and, with the united forces of the clan, they made a desperate onslaught on the Sunnis. The Sunnis fought bravely, but were put to flight, and the Turis reoccupied the lower valley, looting and burning all the Sunni villages there.

Even then the Turis could not hold together. In a few days they began to quarrel. The Upper Kuram men retired with their plunder to the upper valley, and the Lower Kuram Turis, finding themselves left unsupported, evacuated the valley, into which the Sunnis again immediately poured. The usual retaliation began. Turi villages were sacked and burnt, their mosques were defiled, their lands laid waste, and Chikkai assumed the *rôle* of governor of Lower Kuram.

Not content with this success, the Sunni clans next year began to press on the Upper Kuram basin, and made every effort to effect a lodgment therein; but owing to the continued and resolute stand of the Turis at Sangína, the Sunnis were never able to advance farther than Sadda.

Hemmed in by their enemies on all sides, the leading Turis now saw that their only hope of escaping national extinction lay in coming under the protection of a power that was strong enough to save them. Years before they had appealed to the British for protection, and failing us, had fallen back on the Afghans; now

PICKET OF THE 2ND PUNJÁB INFANTRY

again they appealed to us, and, happily, this time with success. The Amír of Kabul, in his own interests, threw no difficulties in the way, and Mr. Merk, who has had such great experience on the frontier, was sent into the valley with a sufficient force to make his will respected, and a new era dawned upon Kuram. Thus ended the ten years of Home Rule.

Naturally the first matter to settle was Chikkai. Merk got him to come and see him, and in a long interview explained to Chikkai his own position, a good deal more clearly than Chikkai understood it himself. Cecil Rhodes has said that, in his experience, he has never yet met a man who could not be "squared." Self-interest is, no doubt, a powerful argument, and if you can put the alternatives clearly enough before a man, he will generally choose what is most advantageous to himself. This Merk did to Chikkai very plainly. He had, after all, much to lose and little to gain by showing enmity to us. If he remained friendly to us, and submitted to our wishes, he was told that, on his own ground at any rate, he would be left to keep the position he had won for himself; the alternative was, of course, to quarrel with us and be "smashed" for his pains. Like a wise man, he chose the former, and has since kept honourably to his bargain.

Into this valley then, so long the scene of trouble and turmoil, Merk and I now rode. Skirting the stony village of Thull, which lies direct in the mouth of the Kuram valley, our little party advanced, consisting as it did of ourselves, followed by Nainu carrying my gun, and a Turi burdened with my camera-case; the rear being closed in by two sowárs of the 5th Punjáb Cavalry and our band of half a dozen wild irregulars.

It was now noon, and the midday sun beat fiercely down on us, being reflected from the barren rocky hills out of which the road is here cut. This is the old road made in the last war, fifteen years ago, and never since touched! The fact of its existence at all, let alone its fair condition, is a testimony to the hardness of the ground and the absence of rain, that destroyer of man's works.

Beyond the fact that it was covered with loose stones, it was still almost passable for wheeled traffic, though no wheel has ever scored it since the last gun rumbled back to India after the war.

The heat did not improve our tempers, and this entrance to the valley is narrow and confined. The stony river-bed below the road has traces of cultivation where possible, but there is not much soil here, and the ground is chiefly grazed over by the Wazírs and the Ghilzais, who drive their flocks down from the higher mountains in winter, into these more sheltered valleys. It is a lonely ride; even for this thinly-inhabited country we met but few people, and on the face of it it is a No-man's Land. Turi, Zaimusht, Wazír, and Bangash, all raid over it, in the happy consciousness that no local witnesses can fix the responsibility of the foray on them.

Towards three o'clock in the afternoon, as we jogged along, we saw a crowd in the distance ahead of us, whom we took to be men engaged in building a tower, as a military post on the road; but on coming up to them a rush was made towards us, and Merk was soon surrounded by a thronging mass of wild and angry ruffians, every one of whom was shouting at his neighbour and appealing to Merk to justify him. The long jezails waved in the air like a forest

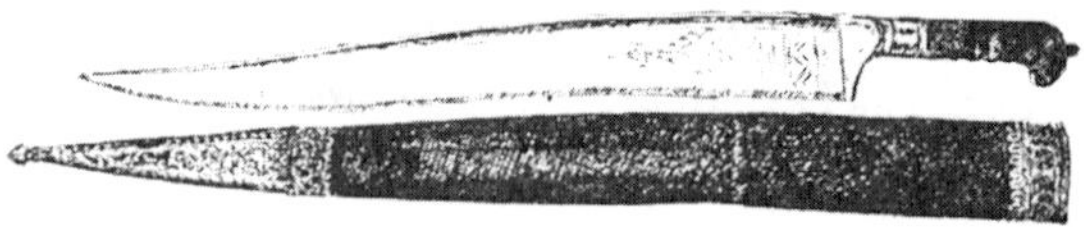

AFGHAN SILVER-MOUNTED KNIFE

of swaying masts, and the murderous Afghan knives offered themselves ready to each man's hand. I sat on my pony, looking on at it all with all the unconcern of ignorance, while Merk dismounted, and handing his pony to one of our Turi guards, stood in the middle of the crowd, pouring oil upon the troubled waters. When it is a case of fifty to one, nonchalance is about the best weapon to be armed with; so I got off my pony, and after inspecting the site of the tower which was to be built here to shelter the new

Turi levies, tried to photograph Merk and his satellites. The angry storm rose and fell, and no doubt scores of eager watchers, hiding like wolves in the rocky hills around us, awaited anxiously the issue, ever ready to swoop down and join the fray!

Life is cheap here; 360 rupees, at 1s. 2d. each, is the price of blood when paid for; but bills here are seldom paid, and the account runs on for generations, being kept open by long shots from behind a rock, or a stab in the dark from a more silent knife.

I waited patiently for the result, which is almost inevitable when an able white man has to do with Asiatics, and soon mounted my pony and rode off behind Merk, who was accompanied by a band of the leading men of each party, one on either side of him, whom he had ordered to accompany him to our night's camp some five miles farther on. Man is but mortal, and even a Pathan finds it hard to keep up his eloquence and his anger while he is walking about six miles an hour on a hot afternoon, and I noticed that Merk's heels did not allow the pace to slacken. By the time we had got to camp, though physically considerably heated, they had decidedly cooled down mentally, and the matter could be settled to the satisfaction of all parties, while the followers who were left behind dispersed, leaving the matter in the hands of their leaders. It was the old story. Every quarrel in the East is over *zan, zar, ya zamín* (women, money, or land); and as there were no women within miles of the spot, and still less wealth or money about the dreary waste, the quarrel must needs turn on the grazing rights over this No-man's Land. The Wazírs, coming down from their hills, had driven their flocks over these stones, which the Bangashes declared were theirs; and the Zaimushts, ever glad to get a dig at their enemies the Wazírs, joined in the argument—which, but for our arrival, would have certainly been ended by bloodshed and the discomfiture of the weakest party on the ground. After sitting in solemn conclave before his tent, Merk delivers judgment, on the basis of the *status quo ante*, and every one is pleased and feels that great is the wisdom of the Hákim.

This bit of road between Thull and Mandúri has always borne a bad name for the above-mentioned reasons, and until the Wazírs on the south have been taught a lesson,[1] it will be more or less in the power of any evilly-disposed ruffian to make his kill and escape over the hills with his booty undetected. It was just here that in 1879 Lieutenant Kinloch of the Punjáb Cavalry, riding along with a couple of sowárs of his regiment, was shot from out of the dwarf palm that lines the road on either side with thick low cover. As Kipling puts it:

> A scrimmage on a Border Station—
> A canter down some dark defile—
> Two thousand pounds of education
> Drops to a ten-rupee *jezail*—
> The Crammer's boast, the squadron's pride,
> Shot like a rabbit in a ride.
>
> . . . .
>
> One sword-knot stolen from the camp
> Will pay for all the school expenses
> Of any Kuram valley scamp
> Who knows no word or moods and tenses,
> But, being blessed with perfect sight,
> Picks off our messmates left and right.

The sun was getting low and the heavy clouds looked threatening as we rode up over a low spur, on the top of which, commanding the road, was a small post of thirty men of the 2nd Punjáb Infantry. A picturesque little walled enclosure stuck against the side of the hill, from the top of which the sentry looked down upon the river below and the country around.

The post all turn out, the guard and sentries alone being in uniform, but all stand at attention with their rifles in their hands and belts over their shoulders. The old Sikh subadár in command comes out and begs us to halt, while he offers us some very sweet milky tea that he has had prepared for us. Just below us in a

[1] Since this was written the late punitive expedition into Wazíristan has been successfully carried through, and the hoped-for result may be consequently realised.

small basin, surrounded by rather a fine outline of rocky hills, we see the village of Mandúri—a square, walled block, with its protecting tower, near to which stand the white tents of our little camp, where the men are already cooking their evening meal and the line of picketed mules are whinnying for their allowance of chopped straw and grain. Merk with his following hurries on, while I stop to take a photo of the little post and to drink the subadár's sweet tea, which is, however, welcome after our ride in the hot sun.

I had just time to canter into our little camp, when the heavy drops began to fall, and the sentries pacing up and down in front of our tents had, I am afraid, a somewhat damp and dreary night of it.

Next morning we cried halt, partly because the rain in the night had saturated our tents, but principally because Merk's arrival had gathered together numbers of villagers who had complaints to make, claims to settle, and petitions to urge; for he had taken over the government of the valley as he found it, and was running it on native lines—an entirely new departure and one which holds out great promise for the future.

Formerly, owing to our ignorance of the frontier tribes, we found great difficulty in dealing with them personally, while they, on their side, looked on us with equal fear and distrust. History repeats itself, and like conditions produce like results all the world over, though the colouring may be different. A close parallel exists between the relations of the Highlanders and Lowlanders in Scotland between the years 1680 and 1745 and our own north-west frontier at the present day. The raids of Rob Roy, the intrigues of Fergus MacIvor, find an exact counterpart in every Pathan clan across the border; and in almost every body of Border Military Police is to be found a Galbraith of Garschattachin, a Lowland khan with friends and connections in the Highlands across the frontier.

The Indian Government was wont to conduct its negotiations with its highland tribes by means of leading native gentlemen, who lived on the frontiers, and who, from long residence on the spot, had intimate knowledge of, and frequent dealings with, the tribes across the border. These gentlemen were employed by the Government as middlemen. The Government dealt with them and they with the tribes. As was only natural, these chiefs frequently used their position of intermediary to forward their own private ends and those of their friends on both sides of the border, frequently to the detriment of both the Government and the tribes concerned. A common form of their procedure was to raise a storm on the border, and then to get credit with the Government for allaying it. They fished in troubled waters, and it was not to their interest that the waters should be unruffled.

In 1877 a very serious raid of this kind was made into the Peshawur valley from the hills across the border, in which many of the unfortunate villagers were killed. This was distinctly traced to the incitement of Ajjab Khan, a leading native gentleman, who happily in this case met his reward on the gallows in Peshawur. Even quite lately also the Miranzai expedition was, no doubt, greatly brought about by the difficulty of dealing with the tribes through middlemen.

It was impossible, however, that this system of ignoring the sensibilities of the surrounding tribes, and of treating them to the cold and impersonal justice that the English love so much, should continue. Happily our exclusiveness has broken down, and more intimate relations have been established, to the mutual advantage of both parties. As we got to know the frontier highlanders better, the time came for the abolition of the middleman, and British officers with an intimate knowledge of the Pushtú language were appointed to the direct charge of the frontier. Under these officers a special border force, called the Border Military Police, was raised from men living on both sides of the border. This force, directly under the control of its British officers, deals immediately with the clans, who thus at once come into contact with English ideas of justice and straight dealing, and much of the mutual distrust disappears; while the Government has, through these officers, its hand

The Shahzáda Sultán Ján. C. I. E    Captain Dallas    W. Merk. C. S. I.

THE POLITICAL OFFICERS IN KURAM

upon the pulse of the feverish highlanders, and is the first to become aware of any coming trouble.

Across the frontier too, in Kuram, as before mentioned, a new system has been started by Merk which, without doubt, has a great future before it in the control of these wild countries, which are so eminently unsuited to the heavy harness of a Western administration. Speaking of the frontier, it is rather difficult to define what the word means. It is easy to paint a red line on a map, but in practice the white man carries the frontier in his pocket, and it is only when the heavy foot of British administration is put down that the native begins to realise that a change has come over the land. British administration to him, looking at it from his microscopic point of view, means first of all discomfort. The new broom, in the form of the mass of native subordinates, begins to sweep, and before it sweeps clean a cloud of dust is raised. He cannot understand the rigid Western laws, with all their technicalities, in spite of the earnest endeavours of an active police to enlighten him. Living in a barren country, he fails to appreciate the strict land-revenue system of the new administration, and above all, wild, free-born mountaineer that he is, he resents his loss of liberty among the host of small native officials who follow in the white man's train, and who fatten on every land into which they are introduced.

From the British point of view also these trans-frontier countries are totally incapable of supporting the cost of such an administration. There is little or no "trade," and the sparse population eke out a scanty subsistence either as nomad pastoralists or as the cultivators of small plots of irrigated ground. Recognising these facts in Kuram, Merk has wisely gone straight to the root of the matter, and has started an administration according to the Oriental method of *personal* government, instead of that of a system. In other words, the people are governed entirely according to their own laws and customs, in so far as these do not come into violent contact with Western ideas of morality and justice. In cases where they do, they are modified by the will of the British officer administering the valley, until they are more in harmony with our accepted traditions.

It is an Oriental system, with a British head. The people are left as much as possible to themselves, while the controlling influence of the British officer, though permeating the whole, is exercised only where necessary, and even then, if possible, through their own jirgas or councils. The result is that the standard of peace and security is sufficiently high; rights and obligations are secured and carried out to the satisfaction of all parties concerned; while this form of administration, by doing away with the hordes of native subordinates, is infinitely cheaper, and far more popular, because, intensely democratic as they are, the Pathans under it practically govern themselves.

Carrying out these ideas then, Merk sat at the door of his tent at Mandúri most of our day's halt there, with his native clerk beside him, his two tall Yusuffzai orderlies, one on each side, and the motley mass of dirty and tattered ragamuffins, who in this country represent the light and leading of the people, in a crowd in front of him. The only alternative to fighting is the jirga, or council of elders, and cases of every kind are tried before them, and judgment given with a wonderful amount of shrewd common-sense. A case in point occurred here. Two men were murdered a few nights before, and the relatives of the victims came to Merk and the jirga, and accused a man of the crime. Now every one present knew that the accused had committed the murder, but the Sharíat, or Mohammedan law, requires two witnesses. If there are no witnesses the law allows a man to clear himself of the charge by an oath upon the Korán. As in this case the prosecutors could produce no reliable evidence, the accused offered to clear himself by the oath. The jirga, while bound to accept the oath, have still a weapon in their hands to use against notorious liars. A man whose oath is disbelieved can be called upon, after the old Anglo-Saxon fashion, to supply compurgators, or men that will swear to the credibility of the party taking the oath. So the jirga in this case, while professing to be convinced by the accused's oath, ruled that he should bring seventy men to swear with him! These he had to produce by the end of the week, and on the appointed day he appeared with his strange retinue, who one and all swore that he was a good man and true and that he was innocent of the crime! We heard afterwards that he had to pay each of these men five rupees to come, as their oaths were false, so that he was practically fined Rs. 350, the price of blood being actually Rs. 360! The law was thus vindicated, the guilty punished, and both prosecutors and accused had an honourable escape from a blood feud, which would otherwise have been incumbent upon them.

Nothing is more remarkable in this country than the way the guilt or innocence of a man is well known to all his neighbours. Killing is frequent, but when a man is killed every one in the village knows who has done it, and by fining the whole village in punishment for an outrage as they do, the Government without doubt brings the guilt home to the authors of the crime.

We spent the afternoons in long tramps through the dwarf palm, which here clothes the stony hillsides in grey patches, in search of the black partridge—that uncertain bird which is never to be found at home when most wanted. Our guard made excellent beaters as they forced their way through the tough growth. Surely a fortune is before the lucky man who turns this mazré, or dwarf palm, to account. The fibre of the leaves is intensely tough, and even in its undressed state the natives make plaited ropes and nets of it that are quite equal in strength to hemp.

We did not get many birds, for the black partridges had shifted, and we could not go up on the hills to look for their cousin the chikór, but a good day's sport can be got in Kuram if you know where to go for it. Higher up in the mountains ourial, the wild sheep, and markhor, the splendid goat, are to be found, and no doubt when the country gets more settled these will be duly looked up by the keen sportsman.

The rain came down again in torrents late in the afternoon, and made us turn our faces again towards camp, and as we splashed along the road, we were surprised to see a number of men riding towards us. These turned out to be none other than the redoubtable Chikkai himself, riding at the head of a band of some twenty-five or thirty dirty and ragged retainers. He had come down to see Merk, hearing that he was on his way up the valley.

Chikkai, who, as far as personal appearance and dress is concerned, was in no way to be distinguished from his followers, dismounted from his well-made Wazíri mare at a little distance, and came to meet us with the usual greeting, "Salám aleikum" ("Peace be with you"), which was answered by us with "Wa aleikum salám" ("And unto you be peace"); and then, as the conversation between him and Merk continued in the incomprehensible Pushtú, I had time to examine this man who had caused so much trouble in these parts. A broad thick-set fellow, with a powerful and active-looking body, dressed in most ordinary dirty clothes, which, no doubt from policy, were in no way different from those of his followers. He wore the loose dust-coloured trousers and linen shirt of the country, the latter pleated at the back almost like a kilt, and on his feet were the common grass sandals. His face was as rugged as his clothes—strong, but with an evil, hunted expression, which, however, quite disappeared when he addressed his followers, whom he treated like dogs. A man's quality in this country is judged much by the arms he carries, and Chikkai's beautiful Winchester repeater and finely-worked Afghan knife alone raised him above his retainers, who all carried Martini-Henry and other rifles that had no doubt at some time been in the hands of the Punjáb garrisons, before they had been carried off across the frontier by the ever-watchful Pathan thieves.[1]

[1] The business of rifle-stealing is a fine art in India, and is practised with much success; for while I was in Kuram, the competitors in the camp of the National Rifle Association, even so far down country as Cawnpore, awoke on the morning of the prize firing to find eight of their match rifles gone from their tents!

TURI NOBLES AND HOLY MEN

Chikkai was most amiable during his interview with Merk, but it was without regret that we saw this assassin and his cut-throat followers ride off before nightfall, while an extra sentry or two was ordered out, to enable our little camp to sleep all the sounder; and after dinner, as I made my way across to my tent through the dark night, all was peaceful enough—the munching of the baggage-mules, the tread of the sentries, and the bubbling of the hookahs being the only earthly sounds, while above, the heavens sparkled with all the blaze of a frosty Eastern night.

# CHAPTER IV

THE never-failing delight of an early Eastern morning sent us on our way from Mandúri with light hearts. The rain had given an unwonted softness to the dry air, which the hot sun had not yet had time to dispel. Everything seemed bright and keen and fresh, and our ponies even were quite skittish as they plunged into the somewhat swollen waters of the Kuram river, which we here forded. Our picturesque Turis rode in front, hunching their knees up almost to their chins as the rushing waters swirled nearly to the horses' bellies; while behind us Nainu, divesting himself of his nether garments and handing my gun to one of the cavalry sowárs, waded across, holding on to the horseman's stirrup.

The camp and baggage with its escort kept along the road on the right-hand side of the valley, while we crossed the river to beat out the patches of cover which afforded such good shelter to the partridges. The valley began to open out a little, and the frequent villages gave the country a peaceful look, which, however, the invariable defensive tower and high mud wall surrounding them belied. From here upwards, in the flat bed of the valley wherever the levels allow, the precious water is brought from the Kuram river in irrigating channels and spread over the fertile soil, which only needs water to make any crop do well upon it. Many of the villages showed signs of the late burnings and pillagings, though in truth, as the country is almost absolutely devoid of architecture, the rebuilding of the mud walls does not entail any great labour, and the fact that a village has been sacked adds no more than another degree to the general poverty and dilapidation of its appearance.

The people were acknowledging the peace that had come over the valley by digging the fields with their long-handled, heart-shaped spades, stopping only to watch our party ride by with the indifferent curiosity that peasants of all countries show to any novelty.

We got off our horses now and again, and taking our guns, waded through the dwarf palm, getting a few shots at the black francolins and seeing a hare or two, which we scandalised our friends, the Shía Turis, by shooting; for owing to the fact that their venerated ancestor, Ali, kept hares as pets, these animals lead a life of happy immunity in a Shía country.

We sat in the shade of a village wall to eat our lunch, and watched with interest a curious game the boys and men were playing here. They had got hard-boiled eggs, coloured just like the familiar German "Easter egg," and each man, holding his egg in his hand, tapped the end of it against his opponent's egg, the victor being he whose egg was not broken in. Many were the artifices used to gain a victory, and on our examining some of the eggs, one young scoundrel with a twinkle in his eye, showed us his champion, which, though outwardly having every appearance of a coloured egg, must from its weight have been some sort of stone—an egg that would have baffled even Columbus himself.

We questioned some of the young men about the positions of the villages in the valley, and it is significant of the insecurity of the district during the last ten years that none of the young men in Kuram know anything about the country more than four or five miles from their villages. The old men still remember an era of peace previous to this, when their movements were less restricted. Any merchants or travellers through the valley were simply escorted from village to village, and with true military instinct, the young Turis took good care to remain always within reach of their supports.

The question of escorts has obtained quite a different meaning in the East from what we are accustomed to give it. While an escort is everywhere in these wild countries necessary to protect the weak from the strong, you can practically insure yourself against any loss by paying a premium to the clan whose happy hunting-ground you are traversing. They give you a policy, in the shape of a nominal guard, which is recognised by any marauder. Should the village under whose protection you are be a strong one, it may be that a little girl even will be considered sufficient, and in answer to a remonstrance an old Pathan once said proudly to us, "Why, my friend, if one of our dogs was tied up here, no one would dare touch you"!

We clambered up the bare hillside after lunch, to inspect some old ruins on a knoll above the river. Traces of a large work, whose walls were built of immense well-cut stones, are here visible, though little of it is now standing; such signs of wealth and power recall a time when a vastly different condition of things from the present must have existed here. The natives know nothing about it, but from coins found at Alizai, on the opposite side of the river, it is no doubt the work of the Ghazni kings, who flourished about the tenth and eleventh centuries, and who built the fort probably to command the cross-roads here, from Kabul to India through the valley, and from Hangu to Khost across the hills.

Scrambling down over the rough stones, we rejoined our ponies and continued up the valley, where the Turis pointed out to us, with pride, a village which had a few months before been the scene of great heroism. Chikkai, with his allies, was conquering the country, and had carried all before him except this village, which bravely held out until they had nothing left to eat. To his credit be it said, quarter was offered by Chikkai if a surrender was made; but though the majority of fighters on both sides had known each other from infancy, the villagers refused to give in, and the tower in which they made their last stand was burned over their heads. The instinct of chivalry is buried deep down in

MARUKHEL VILLAGE AND THE SAFÉD KOH

these rough mediæval warriors, the uncouthness of whose exteriors is probably not greater than was that of the knights of King Arthur's Round Table, though modern romance has clothed the latter in the silks and satins of nineteenth-century civilisation.

Only last year Chikkai was going to pay a visit to his neighbours the Orukzai, but as he suspected treachery, he begged that hostages might be given, and accordingly two sons of one of the Orukzai chiefs were sent to him. As soon as Chikkai got them into his power, he seized the boys and threatened them with death unless their father drove out some enemies of Chikkai's who had claimed and obtained the hospitality of the Orukzais. The boys, nothing daunted, thereupon sent to their father a message, begging him on no account to accede to Chikkai's wishes, for that they would gladly die rather than that the name of the Orukzai hospitality should be disgraced. Wild and rough though they are, there is no doubt that the Pathans, in common with most mountaineers, have a highly-strung fibre running through somewhat uncouth personalities.

We forded the river back again and got on to the road, a short mile taking us into our camp at Marukhel. Just before reaching the village a short rise brought the whole line of the Saféd Koh into view—a glorious white range of mountains some 15,000 feet high, the extreme left-hand peak, Sikaram, being even as high as Mont Blanc. This range, almost overhanging the Upper Kuram basin, is undoubtedly the most beautiful feature of the valley. The glistening snowy mass, hanging in the blue air, is an incessant delight to the eye wearied with the dry and treeless country. The whole way up the lower valley glimpses are caught of it here and there; while, once the Upper Kuram basin is reached, it stands like a wall before one. Looking at the vast snow-fields, it is almost impossible to realise that only a few small patches can last through the heat of the summer sun. But as the snow melts, masses of alpine flowers spring out of the high pastures, and the shepherds drive their flocks of sheep and goats up the deep ravines on to the green hillsides above, where they graze the short summer through, until the autumn storms warn them to seek again shelter lower down. This great range is otherwise quite uninhabited. The Turi is no admirer of scenery, and there is little to tempt him away from his cultivated fields by the river-side. Now and then an enterprising hunter clambers over the rocky slopes in search of ourial, and still more rarely a devotee makes his way to the sacred summit of Sikaram, but otherwise solitude reigns over the whole.

OUR BAGGAGE

We pushed on next day to reach Sangína, where the remaining half of the Kuram force was encamped, passing the many-towered villages which here dot the valley all along. The people were civil enough, coming out often to greet Merk as we rode by, now with a complaint and now with a welcome, while the children, with little on them but a few rags, poured out of the village gates to satisfy their curiosity.

As we neared the big village of Sadda, the sound of artillery-firing and shells bursting at the camp beyond made us ride up a low hill to reconnoitre. Continuing, however, we were somewhat relieved by meeting Lieutenant Molesworth bringing in the two

CAMP AT SANGINA

guns of his mountain battery from practice, and soon came to a picket of the 2nd Punjáb Infantry guarding the watering-place and ford over the stream that here joins the Kuram river. Here a bridge of faggots had been built across the water, from which a soft road was made over the terraced fields into the little basin behind the village of Sangína, in which the camp lay hidden—a sheltered nook off the main valley, down which the bitter wind sweeps almost every winter's afternoon.

We were kindly greeted as usual as we rode through the straight lines of tents to the upper end of the camp, where the politicals reigned supreme. As an honoured guest, I was put up in "the palace" which that man of peace, the chief political officer, had caused to be built as a sign of the permanency of our occupation! It consisted of a square stone and mud hut, ten feet by eight, a mud floor, a flat mud roof, through which the rain leaked, no windows, and a door which had been cut out of a huge deodar tree with an axe. Never was I lodged in such a cold and dismal abode. The warm sun outside even made no impression on it. However, it had the advantage of being dark enough to develop photographs in, and it was soon arranged satisfactorily for that purpose, and was no doubt the first "photographic studio" with which the valley had been honoured.

Sangína, being the headquarters of the occupying force, was a much larger camp than that at Bilandkhel, and lay snugly surrounded by high stony hills, being cut off also from the main valley by the picturesque towered village of the same name, which crowned a low hill. A constant stream of camels brought up supplies from Thull, and there was much movement always on the parade-ground, which formed one side of the little basin. The weather was again gloriously fine after the late rains, and the air was none the less keen from our being some 4000 feet above the sea; for though the road up the valley seems level enough, it is in fact rising steadily all the way.

My mornings were, as usual, busily occupied with photography, the Sikh native officers, as at Bilandkhel, expressing a childish delight at having their pictures taken. I was again favourably impressed by these men. The happy, friendly dispositions, the well-bred courteous manners, and a bright geniality that they possess, make it much easier to get on with them than with their more reserved and silent Pathan comrades. The relations of the English and the native officers of the 2nd Punjáb Infantry were here also of the most friendly description. If the mornings were strictly devoted to drill and musketry, the afternoons always brought round a keen game of football, when the parade-ground was covered with a rushing and excited crowd headed by Lieutenant Elsmie, who often met his match in a very fast little Sikh during the varying fortunes of the game. If the Sikh is a good man to fight, he is equally ready to play you either at football, wrestling, jumping, or any other sporting competition; and with his pagri knocked off, his long black hair and beard streaming wildly in the wind, he looks the picture of keen activity as he careers over the ground.

While we have been watching the players, who are encouraged by the shouts and cries of the long line of sepoys, dressed in their yellow tanned sheepskin postíns, standing round the ground, the sun has dropped behind the hill, and the heavy dusk falls suddenly over all. Silently, before the guard-tent close behind us, the night pickets of some thirty men have formed up, and have been inspected by their officer, while the buglers of the regiment line up alongside of them. "Attention!" rings out into the growing darkness, and the double line stand immovable in their long black greatcoats, with bayonets fixed. There is a pause while the bugles are raised, and then, in perfect time, clear into the still night air sounds the beautiful call—

—which is repeated again and again by the echoing hills around, until the last soft C has faded away into the night, and the tramp of the pickets alone is heard as they march off to their respective posts on the rocks above. It is like an evening prayer to the protecting Deity.

But we have to hurry off, for the football is over and the mess bugle has long since gone, and I have to cross the whole camp before I can reach my "palace," where Nainu is waiting with soap and water to make me fit to appear at the mess of the hospitable 2nd Punjáb Infantry.

The usual camp routine was going on here, and every one was busy during the mornings; but owing to the Turis in this part of the valley being much more peaceably disposed than the Wazírs at Bilandkhel, we were allowed much more liberty, and if accompanied by a guard, were free to go where we liked in the neighbourhood. Just at the corner, where the valley takes the sharp bend and only half a mile from the camp, lay the big village of Sadda—a picturesque, if dirty, conglomeration of mud and stones. From the outside nothing is seen of the houses, for the high wall shuts them all in; but the many towers, which are built of wood filled in with sun-dried brick plastered over with mud, give the village an imposing look. In this country, where there are so few signs of men's skill in raising buildings, one's eye rests with pleasure on the ornamented loopholes of these towers, many of which show signs of great care and taste in their construction.

Accompanied by Nainu carrying my camera-case, and two orderlies, I made sundry excursions to Sadda, and found the people friendly enough—which is surprising when one considers how little they could have understood what I meant when I planted the camera on its legs and, putting my head under a black cloth, begged them to stand still! In the village itself there is absolutely nothing to photograph. The narrow alleys are as usual hedged in on both sides by mud and stone walls, with now and then an opening through them into a muddy yard, flanked by rough sheds, which seem to be used at once by the cattle and their owners. Walking round the outside of the village, I came at last upon a picture in this pictureless country.

An irrigating channel had been brought round from the streams above, and the fall was used here to turn the wheels of two corn-mills.

The water-mills all over this part of the world are sacred to the women. It is they who carry the corn thither in baskets on their heads, grind it, and carry it home again. The mills thus become the centres round which the love stories play. Assignations are made here, and if the ardent lover is bold enough, he carries off the loved one as she returns in the dusk with her load gracefully poised upon her head.

The construction of these mills is curiously enough the same as those in Kulu; the water is brought down in a straight shoot, and impinges upon wooden blades set out at an angle from the vertical shaft which carries and revolves the upper mill-stone. A small shed protects the women from the noonday sun, as they sit gossiping on the open floor beside the spinning-wheels, while the water that has done its work gushes out from under the floor in a sparkling stream that is refreshing, even to look at, in this dry and barren country.

Into this dove-cot I suddenly pounced, to the consternation of the timid ladies. Those whose retreat was open made haste to fly, while those who were cut off drew their sober-coloured shawls across their faces to hide, I am afraid I must confess, their not too attractive features.

It is the next worse thing to being blind for a traveller to be ignorant of the language of the country where his wanderings take

him. A few laughing words, a joke, in Pushtú, would have put these good ladies quite at their ease; as it was I am sure they only attributed it to my shocking manners that I immediately put my head into a black box and told the orderly to tell them that I would not hurt them, if only they would sit still and not be afraid.

Happily there were very few men of their village about, or the attention thus paid to them by a Sahib might have been disconcerting to them; but with patience on my part and curiosity on theirs, the matter was satisfactorily arranged, with the result of the picture on the opposite page. The small arched building above the mill is the village mosque.

Happily for Job, photography was not invented in his day, for the patience required to get such unstable elements as the sun, Eastern women, running water, and Kuram wind to remain still together for even a couple of seconds, would have sorely tried him. When to these are added the photographer's minor cares, of his shutter, his stops, his exposures, his levels, his plates, it is always a marvel to me how his back is broad enough to support the burden!

Sportsmen were plentiful in Sangína camp, and we diligently tramped the valley with our guns, for some swampy, irrigated ground just below Sadda formed a famous lodging-place for snipe. The best of this excellent shooting was over before I reached the valley, but a good day's sport could be got, as well as, alas! many cartridges thrown away, in trying to get the better of these erratic birds. The fishermen too were not idle. Captain Nicholls, the brigade-major, an indefatigable sportsman, spent as much of his time as he could spare trying the merits of spoon bait, Chilwa, and frogs with great success; for, whisper it not abroad, the Kuram river is one of the best of mahseer preserves, and before I left the valley I saw a thirty-five pounder brought to bank.

While in camp at Sangína I made the acquaintance of a gentleman to whose kindness I owed much of my pleasure in Kuram. The Shahzáda Sultán Ján, C.I.E., is a descendant of Ahmedshah, the first king of Afghanistan, whose dynasty was supplanted by the present Barukzais. In the convulsion of the Kabul disaster in 1841, the Shahzáda's father and his household had to fly from Kabul, and took refuge in the British district of Kohat, where they have ever since been one of the leading families, and one most conspicuous for their loyalty. When the mutiny of '57 broke out, the Shahzáda, then a young man, raised a troop of cavalry, and went through the whole of the campaign with great distinction. On his return from the wars the young prince entered the civil administration, in which he has served ever since, rendering most excellent service in the many expeditions that have taken place on the frontier. His intimate knowledge of the people and the country are of great value, and during the last war, when the Afghan district of Khost was occupied, he was left there as governor of Matún—a position from which he had to be hastily rescued just in time to escape being massacred by a large and powerful combination of the tribes. He is a man greatly beloved by the people and thoroughly trusted by every one. He is known affectionately by all English officers on the frontier as "the Prince," while his perfect manners, his breeding, and courtesy, combined with his gentle modesty, have made him an universal favourite. Here in Kuram he was Merk's political assistant, and no doubt by his tact and ability helped to bring many a matter to a successful issue.

It is a real pleasure in a country where one sees almost nothing but the servant class, and now and then a member of an effete and emasculated nobility, to come across such a true specimen of a native gentleman. The Shahzáda's tent was pitched close to mine in the camp, and he was mostly to be seen sitting in judgment at his door, with a crowd of the tatterdom of the country squatting on the ground before him.

The other member of our political corner was Captain Dallas, who was in command of the newly-raised Turi Militia.[1] It was

[1] An almost exact parallel to the Indian Border Military Police and the Kuram

EMBODIMENT OF THE TURI MILITIA

amusing to see these men being broken in and mouthed like colts. The majority had not yet got their uniforms or rifles, and wore the dress and carried the long flint-locks of the country, but upon them was already devolving the responsibility for the peace of the district. The squad of them here illustrated were marched up by Captain Dallas to have their pictures taken. They were under the command of their jemadár, the good-looking boy in uniform, who was none other than the nephew of Chikkai himself, and who lisped the newly-learnt English words of command with a half-shamefaced, blushing smile! Fine big healthy men all of them, enlisted on the spot, they are capable of being made into excellent soldiers as soon as they have learnt the necessary self-control and self-respect. At present they garrison small posts in different parts of the valley, while their headquarters were at Baleshkhel, just opposite Sangína; and they lately evinced their military spirit, on the occasion of some troops being moved up the valley to turn out a party of Afghans who had cut off the water from the irrigating canals, by sending in word from the outposts, that if there was to be any fighting with their hereditary enemies, it was their intention to be present, with or without the necessary orders!

There is no doubt about the personal courage of these frontier tribes, from whom such a number of recruits are enlisted into our native infantry regiments. They are inured to fighting from their boyhood, life is given and taken with little heed on either side, and it is only the want of capable leaders that has prevented them ever being a really powerful combination. They are too democratic in spirit to render implicit obedience for long to any

Levies is to be found in the raising of military companies in the Highlands of Scotland, at the beginning of last century. These were for the protection of the country against evildoers. Among these companies were the Sidier Dhu, or Black Soldiers, out of whom the celebrated regiment of The Black Watch was formed. Just in the same way, without doubt, the Border Military Police, the Khyber Rifles, the Zhob Levies, the Kuram Militia, and the various other local irregular corps, will, fifty years hence, be found amongst our best fighting regiments.

one of their own class; and it is only when they are brought under the guidance and leadership of an Englishman from outside, that they learn to forget their differences in their obedience to him, and so develop their full value as a fighting material. Those who were at the battle of Ahmed Khel know that the 2nd Punjábis can stand when others run, and their grizzled old subadár-major is a type of a north-west frontier soldier. A tall, thin Shinwarri from the Khyber, his long sparse grey beard hanging almost to his waist, active and supple, his bright eyes peer out of his hollowed cheeks with no look of a man of peace—nor has he been bred up in the school of peace.

Wali Khan, as is so often the case, inherited a blood feud at his birth, and grew up with the duty of vengeance upon him, and while a lad his movements at home were never free from the constant anxiety. Like many others, he took service with us in order to escape this harassing life, and enlisted in the 2nd Punjáb Infantry. His visits to his wife at home, however, when on furlough, were always by stealth, and he had to travel by night and across country to avoid his ever-watchful enemies, who would have been only too glad to catch him thus alone on the road if they could.

Some ten years ago these wretches, in disappointment at not getting hold of Wali Khan himself, seized his son, a promising lad, and imprisoned him in one of their towers. The next news that Wali Khan heard was that this favourite son had been brutally murdered by having his throat cut.

This preyed so upon his mind that he never rested until he had got a revolver and the best sporting rifle that he could purchase from England; for at that time the restrictions upon selling arms to Pathans were not as strict as they are now. Every furlough that he could obtain, Wali Khan crossed the frontier and stole up into his mountains to stalk his enemies, and, with an almost religious fervour, to avenge his boy's death. Many were his escapes. On one occasion he was met by a woman, who begged him not to go to his home by a certain road, for that his enemies knew of his coming, and were there lying in wait for him. Wali, profiting by this information, waited until nightfall, and then made his way over the hills to the very track where his enemies were expecting him, and there hid himself in some rocks to await them. He never moved for the whole of next day, till at last his opportunity came, and he saw two men making their way back on the path below him. They had got tired of lying in ambush for him, and thinking that he must have gone by another road, were returning to the village. Wali's rifle-shot echoed through the silent hills, and waiting only to see that his man had fallen, he hurriedly made his escape back to British territory. The man was only wounded, however, and Wali later told his friends in camp how an unaccountable evil fortune frustrated all his efforts. "I have hit my man twice, I have broken his arm, and have shot him in the leg, so that he goes lame, but the man still lives." At last fortune favoured Wali, and he returned after one leave of absence with his mind at rest, for he had avenged his boy's death; but of course by killing his man he had reopened the feud, and his village became an impossible home for him. He had few friends there and many enemies, for he had been a loyal soldier to the Government, and by his help many a deserter and many a stolen rifle had been recovered from across the border. Age, too, was beginning to tell against such a life of incessant hardship; so with his savings, which were considerable for a man of his rank, he bought some land near Peshawur, and thither transplanted his wife and his remaining son, and is now enabled to visit his home under the security of the British ægis.

Such blood feuds as these are characteristic of the country,[1] and have done much to bring about the present Pathan institutions, though it is difficult to trace their origin. They are strictly confined to agnates, or relatives on the male side, and often continue for two or three generations, sometimes blazing up, and then again

[1] See Appendix E.

lapsing into quiet for a few years, only to break out afresh. Should such feuds spread and involve, as they often do, the whole clan, the leading men and the mullahs, seeing the danger of such dissension, interfere and compose the quarrel, after which all honour in killing is lost; for the whole affair is a matter of honour, and it is considered a chivalrous thing to have lost one's life in such a feud, though the means taken to get rid of the enemy are not such as we should esteem highly. But inasmuch as a tally is kept of the number of deaths on each side, there is great advantage in killing your opponent secretly, while the fact that the feud is often carried on by the retainers on both sides tends to spread rather than to limit the quarrel.

Brought up under such circumstances, it is only natural that the Pathan has developed his characteristical contempt of death, and has learnt to look upon life as a serious thing while it lasts; and there is no doubt that many of the young men enlist in our regiments in order to escape the life of unrest and anxiety that these constant feuds entail upon them at home.

Every Pathan male owns his share in the property of the whole clan, and in any new conquest or move of the clan he will always be entitled to his share; hence every male is known and registered in the memories of the leading men of a clan, who have the faculty for genealogy immensely developed and can remember the members of each family for generations. "Peace to you, O much on the father's side!" is the greeting to a stranger; "whence come you?" "Sahib, I am an Orukzai." "Among the Orukzais who are you?" "I am a Massuzai." "Good; among the Massuzais of what kind are you?" "A Mastal Khel, Sahib." "Of the Mastal Khels to which house do you belong, O man of good birth?" "To the Mirbaz Kór, O Sirkar!" "In the Mirbaz Kór who was your grandfather?" "Malik Abdulla Núr" will be his reply, in the pride of possessing an ancestor who was well known.

Any man can sell his birthright in a clan, but as the possession of land is necessary to give him a political status and a voice in

TOWER IN THE VILLAGE OF SADDA

the jirga or council of the tribe, it is seldom done. Though of course Pathans differ in worldly prosperity, yet they are all socially equal in blood, and can intermarry, though in truth marriage to them is rather the "taking unto himself" of a wife by the man. For the women are for the whole of their lives *in manu viri*, the absolute property of their male owner for the time being. While unmarried, girls are the saleable property of their father, and in the event of his death, they are at the disposal of their nearest male relative. On their marriage, women pass out of their own family into that of their husband, and should he die, they become the property of their sons, or if childless, then the property of their husband's nearest male relative.

Thus an enterprising son frequently sells his widowed mother to an eligible buyer, and with the proceeds himself invests in a wife.

Women in consequence have, besides their other charms, an intrinsic market value—which of course fluctuates, as other commodities do, with the desire of the buyer; but *peghlas*, or virgins, are considered cheap at Rs. 100, while an average price is Rs. 250; if, however, the buyer be a khán or leading man, as much as two, three, or even four thousand rupees is asked for by the happy guardian of the damsel.

The poorer classes seldom can afford the expense of more than one wife, and marriages are usually determined by considerations of family and money. A man acquainted with both families will go to the bride's father, mention the suitor's name, and ascertain for what consideration he will part with his fair daughter. In this happy country it is usual for the father to object to overtures for a younger daughter while he still has an elder unmarried one in the house, showing that here, as elsewhere, elderly unmarried ladies are a drug in the market.

The amount fixed by the father will vary according to what he thinks the suitor will give. It will include a sum of money for expenses, another for jewels, while a certain quantity of rice and butter is stipulated for to satisfy the hungry marriage guests.

The haggling that goes on on both sides is conducted with great spirit, the father extolling the beauties and virtues of his unseen daughter with a zeal worthy of a proverb. When the terms are agreed upon and the money has been paid down by the bridegroom, the betrothal is considered made, and the imám may perform the ceremony.

The happy bridegroom now for the first time appears on the scene, and, accompanied by a band of friends, all armed with swords and guns, makes his way through the narrow alleys of the village to the bride's house, where he is received by her friends with showers of mud and stones from the housetops, which before now have caused death!

Undeterred by this somewhat unwelcome reception, he forces his way into the house, feeing liberally all the servants, whose palms are open ready to partake of their share in this festal occasion, and there receives his bride, who is shut up in an enclosed litter! This is carried off by his friends and the procession is re-formed, the bridegroom leading the way to his home mounted on his scraggy pony, his friends celebrating their victory in capturing the damsel by repeatedly letting off their flint-locks. The feasting is then carried on for another night, after which, for the first time, the bridegroom has leisure to ascertain if his bride is all that she has been described.

These facts sound somewhat bald, but differ after all in no great measure, especially from the woman's point of view, from many of our *mariages de convenance*, though we doubt much if our modern young gentleman would care thus to "buy a pig in a poke." We profess pious horror at the revolting idea of a pasha buying a wife abroad, while in the same breath we congratulate our friends upon a "well-arranged" marriage at home.

However, if the Pathans have their *mariages de convenance*, they have the necessary accompaniments too in the frequent elopements. The morality of the women is protected by walled villages and towers, but that their feelings are warm is proved by the constant risk of death incurred by the lovers in carrying off the women on whom they have set their hearts. This is no light matter, for unless the husband can be satisfied by the payment to him of the woman's market value, plus a compensation for his injured honour, the lover will have to suffer the penalty of death if caught. If he escapes to another village he will not be received, as by protecting him they would incur a blood feud with the injured man's village. He becomes, in consequence, an outlaw and wanderer in a country where strangers are looked upon with suspicion, and until his family have stepped in and healed the breach, he cannot return to enjoy his birthright among his own people. Natural selection breaks out as strongly in Kuram as elsewhere, and the old Latin Grammar quotation, *Naturam expellas furca, tamen usque recurret,* still holds good in spite of the locks and bolts of the Turi lord and master.

In spite of this apparently inferior position occupied by the women, there is no doubt that they greatly influence the men by their encouragements, as well as by their taunts. For a Mohammedan country they have a great deal of liberty, and are allowed to go about everywhere unveiled. In riding along the road or shooting across the cultivated land, one frequently passed close to them as they weeded their fields near their villages. They showed no signs of shyness, but greeted one with the usual salutation of "Starai ma sha" ("May you never grow weary"); and one's answer, "Kór di abád" ("May thy house be prosperous"), sealed the friendly greeting; nor did any of the men about seem to resent their women's liberty.

After a week or two of this pleasant life in camp at Sangína, we began to make our preparations for our march farther up the valley. In camp life these do not entail any great loss of time, for one's baggage is already reduced to a minimum in order to be portable, and in one's small mule-trunks there is only one place for each thing and each thing must go into its place.

My preparations, however, always entailed the consideration of the photographic impedimenta, and a decision had to be made as to what was absolutely necessary to take with me and what I could safely leave behind.

With Merk's help I engaged a Turi, who, for the consideration of Rs. 4 a week,[1] agreed to carry my knapsack camera-case behind me wherever I went. He was without doubt one of the most villainous-looking men I have ever met. His black shaggy locks fell from under a dirty piece of cotton, which, wrapped round his head, served as a turban; a sparse black beard and cut moustache partly covered his red sun-scorched face, from out of which two evil-looking bloodshot eyes and a nose of a hue belying his strict adhesion to the laws of the Prophet, peered with evil expression. I never knew him well enough to get at his name, but on one occasion, when he was absent for a few days, he supplied his brother for the work, who ran him very close in good looks. An old blanket, which, like his tattered woollen clothes, had long since hidden its original colour under a layer of mother earth, served him as both day-gown and night-gown, while the whole of his toilet was held together by a powerful and pungent human odour of a kind that is only to be attained by many a month's abstention from water.

To this day my camera-case is tainted with Turi.

However, he was a fine big athletic and willing fellow, and the way that he kept up with my pony in marches of twenty miles over the stony, trackless country, with a load of thirty pounds on his back, was admirable; and it was only when I found him one day, in his excess of zeal, inside my tent endeavouring to make my bed, that I had to delicately insinuate to him that, as the tent was so small, I thought that Nainu alone would be sufficient to attend to its internal economy.

It was arranged that Merk was to come with us, and Captain Dallas, having his militia posts to visit, came also with his body-guard of mounted militia orderlies. Merk had received an invita-

[1] This high pay shows the greater independence of these frontier people. Nainu's services were reckoned at Rs. 10 *a month*.

tion to pay a visit to Mir Akbár, the leader of the Mián Muríd faction of the Turis, whose village, Shakadara, lay up on the lower slopes of the Saféd Koh, some six miles to the northward of Sangína camp, and which from its detached situation was said to be interesting and picturesque. So it was agreed that we should send our camp with the escort up the valley to the first march, Sultán, and riding off ourselves with some orderlies, should visit Shakadara on our way.

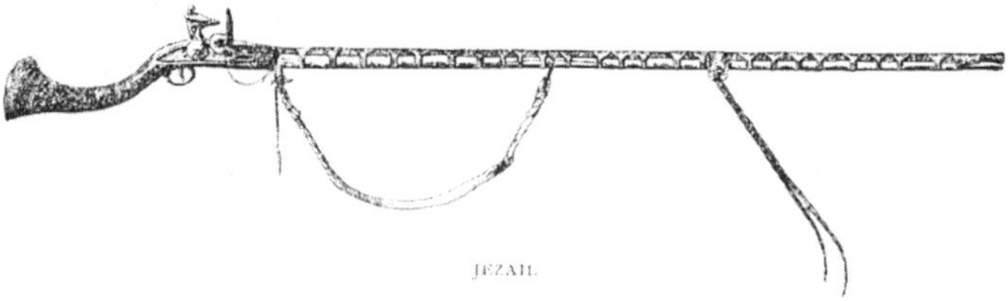

JEZAIL.

# CHAPTER V

THE morning, as usual, was clear and delightfully crisp as we three, accompanied by the usual guard of a couple of Cavalry sowárs and some half-dozen of Captain Dallas's mounted flint-lock warriors, rode down through the broad avenues of the camp, past the lines of picketed battery mules and white horses of the cavalry; and as we crossed under the quaint little Sangína village on its hill, which from its external appearance faintly recalls some of the mediæval Italian walled towns, the inevitable pariah dogs rushed down the slope to bark a farewell.

On our way down over the terraced cultivation to the river long strings of mules met us coming up from the water, and at the slender bridge itself we had to wait for a convoy of sleepily-moving camels, who with slow and slouching steps were bringing stores up from the distant base at Kohat.

Once over the river, we turned to the left up the valley and kept up the old track made during the last war, which here runs through the flat cultivated river-bed. It is difficult to convey an exact impression of this frontier country, for though the whole of it may be described as a stony, barren, treeless wilderness, yet wherever man has brought water, the fields are green with rich crops, and the water-courses are bordered by graceful willows, with here and there a fine plane; but this cultivation is so artificial that you can literally stand with one foot on a green wheat-field and the other on the desert, which may extend without a break for twenty miles. Thus as long as we kept along the river we rode over a fertile soil, cultivated with great care and dotted every half a mile or so with square fort-like villages, which prove the prosperity of the Turis in spite of the many disturbances that have lately occurred.

After a mile or so of this, however, we turned off to our right, and clambering up a steep bank some thirty feet high, found ourselves on a vast, open, stony slope, running right up in one even gradient to the foot of the great snowy range some five miles off. There is nothing to break the long lines, nothing to catch the eye. The dry, barren earth is covered with a gigantic gravel, between the stones of which grows a low, thorny scrub, with here and there patches of the dwarf palm, whose grey-green leaves form the only variety in the widely-stretching brown and sunburnt expanse. Straight in front of us, rising like a wall, towers the Saféd Koh range, some 11,000 feet above us, the upper half of which is white with fields of dazzling snow, resting on a base of dark pine trees which sweep down the ridges until they almost reach the slope we are on.

Mountains never appear their full height when looked at from underneath, and there was indeed little beauty in the scene, but the extent of the landscape and the solitude of the desert are very grand and imposing, for, as I looked around, our little band and its accompaniment of half a dozen wild-looking Turis, with their loose clothes fluttering in the wind and their long-barrelled flint-locks slung over their shoulders, seemed to be the only living things in this vast and stony area.

The distance seemed interminable, for the horses, picking their way, could not go out of a slow walk. Now we had to find a path down into a narrow ravine, cut deep into the general slope, only to climb up the other side—a proceeding which taxed our horses severely as, half walking, half sliding, they descended in a shower of stones, only to scramble up the farther bank panting with the exertion.

Our rise, though gradual, had been at a steady rate, and on turning to look back we could see the whole of the Upper Kuram basin lying open below us, the river like a silver thread stretching away up the valley, backed up by the brown hills that line its farther bank.

At last we seemed to be getting near the mountains, and our guide pointed out a dark clump of trees in a ravine on the hillside as the situation of Shakadara. On nearing this cleft we were greeted by several shots, and looking towards them, saw Mir Akbár's two sons with several followers, who had descended to welcome us and fire a salute in our honour from their long jezails. The usual greetings, "Peace be with you!" "How is your health?" "Is your father well?" "I hope you are not tired," passed, as, mounting their horses, the young men guided us up the narrow boulder-filled ravine. After half a mile of this, we came to a place where the ravine split into two, and on the point between the two, some hundred feet or so above the bed, clustered the little mud and stone houses of the village. Truly a rat-trap for the unwary to be caught in!

As the hill rises again straight up behind the village, the only approach to it is by a narrow winding path up the cliff which is formed of conglomerate, from the ravine bed below. We dismounted in the ravine, and leaving our horses there in charge of one of our sowárs, walked up the zigzag path, all the villagers crowding the flat housetops to look down upon so strange a sight as the invasion of three Sahibs. At the tumble-down wooden gate of the village stood the holy man himself, surrounded by his rough-looking followers—a dignified handsome man in flowing robes, with a full brown beard. Nothing could have been more courteous than his manner, and he led us through the narrow, muddy alleys between the dilapidated sheds which in this country answer to the name of houses, with all the grace of a grand seigneur bowing you through his domain and château. Many were the compliments paid to each other by Merk and Mir Akbár, in true Oriental politeness, as we made our way through the little streets and

Mír Akbár

MÍR AKBÁR OF SHAKADARA AND HIS SONS

courts to the great man's house, which in no respect differed from the other hovels of the village.

Arrived at the courtyard, three rough native beds were placed for us to sit on, but the heat of the sun soon made us pull them into a sort of open shed which formed one side of the building. Here carpets were spread before us, and we sat in state, all the little courtyard before us full of wild-looking fellows squatting on the ground, while children in all states of *déshabillé* and rags swarmed about everywhere and clambered up on to the roofs of the houses round to get a better view of the proceedings. Mir Akbár and his sons of course sat on the carpet nearest to us, and the conversation was carried on between Merk and them, while Dallas kindly interpreted the chief points for my benefit. The people were greatly excited and the conversation was animated, for that very morning shortly before our arrival the Chakmannis, a clan living over the mountain, had raided down and carried off a lad who was shepherding a flock at no great distance from the village—a fact which was somewhat gruesomely impressed on us by the mournful wailing of his poor mother, which continued most of the time we were in Shakadara.

Merk had drilled us in the coming events, by telling us that we should have to partake of Mir Akbár's hospitality, that we would probably be very ill after it, and that if by some good fortune the indigestion should cause us to eructate, we should not hide our faces in shame but fearlessly pay Mir Akbár that greatest compliment to the excellence of his cooking! So after the usual asseverations on our part that we did not want any food, we yielded to Mir Akbár's pressing, and passed into a dark windowless room, where some carpets were again spread; and while we three sat on a bedstead on one side, the holy man sat on the ground opposite, his two sons attending on us. First some tea was brought to us in little Russian cups — dreadfully sweet stuff, diluted with a large quantity of goat's milk which only our long and hot ride enabled us to gulp down. Then, with much pressing that we would do him the honour to eat something in his house, Mir Akbár beckoned to a follower, who brought some water in a long-necked brass Persian vessel, and we, coached by Merk, held out our right hands over a basin, while the servant poured some water over them.

This was evidently the grace before meals.

One of the sons then passed backwards and forwards into the women's apartments, where the food was being cooked, taking good care to squeeze himself through as narrow a space as possible and to close the door at once. I don't know whether it was to prevent our being captivated, or out of fear of the women losing their hearts by a stray glance, that all sight of them was thus denied to us. With many whisperings, however, some eight or ten big trays of brass were passed in, and set upon the carpet before us, each loaded up with eatables. In the centre a huge pile a foot high of pillau—a dish composed of greasy rice, boiled chicken, almonds and raisins—was laid; then trays of curries, trays of vegetables swimming in butter, and several of sweetmeats, and one strange compound of some sort of grain mixed up with honey and butter, not at all bad in spite of its deadly appearance. A dish of kabobs also appeared—long thin sticks of wood with little lumps of roasted mutton and fat alternately strung upon them—and last but not least, an immense cone of snow, looking like the top of Sikaram itself, was placed before us. All these dishes, though not at all bad to taste, were, owing to their richness, eminently qualified to give us that indigestion that was to express our full hearts, as well as stomachs, to our excellent host.

Our difficulties commenced with the opening of the repast. Without knife, fork, spoon, or plate, we were asked to use our right hands only, for it is bad manners to touch food with one's left. To break myself in, I began with the kabobs, which were easy enough, for Mir Akbár, with many expressions of goodwill, held the stick towards me, off which I pulled the lumps of meat and put them into my mouth; but the moral courage required to plunge one's hand first into some honey, then into some curry, with now and then a dip into the snow and the buttery vegetables, was almost more than we could command without flinching. However, we floundered on, stuffing our mouths with whatever came to hand, to hide our laughter from the grave Turis sitting opposite to us, but all the time feeling convinced that the man who can eat greasy rice with his fingers, without depositing the greater part of it on his best shirt-front, not to mention up the sleeve of his coat, may consider himself a juggler of the highest order. Luckily we found salvation in the Pathan bread that was handed to us, big flat brown cakes, which we used as plate, spoon, and table-napkin in turn.

The meal at last over, fresh water was brought and poured over our hands, very ineffectually cleansing them from the greasy traces, while tea was again handed round. We felt quite sorry that our poor friends opposite could touch nothing of this lavish feast, but this being the month of Ramazán, in which the Róza is kept, no good Mohammedan can allow any meat or drink to pass his lips from sunrise to sunset—often a very trying thing in this hot country with the frequent long marches.[1]

The floor was then cleared, and the servants brought in and laid before us a pile of stuffs—Kabul coats, silk brocades (some of them handsome enough), two dried ourial skins from the Saféd Koh, and an old brass helmet, formerly used by the Afghan cavalry. These Mir Akbár, with many apologies for the poorness of his offering, begged us to accept—a thing which of course Merk, with many compliments as to their unheard-of beauty, declined; but I, not being officially employed, was allowed to carry off as a souvenir the old brass helmet and a pair of ourial horns.

The crowd outside, in the meantime, was growing anxious to satisfy their curiosity, and were with difficulty kept back from the door, while Mir Akbár whispered to Merk his plans for

[1] It was a curious sight a few weeks later, when travelling by rail in India, to see the train empty itself at the first station we stopped at after the sun had set. The water-carrier was almost mobbed by the thirsty Mussulmans in their endeavour to quench their thirst after the long day's fast.

making a raid upon the Chakmannis in order to avenge the boy's death, and a scheme was drawn up by which, with the assistance of some guns and ammunition from us, he was to carry war into the enemy's country.

Then we were again taken round all the points of view in the village, the distant Kuram river far down below us glittering like a silver thread in the afternoon sun. Having taken a photograph of Mir Akbár, I told him that in England people would look at his picture, and I would point out to them, "This is the great Mir Akbár of Shakadara"; to which he replied that my condescension was great, that he was my slave, that all I saw was mine—houses, land, and men. Rather an embarrassing possession to have suddenly thrust upon one.

As we made our way down the cliff we stopped repeatedly, in true Oriental fashion, to beg him not to come any farther, while he on his side expressed the impossibility of seeing us go off alone; and so with many compliments we mounted our horses and rode away, accompanied for a mile or two by his sons, whom we at last persuaded to return to their home.

We heard afterwards that the very next morning a party of Chakmannis, no doubt in retaliation for our visit to Shakadara, came over the mountain, and after shooting dead a wretched wood-cutter, who had wandered from the village, and badly wounding another with their knives, had escaped over the pass again before the Shakadara people could organise a pursuit! Such is the respect for life in this country!

It was getting dusk before we got down to the river again and struck the track up the valley; and there was just light enough for us to have a smart gallop over the stones after a fox which Victor, Dallas's little fox-terrier, put up before us. A few miles along the road brought us into camp at Sultán, where the fires were already lighting up the dark figures grouped around them, and the night sentries paced to and fro before our tents.

Next morning, to our regret, an orderly galloped in with a

DECOY DUCKS IN KURAM

message to Merk which necessitated his starting back at once to Bilandkhel, to arrange about the withdrawal of our troops from there, as the Amir had at last agreed to leave that dreary spot alone in peace. So he turned his steps back, while Dallas and I, taking our guns, proceeded to wade through the flooded rice fields all day in search of snipe. These terraced fields are won from the great stony desert by little irrigation cuts, taken from the river all down its course, and afford a delightful contrast to the great brown waste all around. An amusing feature all along the river are the numberless small ponds, made by raising a little dam and filling the space with water from an irrigation channel. In these ponds the water is about a foot deep, and nearly every one of them has its group or two of wild ducks upon it. These are most cleverly and naturally made by the people. A tiny mound of earth is made in the pond, just reaching to the water's level; on this a flat, grey, oval stone from the river is laid for the duck's breast, a little brown mud is then smeared upon it for the back, into which a stick with a cow-dung head upon it is stuck, while a tail of the same material is pinched up into that perky look so peculiar to the mallard. The position and grouping of these ducks, often half hidden in the rushes, is so wonderfully realistic, that though almost every pond has its group, one can never look at them without a momentary inclination to put one's gun to one's shoulder. The people use them as decoys, and in the early morning from behind the banks lie pointing their long flint-locks at the unwary wild birds, who have dropped from their flight overhead to join their less active fellows sitting on the water. With a prolonged "fiz" and a bang, some fifteen square junks of lead are scattered across the pond, and the eager "sportsman" splashes through the shallow water to pick up his spoil.

These long jezails or flint-lock muskets, by the way, are curious things, and in this country of no arts have received, in common with other arms, the only attempt at decoration that there is to be found. The curiously-bent stocks have often a Persian pattern of brass and mother-of-pearl inlaid into them, while bands of silver ornament the barrel. Strangely enough, the flint-locks all have the ancient Government mark of a crown and a figure upon them, and without doubt most of those now in use all over Afghanistan began their lives in the Peninsular campaign and at Waterloo, and drifted to our army in India, where, on the introduction of the Enfield rifle, they were sold to the natives, who

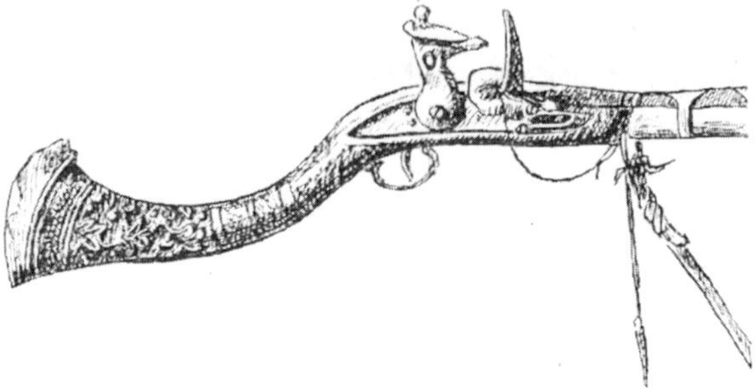

AN OLD "BROWN BESS" LOCK IN A NEW SETTING

picked out the locks and adapted them to their own long-barrelled weapons. The pistol barrels, too, are in many cases really beautifully inlaid with silver, and are handed down from father to son as the most valuable possessions.

We made our way leisurely up the river, shooting on most days, until we came to the village of Ahmedzai, where we had the pleasure of meeting the Shahzáda again. He was here settling some cases in conjunction with Syud Abbàs, the leader of the Dréwandi faction of Turis, and as we made our way through the village gate they both came out to meet us, Syud Abbàs doing us the honours of his village, and taking us to his house, which, having been formerly built as the residence of the Afghan governor of the day, was the only one which I saw in all Kuram that had any pretensions to architecture, though here too there was an utter absence of what we consider comfort. The Shahzáda was, as usual, most kind about helping me to get photographs of the people, and

The Shahzáda        Syud Abbás

AT THE GATE OF AHMEDZAI

to him I am indebted much in this way. The villagers became quite interested in the process, and a look through the camera at their friends caused unbounded astonishment and delight, and with many a laugh and a joke, they willingly grouped themselves into as "unphotographical" positions as I could suggest to them.

We were now right in the middle of Upper Kuram—a wide, stony, treeless basin some fifteen miles across, along the south edge of which the Kuram river runs, leaving the rest a gentle slope up to the foot of the great Saféd Koh range. There is, in truth, nothing beautiful or picturesque in this country; everything, like its inhabitants, has a hard and rough look. The vast stretches of barren waterless country so far outweigh the little patches of irrigated cultivation, that the general impression one gets of "Central Asia" is inhospitable in the extreme; while the snowy range, cold, dreary, and uninhabited, here blocking in all the northern side, is only softened when the long rays of the setting sun suffuse its hard bleakness with pink and opal streaks. This is essentially the home of the Turis, and Syud Abbàs, though somewhat sleepy-looking, is a fitting leader of the clan. He is the best tent-pegger in Kuram, and in one of the fights with Chikkai he went out under fire, to bring in one of his wounded men, with a courage that would have earned him a V.C. in our service.

Shut in thus as they are on all sides by Nature, cut off from all their Sunni neighbours in religion, they have been thrown much upon themselves; and in spite of their private feuds and the detestable Mián Muríd-Dréwandi discord, they are much more to each other than to their surrounding neighbours. They are not connected with any other tribes like the Wazírs or the Afrídis are, for they can look to no other clan with a common ancestor for sympathy and aid. Though life is given and taken with great recklessness it is true, yet for a Pathan people there is far less of the tenacious bloodthirstiness and morose fanaticism than is to be found amongst the clans to the north of them; while amongst themselves they are kindly and hospitable, ready for a joke, as easily pleased as angered, and their open and easy nature is in strong contrast to that of their surrounding Sunni neighbours.

Unlike the Sunnis', too, are their religious observances. The call to prayer is seldom heard in a Turi village, and they use the few mosques they possess rather as rest-houses than places of worship. Kerbela and not Mecca is the object of their pilgrimages, and in the place of fanaticism and intolerance they have a distinct leaning towards Christians, owing to the well-known fact of a Christian ambassador from the Byzantine Emperor to the Arabs having been killed at the battle of Kerbela while fighting on the side of the sons of Ali, the beloved ancestor of the Shias. This Christian martyr is even to this day extolled in the sermons of the Syuds during the Mohurram before the weeping crowds, the earnestness of whose lamentations for Hassan and Hussein is frequently shown by the bleeding backs of the men and the inflamed faces of the women—self-torture inflicted in their religious enthusiasm.

To us they were friendly in the extreme, and there is no doubt that Syud Abbàs realises that only benefits can come from the British occupation of the valley, which has given them peace, without, thanks to the new and popular form of administration, taking away from them any of their cherished customs or institutions.

The only strangers we met in these parts were several large caravans of the nomad Ghilzais, who visit Kuram every winter, passing through it in the autumn and spring. They bring their flocks down to the valley to escape the cold on the higher ground, and thus have become in a way the vassals of their Turi lords. Each section, in return for their lord's protection and permission to graze over his lands, renders him service of various kinds, which has become fixed through long custom—may be the payment of a certain quantity of dry curds, or one per cent of the flock, or a donkey-load of wool.

These Ghilzais are an Afghan tribe whose origin seems rather

GHILZAIS ON THE ROAD TO KÁBUL

doubtful; but from the fact that Kilichí is the Turki word for swordsman, it is probable that they were the mercenaries of the old kings of Ghazni, who, intermarrying with Afghan women, founded the tribe of Ghilzais. Ibn Batuta, a traveller in the 12th century, mentions that he found a nomad tribe, called Ghaléji, speaking Turki in the neighbourhood of Ghazni, and to this day the official Afghan way of writing the name of the Ghilzai tribe is Ghaléji, so that likely enough this theory is a correct one.

One day, out shooting, a number of them passed me, and I got my Turi guard to ask them to stop, as I wished to photograph them; but they were rather turbulent and impatient, and mostly refused to wait, no doubt considering that this performance was not included in their vassal service to the Turis. Wild, picturesque-looking men and women they were, with numbers of ragged children of all sizes playing about like young kids amongst the donkeys heavily laden with the family goods.

In this caravan, too, I saw an instance of maternal affection on the part of an old she-donkey, who, in addition to an immense bundle on her back, carried also her few-days-old progeny. The little fellow, scarcely able to walk, had been stuck into one of the folds of her pack by her master, from out of which his black woolly head and long soft ears peeped in the most interested way on the new world around him, while his fond mother continually bent her head round as she walked along, to lick his white nose and to reassure herself of his safety.

My time in Kuram was now drawing to a close, and I wished to push on to Shalozán and Peiwár before turning my steps down the valley. On the following day, therefore, Captain Dallas and I, accompanied by the Shahzáda and Syud Abbàs, started from Ahmedzai to ride to Shalozán—a distance of some thirteen miles, across as dreary a waste as it has ever been my lot to see; for, on leaving the river behind, not a blade of grass is to be observed until the little dark patch of fruit-trees at Shalozán, seen from so many miles off, has been reached. Still the great circle of mountains around is impressive. Straight in front, now close to us, towers the snowy peak of Sikaram some 10,000 feet above us, being the extreme left-hand peak of the long white range, almost as lofty as himself, that stretches far away to the right. To our left a long spur runs from Sikaram himself in bold outline right down to the river, and it is across this spur that the road to Kabul passes over the Peiwár Kotal, where General Roberts fought his celebrated battle in 1878. It is to avoid the long detour of the river that the road crosses this pass and joins the valley again beyond at Ali Khel, and to this position the Afghans had retired on the advance of our force up the valley in that year. Naturally a strong one, where in a short two miles the track rises 2000 feet to the top of the pass, the Afghans had strengthened the position by placing their guns cleverly on the spurs, and filling the pine-woods which lined either side of the ravine with their sharp-shooters. From six o'clock in the morning until past one o'clock in the day General Cobbe attacked this position in front, without being able to make any impression upon it; and it was only owing to General Roberts' clever turning movement that the Afghans, finding themselves threatened in the rear, retired and allowed the pass to be occupied. General Roberts had led four regiments during the night up the stony Spín Gawai ravine, which leads to a gap in the crest between the Peiwár Kotal and the steep slopes of Sikaram. The Afghans had fortified and occupied this pass also, but were surprised in the dark cold December morning by the sudden appearance of the 5th Gurkhas and 72nd Highlanders, who, after a tiresome and difficult night march, clambered up the steep mountain-side unnoticed, until they were within some fifty yards of the first Afghan picket lining a breast-work of fallen trees. A short and sharp fight in the dark drove the enemy from stockade to stockade, and by the time that the grey dawn broke, our troops had gained the crest and driven the Afghans into the surrounding woods. General Roberts, after a rest, pushed his men on down the ravine towards Ali Khel, thus getting behind the Peiwár Kotal, whereupon the Afghans,

LOOKING DOWN THE KURAM VALLEY NEAR AHMEDZAI

finding their position there untenable, retired. Thus it was in the Spín Gawai ravine that the battle of the Peiwár Kotal was fought and won.

As we rode across the open waste towards Shalozán, the village of Peiwár, some five miles off at the foot of the gap in the ridge, was lit up by the sun's rays, and it was with much regret that I was unable to obtain permission to ride up to the top of the pass; but just at this time our relations with the Amír were rather strained owing to the Bilandkhel affair, and it was considered advisable not to come into contact with the outpost of his troops which held the summit.

## CHAPTER VI

It was with one of those wonderful surprises which are common enough in the East that we rode into Shalozán, stepping out of the dry desert into a lovely English coppice in spring. The village, unlike all others we had seen, without walls, lies scattered in a long bower of trees, which are fed by the life-giving water that here comes rushing in a torrent straight down from the snows of Sikaram. Every lane is the bed of a little stream, which is diverted here and there into the green orchards with fruit-trees of all sorts —walnuts festooned with vines, almond trees bursting forth in all the beauty of their pink blossoms, peaches and plums; while through the brown winter leaves that cover the ground sprout up the bunches of blue violets and little wild red and yellow tulips.[1]

We rode up through the village accompanied by a number of the inhabitants, and soon found our camp—which, as usual, had been sent on ahead with a guard of twenty sepoys—pitched in a delightful grove of walnuts, while all around stood the Turis watching with great curiosity the wondrous details of a Sahibs' camp, often encroaching until they were driven off by the impatient soldiers.

It was like finding oneself in a new world, and it is no wonder that Shalozán has got the name of the Garden of Kuram. On a hot summer's day it must truly be a retreat for the weary, and

[1] *Tulipa stellata.*

SHALOZÁN

even now, though the weather was still cold, we felt sheltered from the wind by the dense growth of trees.

Lying as it does in the very north-west corner of Kuram, Shalozán is protected from its enemies on all sides, except the south, by the huge uninhabited mountains that rise immediately behind it, and it has consequently a less warlike appearance than any other place in the valley; while to the south the open desert stretches away to the Kuram river, and would give ample notice of any advancing foe. The climate, though cold in winter, is delightful, for it is sheltered from the bitter winds that blow down the valley, while its height above the sea (6000 feet) will always prevent its summer heat from being too oppressive. No wonder that all through Afghanistan its praises are sung, not only for its natural beauties, but also for its fair women.

> Sang i Mauláná, ab i Zerán,
> Bad i Kuram, dukhtar i Shalozán,[1]

as the saying here is for the noteworthy things in the valley. The Amírs of Kabul—which, as the crow flies, is only fifty-five miles off—have always been accustomed to get the fairest members of their harems from here, the present Amír himself being the grandson of a woman of this village.

Some day this will no doubt be one of the most popular hill-stations of the Punjáb, while with better communications and the spread of irrigation an immense quantity of fruit will be able to be carried down to the dwellers in the hot plains below. The latitude is only a little to the south of that of Malta, and the climate is such that any English fruit will grow here to perfection, with the addition of the best of grapes.

We had another reminder of England next day in the continued rain that fell without ceasing, sweeping down from the cloud-wreathed mountains above until our little camp was nearly

[1] Stone of Maulána, stream of Zerán,
Wind of Kuram, daughters of Shalozán.

flooded out, which set all the men to the work of digging trenches round the tents in the vain attempt to get rid of the water. I spent the day in writing, but towards evening Dallas and I were able to get out for a walk through the lanes all running with water, and to gather bunches of violets from under the dripping trees. The Turis evidently appreciate flowers, for every young lad who imagined that he had charms enough to captivate a lady-love, added to them by sticking a bunch of the little red and yellow tulips in his turban.

Next morning we, accompanied by the leading men and a motley retinue of hangers-on, went out to see, and were first led up the hillside to the Ziàrat or Saint's Tomb—a poor little building in itself, but with a beautiful view over the flat-topped houses of the village embowered in the mass of trees, to the vast plain of the Kuram valley stretching away down to Sangína some thirty miles distant.

Then we retraced our steps and were led into the bazár, the Regent Street of Shalozán. These were the only "shops" we had seen in Kuram, and consisted merely of open sheds. Neither was there much variety in them, for they were all making the same things—guns, the only saleable commodity apparently in this warlike country.

It was interesting to see the men at work. The finished article, when lying on the ground at a few yards' distance, had every appearance of the Enfield rifle, from which it was copied; but on taking it up, the crude simplicity of the work could be fully realised: the metal was roughly hammered into shape and then scratched over with a file. The barrels were made in short lengths of about a foot; a square iron rod being wrapped round a central mandrel, which was then withdrawn and the whole heated and roughly welded. Three or four of these tubes were then joined together, but as they had no tool to bore out the barrel, a square rimer was inserted, which, being turned round, scraped off any too prominent lumps on the inner surface! Still every detail of the English rifle, from

SIKARAM FROM SHOBLAN VILLAGE

the sights to the sling loops, was as carefully imitated as their coarse tools would allow them. The price asked for these guns was five Kabuli rupees or four Indian ones!

Nainu was enchanted. He had at last found something to stir his admiration. "Sahib," he whispered to me, "never have I seen such beautiful rifles and so cheap! If the Protector of the Poor would only grant his permission? No, Sahib, the police in Hindustan will not take it away from me: see, the Sahib shall say that it is *his* rifle; and when I come to Dehra I will take it to my village in the Tiri state, and all men will envy me. The Sahib says that these rifles are bad and will go broken; but see, there is a man here who has one which has already killed three men, which he will give for only six rupees"! "Very well, my dear Nainu; but if you ever fire it off I can assure you that it will kill a fourth"; and accepting this feeble joke as my consent, he duly brought the murderous weapon to my tent that evening. Nainu, by the way, nearly got locked up, a week or two after this, for firing this blunderbuss near the camp at Sangína without the commanding officer's permission!

From the bazár we went to the school, where some thirty boys and men were gathered together under a teacher sent up by Merk at the request of the Turis a month before.

Up to this time the only means of education open to the Turis consisted in frequenting the mosques, and spelling out the Koran in a monotonous sing-song voice—a sight which is to be seen in every Mohammedan village, where the shrill droning of these "Seekers after Knowledge," as they are called, sounds almost like a swarm of locusts; but already the new order has begun, and here we found in a shed, scarcely, however, worthy of a London board-school, the boys sitting round their master, an eager-looking young Mohammedan from Peshawur. He evidently had his hands full, for the Turi boys were not accustomed to much discipline, but crowded round us without the slightest shyness, eager to show off their proficiency.

A bed was brought and we sat down, Dallas beginning the

examination. The show boys were trotted out, and read fluently out of illustrated picture-books (supplied from India) simple Persian tales—for Persian is the French of Central Asia and the official language in Afghanistan, just as Hindustani is the official language in British territory.

Then the small boys brought out their Hindustani books, getting through their pages with but little stumbling, the teacher telling us that he had no complaint to make on the score of their dullness. After this we tried arithmetic. They had no slates, only pieces of wood chalked over, on which they wrote the Persian figures with a stick of charcoal, and did sums of addition and subtraction for our edification. The whole gave one the impression of great quickness of mind in these sharp little fellows, who looked quite turbulent enough, when not occupied with their books, to have made things very uncomfortable for any one who crossed them.

I was anxious to give them some money for prizes, but the teacher begged us not to do so, for he explained that they would fight bitterly for the possession of it after school, having as yet evidently no respect for the trial by competitive examination. So a sheep was bought, and divided amongst these young wolves, on the principle that what they had eaten, could alone not be taken from them by force.

There is a magnificent clump of chinárs, or Oriental planes, in Shalozán—really immense trees. Dotted about the valley, nearly every village has its chinár, which has the same sort of character as the pepul tree has to the Hindu. They are generally planted by the side of an irrigation cut, and grow into stately shapes, it being considered wicked to cut them in any way. As we stood under this big clump, Syud Abbàs, pointing to the broken bough above our heads (which can be seen in the photograph), told us the story of his father, Badsháh Gul's, death. Two years before, his father was staying at the house of a friend where a drooping limb of a chinár had grown so as to cause every one to stoop on entering. Badsháh

THE CHINÁR TREES AT SHALOZÁN

Gul, being a practical man and not given to superstition, got permission to cut it off, and thus was able to enter the house without bowing his proud head. Three weeks afterwards, as he was sitting in council with the elders of Shalozán under these big trees, suddenly without warning the heavy branch above, breaking off, fell crashing down on Badsháh Gul, killing him on the spot. A strange coincidence, which naturally confirmed the devout Turis in their respect for the chinárs.

I had come now as far as British influence had made itself felt, and as April was now well advanced, I had to think about getting back to India; so with many regrets at having to leave this charming spot, Dallas and I mounted our ponies one morning and rode through the flowering orchards out on to the great bare stony flat. We had given orders for the camp to march down the valley direct to Shoblán, while we ourselves with a few men, instead of going back to the river as we had come, kept along close under the Saféd Koh. The whole force of the Kuram wind was blowing this day. Though we had our sheepskin postíns on all day and there was never a tree to shade us from the burning sun, the bitter cold wind seemed almost to whistle through us. The men felt it intensely, many losing the skin off their faces, and Nainu registered this as one of the many black days in this wicked country.

The Saféd Koh rises straight up here on our left without any intervening ridges, and the face of the range is only broken by deep ravines and gullies which cut through the scanty pine-woods on the lower slopes. At the mouths of these short valleys, where the streams issue, villages have been built to take advantage of the water, and the ground around is cultivated. Mauláana is the first passed, nestling in its little bower of trees, and some miles farther on, Zerán. In winter-time all intercourse with the other side of the Saféd Koh is stopped, but in summer communication is not unfrequent between Kuram and Ningrahár, the name of the Afghan country on the other side of the passes. The shepherds who then drive their flocks up the narrow paths are ready guides to the few travellers wishing to make their way to Jellalabad, but, as usual in this country, no merchant could make this journey unless conducted by friends who, no doubt in return for an ample consideration, would insure him against pillage and robbery by the numerous border raiders. As on the Scottish Borders in the old days, the people on both sides of this great range are acquainted with each other, and though remaining outwardly friends, are always ready to make a foray if the chances of lifting a flock or two are favourable, and fortune favours the strong in this country.

The villages of Zerán, surrounded too by their fruit-trees, are prettily situated at the mouth of a glen, out of which flows an excellent stream. I tried in vain to take some photographs this day, but the wind was so strong that I feared to put my camera up, lest it should be blown away. Up on the Saféd Koh above us, great wreaths of snow, like clouds of smoke, were blown from every peak; and we hurried on to Shoblán, glad at last to get into the shelter of our cosy tents, which were pitched under the lee of the high mud village wall.

Here we were delighted to meet Merk again, who, having settled matters with the Kabul Khel Wazírs near Bilandkhel, had hurried back to Upper Kuram, in order to settle the site of the new cantonment and fort which are to be the headquarters of our future force occupying the valley.

He agreed to come with us for an excursion to Kirmán, a valley running out of the Saféd Koh a few miles to the north of us. We were anxious to see if we could discover any traces of the former occupation of the valley by the early Mohammedan conquerors, who in the tenth century established a mint here, many coins being found in this neighbourhood with the impress of the Kirmán mint upon them in the letters KRMN—from which we gathered that in those early days it must have been a place of great importance.

We shifted camp next morning to the picturesque little fort-like village of Tezána, in a basin of the hills, above which the snow

OUR CAMP AT TEZÁNA. LOOKING DOWN KURAM VALLEY

peaks shone out clear in the morning sun. A ride of a few miles up the narrow valley brought us to the edge of the Chakmanni confines, and dismounting, we were carried across the rushing little torrent on the broad backs of our Turis. After a steep climb for half an hour over the huge boulders, we reached a knoll, which the natives pointed out as the site of a place they had heard was once famous.

The ground was covered with huge boulders, which lay here only rather more thickly than on the other slopes of the hill; but on one side of the knoll there stood the remains of a wall of immense stones carefully dressed and laid upon each other, very much of the same character as the ruins we had previously visited farther down the valley opposite Alizai. Whether these ruins had any connection with the era of the Kirmán mint it is impossible to say, but it is difficult to imagine how any prosperous collection of human habitations could ever have existed in such an inhospitable and out-of-the-way spot.

On our way back to camp we passed under the picturesque border village of Kanda, which, perched on a rock over the river, is typical of the unsettled state of the country. Across the face of the cliff on which it stands, the water is carried in wooden troughs to irrigate a little flat patch of ground that has been won from the surrounding rocks, and which provides a scanty sustenance to the villagers above. The other object of interest here is the Ziárat or Shrine of Fakhr-i-álam, a holy man who received this title of the "Pride of the World" as a reward for his good deeds. It probably is the oldest building in Kuram, and has most likely stood for over 600 years—a long time in a country where the constant lootings and burnings of successive conquerors destroy all trace of permanency in buildings.

It is one of the very few pieces of architecture in Kuram, and even as such is poor in design and execution. The inner dome is hidden by a flat roof that has been built round it, and the frescoes with which it is ornamented are more Hindu in design than

Mohammedan, and are somewhat crude in colouring. The whole is in that dilapidated condition which is almost universal in the case of monuments in the East, and which is partly due to a religious dislike to altering a sacred building in any way, and more to the general flourishing condition of the local "anti-restoration societies."

This shrine, being the oldest and certainly the most ornamental in Kuram, ought, if the people had any religious inclination in this way, to have had at least the same attention paid to it as the Hindu temples in India have to theirs; but as a matter of fact it has a dead-world look, and the old mullah with his long white beard who received us, looked more like a hermit than the priest of a living religion. He did not seem to have any objection to my wandering about with my camera, and even himself stood immovable at the gate of the shrine for a most unconscionably long exposure, which the setting sun obliged me to give! A fine old Scotch fir, and the rushing water of an irrigation channel just outside the gate, before which stood a spreading walnut tree, gave a picturesque look to the otherwise forlorn appearance of the place; while the group of people who by this time had flocked out of the little walled village near to watch our movements, gave an animation to the scene which it lacked on our arrival.

If the Parsís can satisfy themselves with sun-worship, surely this would have been the country to start a religion of the water-god; for this commodity is the source and fountain of all nourishment, as well as of all beauty, and it alone supplies the food for the people, as well as the grateful shade under which they can sit to eat it.

However, pleasant as was the rushing water of Kirmán with its copses of blossoming fruit-trees and green terraces, happy as was the companionship of the kind friends whose little camp I was sharing, yet my free time had drawn to its close, and next morning my plans compelled me to ride off alone across the open desert, which in some twenty miles would bring me back to Sangína.

THE ZIÁRAT OF FAKHR-I-ÁLAM

Nainu had already started back, taking all my baggage with him under an escort that was going down to Thull; and I had given him instructions to meet me at Khushalgarh railway-station on the Indus, some 150 miles distant. He was quite incapable of getting there by himself, I knew, but Merk most kindly sent one of his orderlies with him, in whose hands I could safely leave everything. The Assistant Commissioner had been written to, to have two ekhas sent to Thull for the use of Nainu, the orderly, and the baggage, and in these they were to proceed *viâ* Hangu and Kohat to Khushalgarh—stages of thirty-eight, twenty-six, and thirty-one miles respectively; and as I had given them three days from Thull to accomplish this in, I expected to overtake them at Khushalgarh in time to catch the train that leaves there at nine o'clock in the morning for Rawal Pindi. By travelling down with the mail the whole way from Sangína, I could thus do in two and a half days what would take them five, an arrangement that, besides giving me three more days in Kuram, took me over the rough part of the journey in the shortest time—a thing always to be desired.

So the last evening came, and as Merk and I, sitting wrapped in our sheepskin postíns in his comfortable little Kabul tent, imbibed our after-dinner whisky and water, we drank to our happy past and the successful future of the Kuram valley. If it has lived through some troublous times, surely a bright future is before it now that it has come definitely under British influence. India is a great collection of countries and races. The wisdom and resource of the governors of India have often been tried, but it is with pride that one can say that they have never yet been found wanting. The fact that such utterly different types of the human race as the Burman, the Rajput, the Sikh, and the Tamil, the Bengáli and the Pathan all flourish and thrive under one beneficent administration, is a proof, which needs no words to emphasise it, that the system of government is as sound as the men are able who carry it out. Force and elasticity are its watchwords. The just appreciation of the fact that it is the duty of the white race to spread its superior civilisation, is the driving power. In the East, where from time immemorial the weak have been oppressed by the strong, it is absolutely necessary for the Government, if it wishes to be just, to be the strongest of all. The elasticity is found in the capacity the English rulers have always shown in working on the spot, with the best tools they can command; and, while bearing in mind the high end they have in view, they have always with ready resource adapted the rules and the regulations to the wholly different conditions in which their work may lie. The Government thus sits far above all these different peoples, holding the scales of justice equally above all. Long may it be before we abdicate this position, won with such noble labour. "India for the Indians" has a plausible sound to some minds, but before this can be realised the lion must be taught to lie down with the lamb, the Pathan with the Bengáli, and the Sikh with the Burman—a consummation devoutly to be wished for, no doubt, but which even a blind man can see is still far remote.

I was up early in the glorious morning, which still had little of the softness of spring about it, and soon had my limited kit packed. Merk was going to move camp that day, for he was off to inspect the site of the new station at Parachinár, just below Maulána, so the sound of packing was going on all round. Tent-pegs were being knocked out of the hard ground, and tents folded up; the baggage-mules squealed their remonstrances to the loading, while the camels groaned and gurgled as each huge bundle was thrown across them by the guard; every one was busy getting ready to start. As I stand with Merk exchanging a few last words the servants bring us our revolvers, the native officer comes to announce that my sowárs are ready, and at last with another hearty farewell to Merk, I ride off with my two men of the 5th Punjáb Cavalry, and am soon out of sight as I descend into the wide stony bed of the Kirmán stream. There are no hedges or ditches in this country to stop you, so I rode in a straight line across the stony flat, bearing rather to the right, until in some

BORDER VILLAGE OF KANDA. KIRMÁN.

miles I joined the road running along the river, down which I kept for some distance, till I reached a ford at the village of Yakúbi, which took me to the Sangína side of the river and saved me a mile or two's detour by the bridge below the camp. The narrow and rough track leads on this side of the river over some wild rocky and broken ground, till you suddenly drop out of a little ravine on to the upper end of the camp. It was about three o'clock when I got in, hot and thirsty, and on riding up to the politicals' tents, I found Dallas sitting in judgment, but not too busy to come to my assistance.

We walked together down to the other end of the camp, where the post-office babu reigned supreme in the tent that did duty for receiving and despatching Her Majesty's mails. A dâk ekha had been started on the Thull-Sangína road, and I was to share its fortunes to-morrow with the driver, so the seat was "booked for His Honour," as the babu officially noted, and I had time for a last walk down to the parade-ground, where the football was again in full swing.

A last dinner in the mess of the hospitable 2nd P.I., and with many thanks on my part and good wishes on theirs, I stumbled in the dark through the innumerable tent-ropes to the "palace," where the political sentry—one of the new Turi militiamen—duly challenged. He seemed quite happy that he had done his duty in accomplishing thus much, for I never heard any one answer him, and he never pursued the argument any farther!

The sun had not risen over the hill next morning when Dallas' servant came and called me, and after a somewhat hasty toilet, I swallowed some tea and bundled my scanty wardrobe into my valise, which we carried down to the place where the ekha was standing ready. A couple of Turi sowárs, sitting bunched up on their ragged ponies to keep out the cold, with nothing but the muzzles of their Sniders appearing out of their voluminous wraps, stood by ready to escort us. With a farewell wave to Dallas and a fiendish blast of a bugle from the driver, Her Majesty's mails got under weigh, and soon we were rolling and pitching over the stony billows and earthy hollows. However, a dâk ekha is an instrument of torture that spares neither age nor sex, and as I was in for thirty-eight miles of it before I could get out at Thull, there was nothing for it but to sit well down in the saddle.

The hot sun came over the hill as we clattered past Sadda and continued straight down the valley past the familiar snipe jhíl and the towers of Darani village. The road is passable when it follows the terraced earthen ground, it is endurable when the pony climbs the stony hillside at a walking pace, but when gravity and the driver's whip compel the machine down a slope of small boulders at

PISTOL WITH SILVER-INLAID BARREL

about nine miles an hour, body and soul can scarcely hold together. I remained conscious as far as Alizai, the "half-way house," where we changed ekhas, and where the kind old Shahzáda had come to bid me farewell. He was working in this part of the valley, and hearing that I was coming down, had waited to meet me. I was glad to have the opportunity of seeing him again, and of thanking him for his many kindnesses to me. Knowing my taste for curiosities, he brought me a pistol beautifully inlaid on the barrel with silver, as a specimen of the work of the valley. With the exception of these inlaid pistols and the jezails, which from their long barrels and curved stocks are curiosities, there is little or nothing of interest to be brought away from Kuram. It is possible that the women have silver jewels of some sort, but as these are only made

EARLY MORNING AT THE VILLAGES OF SHOBLÁN

to order, one never has an opportunity of seeing them anywhere. I took the precaution of getting a Turi to discharge the pistol at a safe distance from me, for, needless to say, every weapon is kept loaded in this country where they may be needed at any moment. After stretching my cramped legs before Alizai, and bidding a hearty farewell to the Prince, I climbed into my box again and we proceeded. I will draw a kindly veil over the rest of this drive, and only mention that I was in a terribly bruised condition of mind and body when we drove at last into the camp at Thull and I was greeted by my Bilandkhel friends, who had moved up here and were now encamped under the walls of the fort pending further developments.

Colonel Brownlow very kindly allowed me the use of a tent of his for the night, where I turned in thankfully after a pleasant dinner at the mess. I heard here, rather to my dismay, that owing to the ekhas not having been sent up from Kohat in time, Nainu had left Thull only that very morning! So I looked forward to picking them up on the road, especially as, owing to some late showers, the earthen track was very sticky.

I was still in my tent at half-past four next morning, hastily swallowing some eggs that Colonel Brownlow's servant brought me by the light of a candle, when the dâk bugler, standing beside the fort above, blew his mournful blasts into the cold grey morning to call my attention to the fact that he was ready. It was not much past five when I stumbled in the dusk across the wide dry stony bed of the river, which lay between the camp and the fort, and clambered up the steep bank to where the dâk driver stood, a black silhouette against the lighter sky. After yesterday's experience this Thull-Kohat road seemed like a billiard-table, and, taught by bitter experience, I had learnt the positions in which rest could be found for a few moments, and religiously adopted each in succession.

It is wonderful how these rough ekha ponies get over the ground, and travelling with the mail-bags in this way, you change ekhas every twelve miles—a journey that seems nothing to them. By eleven o'clock I had done thirty-eight miles, and drove up to Hangu dâk bungalow in time for a late breakfast; and, after an hour's rest there, started again and reached Kohat, twenty-six miles farther on, by three o'clock. At Hangu I heard that Nainu and the baggage had spent the night there, and had started on some four or five hours before I reached it; and, to my delight, I found on my arrival at Kohat that they were not there, so that they must be still ahead of me.

The mail tonga, the strong, low, two-wheeled cart of India, drawn by a pair of horses abreast, only leaves Kohat bungalow at four o'clock in the morning to catch the nine o'clock train at Khushalgarh on the Indus, so that I could throw myself on a bed for a good sleep before going on again. A visit overnight to the post-office had secured my place in the tonga, and as I had telegraphed on to the bungalow at Khushalgarh to have breakfast ready for me, I had nothing to do next morning but to get up at the blast of the dâk bugle and grope my way to the tonga which stood at the door.

I have heard that ice yachting is exciting, and the nearest thing I can imagine to it is a tonga drive on a dark morning, without lights and with a pair of good, jibbing, galloping ponies. After the usual preliminary difficulties about getting the ponies to start, we sailed down the broad Kohat road at a furious gallop. The white gate pillars of the bungalows could just be made out as we dashed by in the dark; the noise of the tonga, the pole of which by the jerking cracked the pole chains in time to the ponies' strides, made it impossible to hear anything. Driving there was none: the ponies knew the road, and knew that they had to go five miles to their stopping-place, and they *went*, never for a moment slackening the pace. The driver, powerless to guide or control his steeds, spent all his energies in prolonged blasts on his bugle, which, with the thunder of the tonga, effectually scared every living thing off the road, so that the course was clear, and nothing checked us

THE SHAHZÁDA AND HIS ESCORT

until the ponies stopped dead, and we realised that another five miles was over; a new pair of ponies being brought out to repeat this performance over and over again. In one of these mad gallops I became aware that we had got off the road in the dark, and were taking a short cut across country; but the pace never slackened for a moment, and by some good fortune we were still right side uppermost when the ring of the ponies' feet on the hard metalled track announced that we had found our way on to the road again.

The grey still day was breaking over the hot dry land as we neared the low line of hills which borders the Indus at a distance of some five miles, and reached a large village, where we again changed ponies. Up to this point, some fifteen miles from Kohat, we had raced two ekhas with four natives on each, who had kept company with us the whole way! We galloped past them when once under weigh, but during the few minutes that we halted to change horses their brave ponies invariably passed us again, bowling along at a hard swinging trot. When we drove off from the village the owners of the plucky little beasts were walking them up and down to cool them, as is their custom always on finishing a journey.

A long ascent through these low red treeless hills at only a slightly diminished pace brought us to the top of the rise, and away before us stretched the almost limitless plains of India, which faded away into the haze that presaged the scorching heat of the coming day. The Indus itself could not be made out, for it runs here in a deep, narrow bed. I had promised the driver an addition to his wages if we got in in time for breakfast, and he certainly intended to earn it, as we raced down the long five miles to the river. The road is kept in splendid order, and we swept along at a royal speed. It was exactly seven o'clock when we pulled up at the Khushalgarh bungalow, having left Kohat at twenty minutes past four—thirty-one miles in two hours and forty minutes. The Kohatis pride themselves on their tonga service, but I think they cannot often do better than this.

After a good rest and a well-earned breakfast we made our way down the river, which here flows in a deep and narrow channel with high, steep, red-earth banks. A most curious-looking place. The mud houses of the village high up on the right bank, the little railway-station on the same level on the opposite shore, with the great bridge of boats spanning the river deep down between them; the huge steel hawsers that strengthen the bridge, stretched from cliff to cliff, looking like spiders' webs hung across the abyss.

The tonga rumbled slowly down the zigzag road to the water, and then across the creaking, swaying bridge, past the huge country carts drawn by the patient bullocks, and up to the station standing in the desert on the other side. On the platform stood Nainu and Ghunni the orderly, salāming and smiling. "How on earth did you get here, Nainu?" "It was the Sahib's orders that we should be here; all the baggage is safe." Each pony had drawn an ekha, two men, and a hundredweight of baggage ninety-five miles in two days!

Nainu was in delight at seeing a train again. "Sahib, that Kuram is a bad country and the people are altogether wicked. Never more will we visit it, Sahib. Last night even, as we were passing a village, the ponies going very slow, for they were very tired, the budmashes came out and threw stones at us, hoping to drive us away; but Ghunni fired quickly with his rifle at them, and they fled." "How many men were killed in the battle, O Nainu?" "Nay, Sahib, do not laugh, it was no battle; but what I say is true talk: the people of this country are altogether bad men and wicked"; and with that he proceeded to stow my baggage into the railway-carriage, with the complacent satisfaction that he was at last on his way home again.

The engine whistles and the train drags itself slowly out into the burning desert, and as we sit in this comfortable product of nineteenth-century civilisation, rumbling back towards "India" with its teeming millions, we have time to think over the wild mediæval highlanders that we have only just left behind.

Here my journey, as far as the reader is concerned, is over. Smart soldierly Pindi, the hot stifling days at Lahore throbbing with its countless life, Delhi in May surrounded by its fiery plains —all these belong to another story. It is only hoped that this short description of two valleys less frequently visited by travellers may have some interest, as showing only one of the many contrasts that meet the eye, the ear, and the brain in that great empire of ours we know as India. How superficial is this account of these two peoples no one knows better than the author; but he will feel more than rewarded if he has enabled those who are obliged to stay in England, to gain in however slight a measure, a clearer insight into that vast dependency, the safety as well as the peace and progress of which depends ultimately upon their intelligent appreciation of their responsibilities.

KURAM SILVER AMULET

# APPENDIX A

THE following photographic notes, it is hoped, may be of use to those who wish to take their camera with them to distant countries.

*Size.* The first consideration must always be the size of the plate to be used. The more certain a man is in his results, the larger the plate he can take, naturally will give him the finest picture. It is worth while, for instance, for Signor Sella, whose most exquisite Alpine photographs so far surpass all others, to take with him to the Caucasus 120 15 x 12 plates, for he knows he will bring back 120 good negatives, and the extra weight and difficulty of carriage involved in using these large plates is amply repaid by the perfection of the result. I would, then, always advise any one aiming at high results to take with him the largest plates that he can ; and the size of his plates will depend then, first upon his confidence in himself to produce good results, and secondly upon the equally important question of carriage.

*Carriage.* In journeys off the beaten track one's means of transport always consist of either mule carriage or kulis, and the loads have often to be made up so that they are capable of being carried either by one or the other as they may offer. A mule in the Himalayas will carry 160 lbs., and a kuli 50 lbs., the former costing 12 annas a day (say 1s.), while the latter are paid 4, 5, or 6 annas a day, according to the length of the march. Mules, consequently, are rather cheaper, and as they are hired for a fixed period, they relieve one of the daily bother of engaging kulis. Against these advantages you have to set the facts that the mule can go only where there is a mule road ; secondly, that you carry many more of the precious eggs in one basket ; and, thirdly, that on the rough hill paths kuli carriage is much safer than mule carriage. Never once did I see any of the wild hill men ever falter or stumble on the worst of paths, and his load on his back was as carefully carried as himself ; whereas the frequent sight of the string of mules staggering down a steep hillside, bumping their loads against overhanging rocks, plunging over the slippery boulders as they forded the stream and scrambling in rushes up the stony opposite bank, was a picture that often made one tremble for the fate of one's plates.

*Films.* Many will say, Why not avoid all this by carrying celluloid films instead of glass plates? and I must confess that, after my own experience, I find it extremely difficult to give any definite reason, except that I fancy, and it may be only a fancy, that on the whole there is less liability to error in working with glass plates. My experience in this trip was confined to six dozen films and eighteen dozen plates. The weight of the former is 4 lbs., the weight of six dozen of the latter 27 lbs. The films require no packing: they are most easily taken out of their envelopes one by one, as required, exposed, and put back with the same ease; whereas the hours spent by night in one's tent after a long day's march, taking plates out of the slides, numbering, packing away in their paper wrapping and boxes, unpacking the fresh plates (which are always required in broken numbers), and filling the slides, will never be forgotten. It used to take me two hours to get this properly done, and yet, in spite of all this, when it comes to developing the negative in the dark room, I am always hopeful of better results from a plate than from a film. The chief practical difficulty with a film is the want of a really good film-carrier which, while simple and easy to use, will keep the film absolutely flat. After searching in vain for this in London, I went without any carrier, simply trusting to the dryness of the Indian air to keep the emulsion side of the film concave, while a thin sheet of wood backing (such as was formerly used in Eastman paper negative-carriers) nipped the edges of the film against the rebates of the slide and pressed it flat. A detail must, however, here be noted—that the single spring, as fitted to most metal dividing flaps of the dark slides, must be removed, as its pressure will bulge out the thin wood backing and the film in the centre, and springs on each edge, to press against the rebate of the slide, must be substituted.

This arrangement will answer in a dry climate with sizes up to whole-plate, though, in spite of special care being given to putting the films in quite flat, two or three of my film negatives were much spoilt owing to the buckling of the film throwing certain portions of the emulsion out of focus. I used glass plates as a rule for the most difficult and delicate scenes, and the films (which were more rapid) for strong and close subjects; and, though I fancied that the films were less successful in the difficult subjects, yet I must admit that many of them are quite as beautiful in detail and delicacy as those on glass, and, given a good film-carrier, there ought to be no reason why a well-coated film should not equal a well-coated glass plate.

The size of the plates that I took was whole-plate; perhaps the most suitable all-round size, though, as I said before, I regret sometimes, in view of the negatives that I brought back, that I did not take a larger size.

*Quantity of Plates.* The number of plates to be carried is the next consideration. I made a rough guess, and took with me two gross—one gross of Wratten's ordinary (a plate which never fails in its high standard of excellence for all landscape work), and half a gross each of Edwards's XL (orange label) celluloid films and Edwards's XL plates. I used the latter for all figure and close subjects, it being a plate to which I had always been accustomed, and of which I never had any cause to complain. This was a rough guess, but it turned out fairly correct, as of the lot, only one dozen Wratten's were broken while being carried on a mule, and one dozen of each kind were left in India on my return, I not having required them. I found that, though in the Himalayas I took pictures of everything that I thought would be interesting, to give a complete idea of the country, the number of plates I exposed in one day never exceeded eight, and the average over three months' marching was under two a day.

*Camera.* I will now endeavour to give some idea of the details of the kit I used, and which, speaking from experience, I may say I found complete in every respect. I took a whole-plate camera of Chapman's (Manchester), which I have had in continual use for eight years, having used it out yachting in Scotland, in the plains of Italy, and in the mountains of Switzerland. It is of the simplest construction, having no especial struts, and is not brass-bound, and, though it will not carry a heavy lens when racked out to eighteen inches in a high wind (what camera will?), yet not one single picture of the 250 I have taken in India has been spoilt by any break-down or shake in the camera or its three double-backs. The camera design has one fault, in that the bellows do not rise and fall with the rising front, and in extreme cases the corners of the picture are cut off when a wide-angle lens is used. When, however, one has to put up and take down the camera so constantly on the march, simplicity and absence of all fancy springs, stays, and screws are the things one values most, providing no efficiency is sacrificed thereby. Certainly this camera, with its three double-backs, speaks well for the soundness of first-class English work, being still practically as good as new, while it has never in any way been repaired since I had it.

*Slides.* The only addition I made to my kit was to get three more double slides, numbered from 7 to 12, which fitted tight into a tin velvet-lined box. This was carried by my gun-bearer, always slung over one shoulder by a strap, and was only used to contain Edwards's rapid plates or films, the slow plates always being in slides 1 to 6 in the camera-case. I was thus always ready for either landscape or figure subject as it came.

*Stand.* On a march of this kind the portability of the camera legs is not a necessity. Before leaving London I looked everywhere for a strong, simple set of legs, with a single sliding joint. Not finding anything suitable, I fell back on my old ones, which, though theoretically weak, yet were strong enough to stand the keen winds on the high passes without shaking. The legs were always carried ready fixed to the triangle, with their joints slid in to reduce them to half their length, the whole being carried on the top of the camera-case as it rested knapsack-like on the man's back. In this way I could erect the legs at once, put on the camera, and I found from eight to ten minutes' halt was all that was necessary to get a picture.

*Lenses.* Of lenses I took three—an eight-and-a-half-inch focus Dallmeyer landscape, a twelve-inch Ross's rapid symmetrical, and an eighteen-inch Swift's landscape. All were fitted with carriers to go into the same flange on the camera front, and all were bayonet-jointed, so that they required only a quarter turn to screw them home. Much as wide-angle lenses destroy the artistic sense of a picture, the eight-and-a-half-inch lens is a necessity for all mountainous countries. The angles from the heights to the depths are so enormous, that frequently one can get no picture on one's plate at all unless a wide angle is included. The rapid symmetrical remains the most useful all-round lens, and a long-focus 18-inch lens enables you to take many a beautiful and effective picture of distant mountains, embracing as it does an angle much more nearly resembling that which is taken in by one's eyes. All my lenses were fitted with iris diaphragms, and the slight extra expense will be amply repaid in the saving of time these little conveniences effect. I used a shutter of my own making, but any time-and-instantaneous shutter, such as Thornton-Pickard's, will do, though without doubt it is an advantage to have one's shutter behind the lens. Each lens was carried in a little chamois leather bag, differently coloured, so that the men, in opening the camera-case, were always able to hand me out the one I required.

*Focussing Cloth.* Last, but not least, comes the focussing cloth, which should be of thin white mackintosh, lined with some thin non-slippery cloth. The white colour keeps off the great heat of the sun's rays at high altitudes, and often prevents the heating of the camera and condensing of the damp on the cold lens. The mackintosh is an excellent cover to the camera, and, if buttons and loops are sewn on the front edges, in rainy weather the kuli can take it out of the camera-case, and throwing it over the whole knapsack, can, by buttoning it in front round his neck, use it as a complete waterproof for the camera-case on his back and himself.

*Weight.* The whole kit in the camera-case, including the six plates and the camera legs, made up a load of 23 lbs., which is a fair weight for a man who marches behind you all day. The other three double-backs, filled, in their tin case, weighed 7 lbs., and were, as mentioned above, carried by my gun-bearer. Both these men were permanently engaged, and became soon experts at helping me to set up and pack away the camera, the gun-bearer going even so far as to pick up an idea of posing the villagers naturally in the picture—always a work of some difficulty, for, needless to say, the natives' idea is always to stand in a row, at attention, facing the camera. In no country, however, are figure subjects easier than in India; the patience of the natives far exceeds one's own, and they will stand any length of time immovable if carefully posed. Even with the wilder Pathans across the frontier, I had no difficulty in photographing either them or their villages; they seemed only surprised that the operation was over so soon, and a peep through the camera, under the focussing cloth, was the greatest reward to them.

*View-Meter.* I made for myself a small view-meter, consisting of a small frame of brass, the opening of which was in the proportion of $8\frac{1}{2}$ to $6\frac{1}{2}$. Through, and at right angles to the longest side, ran a stiff well-fitting brass wire, the end of which was held against the bone just under the eye. By sliding the frame along the wire, which was marked in three places for the three lenses I used, the different angle on the landscape which each lens would embrace was shown at a glance, so that, by the time the camera was on its legs, I knew which lens would be required. This view-meter I always carried loose in my pocket, and I found it an invaluable time-saver.

*Packing.* For the sea journey to India all my plates were packed as the boxes came from the makers, on edge, in two tin-lined cases, each holding about nine dozen plates. This kept the weight of each case down to 50 lbs. I made a depot of these in India, and took with me on the march as many plates as I required, packing some four or five of the makers' boxes in each yakdàn, or wooden mule-trunk, filling the intervening spaces with clothes. By keeping the weight of each yakdàn below 50 lbs. it can either be carried by a kuli or by mule. The most important packing was, however, the repacking after exposure. In order to be quite safe in this respect, I had prepared, at the kind suggestion of Signor Sella, whose great experience in the Caucasus made his advice invaluable, a number of whole-plate cut sheets of Rives's plain paper. These were dipped in a weak solution of Nelson's gelatine, in which enough chromate of alum was mixed to render the solution a pale greenish colour. The solution must be weak enough not to glaze the paper when dry. Exposed plates, packed face to face with this paper between them, will keep an indefinite time, and those I have exposed six months ago when unpacked develop as freshly as if only just exposed. It is a long business packing away exposed plates. It is most difficult to get a dozen Wratten's plates, with all their paper wrappers, back into the cardboard boxes again. It can be done, however, and it is worth while expending every effort to pack the exposed plates carefully once for all. A grooved light-tight wooden box, to hold one dozen plates, will be found the greatest help, so that a whole dozen may be opened at once, worked through the slides as required, numbered, and put back into the box. As soon as the whole dozen is worked through, repack all of them, at one operation, into their cardboard boxes. If only one rapidity of plate is carried, one wooden box will suffice; but each rapidity of plate requires its own box, which had better, for convenience' sake, be painted a different colour. I wrapped each cardboard box, when thus filled with a dozen exposed plates, in brown paper, and then in a sheet of that most excellent Indian Momjáma (cheap waxed calico, bought in every bazár), which is a good waterproof. Each dozen plates had a label on the outside of the box, with the numbers corresponding to those in the exposure-book. I had no difficulty, in this way, in finding those that I wished to develop first. Finally, on my return to India from across the border, I packed all the boxes of exposed plates again in the tin-lined cases in which they came out, and, for safety's sake, inclosed each of these small heavy cases in a larger packing-case, hay being well stuffed between the two.

I will conclude with this advice. Aim at uniformity of result, which can only be acquired by constant attention to the smallest details. Nothing is so disheartening as the discovery on development, that the most wished for negative has been spoilt through some trifling neglect or other. Secondly, let those who go out to bring back a series of photographs of a new country not confine their pictures only to the prettiest subjects, but endeavour to take every landscape that is characteristic, even though it be ugly. For instance, all Central Asia (including in this Afghanistan and our own north-west frontier) is a vast barren, stony desert, in which, here and there where there is irrigation, you find green and fertile valleys, cultivation, fruit-trees of all sorts, many of which bowers remind you of an English coppice. One is tempted to pick out these refreshing bits, to leave alone the twenty miles' march over the barren, stony waste, and so bring back to England a number of pictures which convey the idea that Central Asia is a veritable Garden of Eden. In landscapes, as often as possible, get some of the natives of the country to make a foreground, making them look away from the camera, and stand or sit in their natural attitudes. A group of such figures will always localise a picture, add the human interest, and throw back the distance in your landscape by making a bold foreground.

Nothing can add to the interest of travel so much as the wise use of a camera. It makes you observe so much more the characteristics of the country; it takes you off the beaten track in search of something more novel; it is an excellent passport into native villages and corners, for, children-like, they are all interested in the "picture man," and in return for a few kind words they do all they can to offer assistance; and, finally, it is the best school of all for patience, without which a photographer is no photographer.

# APPENDIX B

## ROUGH SKETCH OF THE DISTRIBUTION OF ADMINISTRATIVE POWER FROM THE VICEROY DOWNWARDS

- VICEROY IN COUNCIL.
  - Governor of Bombay (co-ordinate and subordinate).
  - Governor of Madras (co-ordinate and subordinate).
  - Lieut.-Governor of Bengal.
  - Lieut.-Governor of N.W. Provinces.
  - Lieut.-Governor of the Punjáb.
    - Commissioner of Jalandur.
      - Deputy Commissioner of Kangra.
        - Assistant Commissioner in charge of KULU Subdivision.
          - One *Tehsildár.*
            - The *Neghis.*
              - The *Lumbadárs*, or Village Headmen.
                - The *Chaukidár*, or Watchman.
          - One *Naib Tehsildár.*
        - Several others.
      - Four other Deputy Commissioners.
    - Commissioner of Peshawur.
      - Deputy Commissioners of Peshawur.
        - Three Assistant Commissioners.
          - Six *Tehsildárs.*
            - The *Zaildárs.*
              - The *Lumbadárs.*
      - Two others.
      - Officer on special duty in KURAM.
        - Two *Naib Hákims* or Deputies.
    - Four other Commissioners.
  - Chief Commissioner of the Central Provinces.
  - Chief Commissioner of Assam.
  - Chief Commissioner of Burmah.

NOTE.—Those printed in italics are natives.

# APPENDIX C

THE following kit was found necessary for one person on a six weeks' march into the Himalayas, and may perhaps serve as a guide to others :—

2 homespun Norfolk jackets.
1 knitted Cardigan.
1 sailor's blue knitted jersey.
3 white flannel shirts, with collars.
3 pairs of flannel trousers.
4 merino jerseys.
6 pairs of woollen socks.
3 pairs of cotton socks.
2 pairs of putties.
2 pairs of boots.
1 pair of tennis shoes.
1 pair of slippers.
1 helmet.
2 cloth caps.
1 thick overcoat.
1 mackintosh cape.
4 blankets.
1 pillow.
1 waterproof sheet, to cover bedding.
4 towels.
Sponge, brush, shaving kit, soap, belt, writing materials, looking-glass.

The following stores were taken for one person :—

| | |
|---|---|
| Bread | 10 loaves |
| Onions | 2 seers |
| Potatoes | 12 ,, |
| Rice | 12 ,, |
| Flour | 10 ,, |
| Sugar | 5 ,, |
| Tea | 1½ ,, |
| Soda | 1 bottle |
| Biscuits | 3 tins |
| Candles | 4 lbs. |
| Oatmeal | 3 tins |
| Butter | 1 tin |
| Marmalade | 1 tin |
| Cheese | 1 tin |
| Kopp beef-tea | 4 tins |
| Corn-flour | 1 tin |
| Cocoa | 2 tins |
| Sago | 1 tin |
| Corned beef | 3 tins |
| Mustard | 1 tin |
| Salt | 1 bottle |
| Pepper. | |
| One salted hump of beef. | |
| Whisky | 3 bottles |
| Hatchet, matches, rope, lantern, sewing things, duster, medicine, ammunition. | |

Minimum number of kulis required for the above :—

| | |
|---|---|
| Light drill double fly tent and some pegs | 1 kuli. |
| Servant's pal and remaining pegs | 1 ,, |
| All the tent poles and camp bed | 1 ,, |
| 4 kiltas of stores, etc. | 4 ,, |
| Kit and bedding | 1 ,, |
| Light wooden tub containing books, etc., writing materials, rifle in case | 1 ,, |
| Servant's kit, hatchet, and some ammunition | 1 ,, |
| | 10 |
| Tindal, or headman | 1 |
| Shikari carrying gun | 1 |
| Khansamah (cook) | 1 |
| | 13 in all. |

# APPENDIX D

## MEDICINES FOUND TO BE MOST NEEDED

Bottle of quinine, or 5-grain quinine tabloids.
4 boxes of Cockle's pills.
1 bottle of chlorodyne.
Dover's powder in 5-grain tabloids.
Camphor, opium, and capsicum pills.
1 lb. tin of boracic acid ointment.
1 bandage, soap plaster, linen, 1 pair of scissors.
1 tin of corn-flour.
1 tin of sago.

# APPENDIX E

A CURIOUS instance of the strong duty that is imposed by blood feuds upon the relatives of the deceased man is related by Mr. Forbes-Mitchell in his interesting *Reminiscences of the Mutiny.* It is well known that the necessity of inflicting punishment for the Cawnpore massacres during the mutiny of 1857 fell upon Brigadier-General Neill, who arrived upon the scene while the blood of the 210 women and children still saturated the floor and the walls of the house in which they were slaughtered under circumstances of most fiendish cruelty. The times called for a correspondingly severe retribution, for it was General Neill's wish to show the natives, once and for all, that butchers of women and children would be unrelentingly stamped out by a process which should be as odious to them as their deeds were to Englishmen.

Now amongst those who were caught at Cawnpore was one Safar Ali, of the 2nd Regiment of light cavalry. He was tried by General Neill's orders, found guilty of participating in the massacre, and before he was hanged, was compelled under the lash to clean up a portion of the floor which he had stained with innocent blood. On the gallows Safar Ali adjured every Mussulman in the crowd to carry the news of his death to his infant son, Mazar Ali by name, who was in his home at Rothak in the Punjáb, and to beg him to avenge his father's death on General Neill or his descendants.

The message was apparently never delivered. General Neill was himself killed in the fighting a short time afterwards, and the matter seemed to have been completely forgotten.

When the boy Mazar Ali grew up, he took service in the Central India Horse, in which, by a most curious coincidence, the son of General Neill was also an officer; and the year 1887, just thirty years after the above-mentioned tragic events, found Major Neill in command of his regiment at Augur, in which Mazar Ali was a faithful and loyal trooper.

Suddenly one morning, without any apparent motive, Major Neill was shot down on parade by sowár Mazar Ali. Nothing was elicited at the trial of Mazar Ali, who was in due course condemned and executed for the murder of his commanding officer. Since then Mr. Forbes-Mitchell, by careful inquiries on the spot, has been able to ascertain that shortly before the murder, Mazar Ali was visited by a fakír, or holy mendicant, who for the first time made him aware of Major Neill's relationship to General Neill, and also communicated to him his father's dying message calling upon him to avenge his death.

Mazar Ali then, overcome with his religious duty of vengeance, carried out his father's injunctions in implicit obedience.

Mr. Forbes-Mitchell was able to secure also the following leaflet printed in Úrdú, which was circulated amongst the descendants of Safar Ali, inciting them to vengeance and purposing to be Safar Ali's dying imprecation :—

"O Mahomet Prophet, be pleased to receive into Paradise the soul of your humble servant, whose body Major Bruce's Mehtur police are now defiling by lashes, forced to lick a space of the blood-stained floor of the slaughter-house, and hereafter to be hanged, by the order of General Neill. And, O Prophet, in due time inspire my infant son, Mazar Ali of Rothak, that he may revenge this desecration on General Neill and his descendants."

THE END

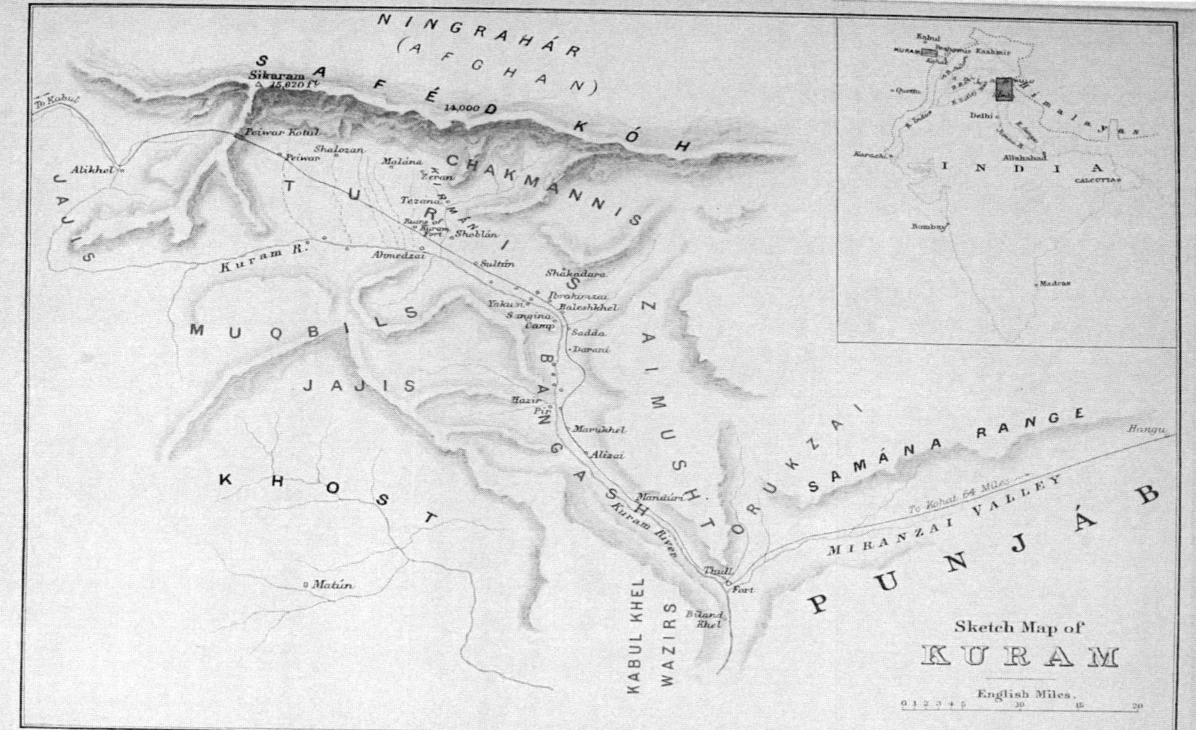


London: John Murray.

Stanford's Geog. Estab.